Bringing It All Back Home

Class, Gender and Power in the Modern Household

Harriet Fraad, Stephen Resnick and Richard Wolff

A New Directions/Rethinking Marxism title

Pluto  **Press**

LONDON • BOULDER, COLORADO

First published 1994 by Pluto Press
345 Archway Road, London N6 5AA
and 5500 Central Avenue
Boulder, Colorado 80301, USA

British Library Cataloguing in Publication Data
A catalogue record for this title is available from the British Library

Library of Congress Cataloging in Publication Data
Fraad, Harriet. 1941–
    Bringing it all back home : class, gender and power in the modern
household / Harriet Fraad, Stephen Resnick, and Richard Wolff;
introduction by Gayatri Spivak.
    p.   cm. – (A new directions/rethinking Marxism title)
Includes bibliographical references and index.
ISBN 0-7453-0707-8
    1. Sex role–Economic aspects. 2. Sexual division of labor.
3. Marxian economics. 4. Households. 5. Feminist theory.
I. Resnick, Stephen A. II. Wolff, Richard D. III. Title.
IV Series: New directions/rethinking Marxism.
HQ1075.F7   1994
305.3–dc20   93-51060
                                                                        CIP

ISBN 0 7453 0707 8 hbk

Designed and produced for Pluto Press by
Chase Production Services, Chipping Norton, 0X7 5QR
Typeset from authors' disk by
Stanford Desktop Publishing Services, Milton Keynes
Printed in Finland by WSOY

Contents

Acknowledgements

The authors thank Jack Amariglio, Julie Graham, and Kim Lane Scheppele for their close readings and helpful criticisms of original drafts of Chapter 1. We also benefited from comments on Chapter 1 and our 'Reply' in Chapter 2 that were made by anonymous reviewers for *Rethinking Marxism* which published them in Volume 2 (Winter 1989) and Volume 3 (Summer 1990). Drafts of various chapters were presented at several meetings and conferences of the Association for Economic and Social Analysis (AESA); we are grateful for especially valuable comments and criticisms from many AESA members which we have incorporated into this book. Helpful suggestions were also obtained in response to presentations of parts of the book at meetings of the Socialist Scholars Conference, National Women's Studies Association, Union of Radical Political Economics, and the Conference on Gender and Class at the University of Antwerp, Belgium. Frank Annunziato, Rosalyn Baxandall, Barbara Ehrenreich, and Richard Lichtman made useful and much appreciated suggestions for revisions, as did many students in classes at the University of Massachusetts where many of the arguments in this book were presented and subject to critical scrutiny. Bruce Norton, the editor of the series of which this book is a part, was helpful in many ways in bringing this book to completion. Lastly, we wish to thank Gayatri Chakravarty Spivak for preparing a valuable and provocative introduction.

Editor's Preface

We are proud to present the work which follows as the first entry in the *New Directions/Rethinking Marxism* series. We are especially proud because, in line with our aspirations for the series, the book measures new ground. While households are well-established concerns in Feminist thought, Marxist analysts have generally not brought them to the forefront of theory as Fraad, Resnick and Wolff do here. Nor have either Marxist or Feminist analysts envisioned households in quite these terms. Opening new paths into a domain in which much of life transpires, the book promotes a radically new understanding of gender, class and power processes at home and abroad.

It may be helpful to call attention in advance to a general characteristic of the analysis. As the authors insist, no *a priori* necessities link household labor and surplus labor to the needs of capitalist firms. Nor do such necessities bind household power relations, gender identifications, and class processes outside the household. Yet these things are related and interdependent, in contradictory ways which will change as other social processes change. In this respect the book participates in the movement away from economic and other determinisms to which many Feminists, Marxists, postmodernists and others have contributed. Fraad, Resnick and Wolff refuse to deduce linkages from abstractly posited characteristics of either capitalism or patriarchy. They urge us first of all to distinguish between different aspects of life and to recognize the ever-changing ways in which these distinct aspects shape one another.

Having done so, new relationships can be seen and new hypotheses advanced. The authors indeed outline a revolution in the configuration of gender and class within households in the United States. They also link the crisis in contemporary US. households to phenomena ranging from anorexia nervosa to Reaganomics and crisis in capitalist enterprises. Along with other recent papers which draw on Fraad, Resnick and Wolff's work,[1] these arguments begin to identify new patterns and possibilities in the turmoil of contemporary change.

Because both its general approach and particular claims are innovative and controversial, the initial argument the authors present (Chapter 1) is followed by the comments of six prominent Feminist theorists (Chapter 2, which also includes a response by Fraad, Resnick and Wolff). While Chapters 3 and 4 are new, all the material in Chapters 1 and 2 originally appeared in *Rethinking Marxism*. We would like to thank the commentators – Julie Matthaei, Zillah Eisenstein, Kim Lane Scheppele, Nancy Folbre, Heidi Hartmann, and Stephanie Coontz – for permission to reproduce their contributions here. Jack Amariglio, *Rethinking Marxism*'s editor, arranged the interchange and oversaw its original appearance.

To provide further commentary we asked another prominent Feminist scholar, Gayatri Spivak, to introduce the book. As will be seen, the introduction Professor Spivak furnished not only provides context for what follows but pushes in new directions as well. Embracing Fraad, Resnick and Wolff's separation of class concepts from a progressive narrative of historical development, she explores various possibilities which this move enables – for a better start towards understanding gender and other processes within households, for solidarity among people living in different areas of the world, and for a new kind of interaction between Feminist and Marxist ideas. We are grateful for the new dimensions her introduction provides.

Finally, we would very much like to thank Anne Beech, who assisted and encouraged the book throughout its long development.

Bruce Norton
Series Editor

Introduction

Gayatri Chakravorty Spivak

This book is an opening for a way to take Marxist-Feminism into new directions, away from some of the problems that it has had. It may be difficult for some of us to understand that Harriet Fraad, Stephen Resnick and Richard Wolff are not trying to deny the historical. They are trying to look at the relatively autonomous sphere of the household and the set of class processes as an explanatory model. In such an attempt the household can be seen as what they are calling 'feudal'. To be able to see that in capitalist society there is an important element that can be described as 'feudal' at work in the household is of course an absurdity as big as chattel slavery within nascent industrial capitalism. We have to come to terms with the idea that this is not the historically 'feudal', in its proper place. We do not want to replay, among Marxist-Feminists, the old battle between E.P. Thompson and Althusser in Thompson's *Poverty of Theory*. This is a new way of looking at the household, and it can give an impetus to struggles within and about households. To say that 'actual feudal societies' were not like this does not take away the strength of what is being offered.

The book offers us a way of looking at the misfit between the household and the larger society which may allow us to go into areas, or countries, where the misfit is not precisely this one. One might see this feudal model of the household as operative in various other kinds of conjunctures. So it can in fact produce a certain sort of commonality between different areas of the world, which is going to be very useful, without necessarily looking at other areas as less advanced, the United States as more advanced, Europe as the proper model, and so on.

From such a strategic viewpoint we can look at the goal of Feminism when we focus on the household. It suggests that to look at the liberal bourgeois household as a goal from within which you make reforms is not sufficient. Fraad, Resnick and Wolff's analysis shows us that that is not a *telos*, and there are no invariable connections between the broader capitalist society. Many activists think that what one should bring into the African–American community is the possibility of what one can call a stable bourgeois household. In other kinds of contexts, for the world's women, in planning within 'Women in Development', within Feminisms in various countries, attention is often focused on the establishment of the safe nuclear

family as a goal. The analysis in this book, which uses the household as a
space for class struggle, also undermines that teleological move.

This is of course the typical gain of a point of view which detaches explanatory models from a *necessary* historical scenario. It is quite correct that this
sort of analysis does not want to align itself with a historical story. As the
authors themselves put it, history need not always be thought in sequence.

Apart from the criticism that the truly feudal had a different historical
manifestation, we might also be puzzled because the sort of family situation
the book describes seems to have emerged in what is called, in the
Anglo–US context, the Victorian era. The point has been made that
certain kinds of possibilities of legal redress emerged by the very processes
that constituted the Victorian domesticated bourgeois nuclear family. If we
hang on to the analysis provided here, we may be able to see the limits of
those legal redresses. The gender arena is productive of meanings. And the
meanings produced by the domestication of love assisted the very denial
of investigating the household in feudal terms. (We must keep in mind
that, in the authors' understanding, 'feudal' is the site of coding of affective
value, not just economic value.) And that denial is part of the reason why
just those possibilities of legal redress are not enough. If we do not investigate this paradox, there is a certain sort of legitimation-by-reversal of the
ideal of domesticity that came with the Victorian emergence of the kind
of family that the writers of this book are pointing at as the habitation of
feudal values, not just of feudal class processes.

What we are looking at is the kind of fine practical gain made when the
connection between history and theory is strategically loosened. You do
not destroy it, but you loosen that connection, as an alternative way of
approaching a problem. If you inevitably tie theory to history understood
as narrative sequence, it remains so situation-specific that it has no use any
more. It will be a little difficult to think such a loosening through so that
we can use it, because it is counterintuitive. Sometimes analytical tools are
useful *when* they are counterintuitive.

Now this book has laid out these conflicts and these debates for all readers
to see. It is a collective project, so that we actually look at the conflict as
it exists and therefore we can read ourselves into it, make up our minds
about how to deal with what may be our own problems with the text. I
think that is a bold way of setting out such a project.

We have considered how important this book is as a beginning, so that,
analytically loosening the connection between historical authority and
theoretical robustness, as it were, we can actually use the approach it
develops for purposes of a struggle which is not situation-specific. Having
said this, I want to point out a few ways in which this model can be, as I

would say in my own kind of language, set to work. Because it seems to me, and I think it is also clear from the nature of the text, that the judgement on this theoretical model will come in its setting to work.

Now, in order for its setting-to-work, we will have to consider the *appropriately historical* in its very differences. One of the big points that I am sure a traditional historicist critic would make is that the ideologies which serfs had toward their feudal lord, and the ways in which feudal resistances were organized and were effective, do not resemble the ideologies at work within the domestic space described here. I think that this historical difference can in fact give a certain kind of impetus precisely to the understanding of gendering as a locus of meaning. Why is it that the structures within which the male model of feudalism developed are taken as the historically correct model? After the attempt to separate into relatively autonomous spheres, and to loosen 'history' from 'theory' which Fraad, Resnick and Wolff propose – risky and imperfect procedures, of course – if we look again at the historical workings of the model which even Feminist historians accept as the workings that can be appropriately called feudal, we may capture the operation of those ideological remnants that survived right through all the models of resistance that are 'correctly' called 'feudal', and have residually come to roost in the 'Victorian'-model household. Men's and women's histories cannot share the same sequential labels. Of course, we cannot have the *same* kind of patriarchal loyalty structures, and the *same* possibilities of resistance, within this persistence of the feudal residual structure, unmoored from its recognizable so-called historical connection. When our risky delinking procedure is 'set to work', we could learn something by allowing the historical narrative back in again, but in this new way, rather than protecting the correct sequence as *the* historical and the delinking itself as *the* theoretical. I will look forward to that. And this book will allow us to go in that direction.

I do think however that if one rehearses the old objections that US Feminism has had against Marxist analysis, then this project is going to founder. It is then going to look as if this is too 'Marxist,' and therefore it denies female realities. That is not the nature of the enterprise here. The nature of the enterprise is simply to unmoor the explanatory model from the narrative. Of course the model has not been developed to a high degree of sophistication. This is a beginning. Nothing is to be gained by insisting that within 'feudalism' as such the relationships within what could be called the household were not the same. That is precisely the point. The differences are gendered. Why call it 'feudal'? Because the ideological support for the economic resembles the feudal sufficiently.

The use of the word 'feudal' may be powerful as a tool of struggle. The domesticated notion of love is not often questioned by mainstream women. The idea of love and affect, even within the mainstream gay movement, remains more and more an unquestioned good. If it is possible to show that this ideology is underpinned by the feudal class process, and is a condition and effect of feudal class processes, then quite apart from its scholarly appropriateness, as a tool of struggle it can be useful. Since internalized gendering is something that stands a good deal in the way of the Feminist struggle, I think looking at class struggles within the household, rather than always seeing the latter as outside, can be very useful. I don't think this is *supposed to be* an exhaustive and rich and full analysis. This is a strategic use of theory for a better understanding of the stakes in a struggle.

And this may also allow us to complicate the model by bringing in the question, not only of labor, but of pleasure. The question of pleasure, and the question of childbearing and childrearing, undermines theoretical explanations of exchange and surplus. The undermining is not a negative critique. If you attempt to do what I have been calling a delinking separation between history and theory, you may get a chance to look at the affective value coding – what our authors call gender as the locus of meaning – internalized as gendering. This gives us a breathing space, temporary if you will, not to produce the coded alibis ourselves, overflowing the limits of theoretical analysis. It does seem to me that questions of pleasure and affect and the peculiar nature of childbearing and childrearing are issues which can be added back in. I am looking at it on the model of letting history and affect seep back in after we have made the first analytical separation, so that we can complicate our analysis and set it to work.

As for the matter of the production of 'feudal' loyalty. In the future when we use the model we will have to think about what is called psychoanalysis. Of course psychoanalysis may not apply all over the world, although it *can* be institutionally imposed by begging the question. But we are writing of the white western middle-class or of those who want access into its civil society. Let us, therefore, consider psychoanalysis, which may help us in plotting the production of affect, and the manipulation of loyalty.

The writers of this book want future Feminists, the readers of this work, to broaden the focus themselves in forthcoming work, I think. If one did indeed broaden this project transnationally (and I've already touched upon this question briefly when I said that the notion of feudality can allow us to see it at work in places which, by the old 'historical' model, are not in the same place on the evolutionary grid), one could perhaps look at the worldwide phenomenon of what is called 'homeworking'. Sweated labor at home, absorbing the cost of workplace safety, health, management, etc., is peripheralized within Feminist analysis, as is quite clearly recognized by many Feminist activists. But one of the major phenomena in the support of transnational capitalism. This extremely diversified phenomenon can continue because organization here is almost impossible as a result of varieties of internalized gendering. Work like this might make it possible to discover structures of complicity between our resistance to theory and the internalized gendering of these kinds of workers that would undermine the usual sort of benevolent cultural supremacist presuppositions that many activists carry with them into this arena. Both work to assure the continuity of 'feudalism'. Those who 'set to work' do perhaps 'know' this, but it does not infiltrate into academic definitions.

As I said in the beginning, this approach, in breaking class process in the household from the 'historical' sequence, makes visible a scandal analogic to the existence of chattel slavery within nascent industrial capitalism. Thus one might look at debt bondage today, where the alibi is 'Women in Development,' or 'Population Control,' with *its* manipulation, pro and contra, of the relationship between gendered 'feudal' meaning, and finance capital. I mean by this the pattern of debt bondage within development, in the so-called 'developing countries'. The way in which the International Monetary Fund and the World Bank and the transnational agencies and the subcontracting agencies and the donor countries, and so on, play the game is by mortgaging the future: debt bondage. And Feminists stuck on the European mode of production *sequence* might be surprised how often feudal household class processes are imbricated here. 'Feudalization of the periphery' is hand in glove with the 'central' household in the gendered sphere. We need to become aware of this, rather than rehearse New Left debates local to the US. Then we can look at how debt bondage actually connects with existing practices and so-called traditions of bond slavery and bonded prostitution. This kind of analysis, which unhinges the narrative of history from a Marxist analysis of class process, could be extremely useful. As we know, traditional class analysis has not been able to cope with these phenomena. I'm not suggesting that this is the only way to look at it. But the argument, often advanced, that 'traditional' practices belong to another discursive formation, and therefore – especially when it comes to the struggle – are not commensurate with or coherent with our own arena, the fully developed capitalist arena, can be set aside, for a little, if we went into it with this sort of project in mind. This is something that one looks forward to, and I think an analysis such as this can take it on board.

Having talked now at some length about the kinds of ways in which the project this book develops can help us rethink the problems of Marxist-Feminism, and in which it can be set to work, I would like to suggest also that it would be useful for masculinist Marxism (which is sometimes called Marxism as such). The latter has of course worked on the separation of the private and the public, and has seen class struggles as belonging to the public sphere. So it should be understood that, in analytical terms, for the workings of class to be seen in the domestic sphere is in itself a Feminist

gesture. It is not giving over gendered space to class, but in fact understanding class through gendering. We have been so involved in fighting
the idea of class restricted to the public that it may be difficult for us to
recognize what is at work here. But that very defamiliarization, that recon-
stellation of the conceptual tool that is class will, I think, be very useful. It
is, in other words, a rewriting of the category of class in Feminist terms. I
don't think there is in this book an acceptance of the old-fashioned understanding of class as the privileged instance at all – unless one wants to see
it that way. It is not factoring gender into class. It is rather a certain
expansion, or opening up, of the concept of class. It does not resemble
what class has been understood to be. I think it is up to us to think this
through, with its implications.

In the essay by Stephen Resnick and Richard Wolff in Chapter 3, we
see how difficult it is to make the analysis equal to the possibilities of this
move. It is a very fine essay, which does show us how, if you consider
gender issues, the economic description of the Reagan–Bush years is rather
different. But I would venture to say that here, too, we have not really
seen what can be done once we become more habituated to this change
in the concept of class. It seems to me that much more can be done than
gendered descriptions of economic *events/processes/reality*. Although in the
case of both the first chapter and the third I am fully aware of the importance
of what the authors are doing, in both cases I am really looking forward
to what this model of analysis can do (in the future), as indeed I think the
writers are as well. I do feel that there are ways in which the conceptualization, or the thinking of economic reality, might change if class is
unmoored from the public sphere. That I look forward to.

When 'communist' and 'ancient' class processes are thought, there are
two ways of looking at the use of these terms. I think this is the boldest
part of the first chapter – I think the writers are taking the greatest risk in
using these terms. But we have to keep in mind, it seems to me, if we want
to make this useful, that they are using them in the way in which I have
suggested in the case of the word 'feudal'. That is to say, unmooring the
words from a historical progression of cause and effect, or determination.
And just as I suggested in connection with the 'feudal' that at a certain point
you let history seep back in to learn new lessons, I think we can look forward
to new lessons here – at the time of the setting-to-work of the ideas. If we
let the public sphere seep back in, I think we will begin to consider how
these ancient and communist structures work or do not work within the
state. Then, it seems to me, we might do something rather unusual.
Because we will have said that we have seen what we are calling a
'communist' and an 'ancient' model at work, and on that basis we can take
the household as a model for the state. Rather than, as in the evolutionary narrative, always putting the family as before the process of thinking

'state'. Consider this in a global focus! This would also be extremely useful in situations in the developing world where the state is being substituted for the old patriarchal family as the locus of patriarchal oppression, because the state is 'rational'. And, since in the new world order transnational capital is beginning to restrict and constrict the redistributive project of the state, the state is obeying the *rationale* of transnational capital. It is an evolutionary historical narrative at work to justify this ruse of reason, even in the words 'developing' and 'developed'. The possibilities for this unmooring of class from the public and rational are rich for future work, which may not be constantly put in its place because, in gendered space, it dares to situate the so-called gains made by the bourgeois revolution as a profound and surreptitious anchoring of the 'feudal'.

In Harriet Fraad's study of anorexia (Chapter 4) the two aspects of this project are visible. First, it attempts to rewrite the idea that class operates only in the economic sphere or the public sphere or the 'world', whereas gender operates in the private sphere or the domestic sphere or the 'home'. And, secondly, it tries to question the idea that when you actually bring Feminism to bear on Marxism, you consider the gender analysis as subsuming the class analysis; whereas, when you bring Marxism to bear on Feminism, you consider the class analysis as subsuming the gender analysis. The failure of such theoretical enterprises, Fraad seems to suggest, is acted out in anorexia. It is almost as if the need for the book's theoretical enterprise is written in the body of the anorectic. My own predilections are to a brand of psychoanalysis which is less committed to subjective agency, or expressive intention. Nonetheless I think Harriet Fraad's study of anorexia is so revealing because there are clues all through the study that in fact what she is really talking about is the body as a kind of textualized agency that the anorectic is not able to read correctly. Again and again – in her notion of anorexia as a hunger strike, which leads to the contradiction of obsession with the flesh, for example – the contradiction points at the notion of the body's textuality, uses the idea that we are constituted as subjective agents by reading the body's signals right. That itself has come unhinged because – and this is a fascinating argument – the two are inscribed in the class processes of two separate spheres: the public as capitalist and the private as feudal (in the book's terms). So that the scandal, again, of chattel slavery within nascent industrial capitalism, the scandal inscribed in the phantom of *Beloved* – the scandal of the feudal (in the special sense) within post-industrial capitalism – is carried by the anorexic body. This, to me, is the virtue of Chapter 4. I think this too can lead us in further directions, seeing how this theoretical enterprise is not just simply something to apply to the *socius*, but something the failure of which is inscribed in the *socius*.

Perhaps this is going beyond strict adherence to Althusser into more decon-
structive views of the relationship between theory and its setting-to-work.
But I believe that the writers of the book had hoped that I would bring
some of those considerations into the reading of this book.

There are questions which remain, for example about the apparent
emergence of male anorexics today, or issues concerning homosexual
households. I hope one of the implications of this kind of study is to show
that sexuality and gendering are not identical. That may be the greatest
advantage of unhinging history and theory in order to reconstellate them,
concatenate them, after seeing how their securely hinged closure can help
to keep old wounds forever open.

Gayatri Chakravorty Spivak
Avalon Foundation Professor
in the Humanities
Columbia University

For Every Knight in Shining Armor, There's a Castle Waiting To Be Cleaned: A Marxist-Feminist Analysis of the Household

Question: What in your view is the exact connection between patriarchal oppression and capitalist oppression?
Answer: Of course housework doesn't produce any (capitalist) surplus value. It's a different condition to that of the worker who is robbed of the surplus value of his work. I'd like to know exactly what the relationship is between the two. Women's entire future strategy depends on it.

Simone de Beauvoir (Schwarzer 1984, 38)

Today, nonfamily households (people who live alone or with unrelated people) outnumber married couples with children. The pundits may be saying Americans are returning to traditional lifestyles, but the numbers show that it just isn't so.

Judith Waldrop (1989, 22)

Households and their profound influence upon modern society have been badly and unjustifiably neglected in social analysis. Marxist theory, and particularly its class analytics, can be applied to contemporary households to help remedy that neglect. Feminist theories of gender, of the social construction of what 'male' and 'female' are supposed to mean, can likewise yield original insights into the dynamics of households today. We propose here to combine the two approaches into a distinctive Marxist-Feminist theory of the household.

Instead of observing the unwritten rule that Marxist class analysis must stop at the doorstep and must not address what happens inside the household, we investigate the class processes inside. Similarly, we extend some Feminist discussions of the interaction between class and gender in markets and enterprises to an examination of their interactions within households. The resulting analysis shows that households in general, and contemporary US

1

households in particular, display specific kinds of interwoven class structures and gender identifications. The class positions occupied within households depend upon and shape the definitions of gender lived by the members of such households. Moreover, the class and gender positions within households operate as both causes and effects of those positions outside households.

Finally, our theoretical argument and the empirical evidence that we offer will claim that basic class and gender transformations (revolutions) are underway in the United States today. They are occurring inside households – precisely where too many theorists and activists overlook them. Class and gender struggles are fought inside households as well as at other social sites (enterprises, the state, etc.). We shall suggest how those struggles within the households can influence virtually every other aspect of contemporary social life.

Marxist-Feminists have taken the lead in recognizing the importance of the household for social analysis. Unlike more traditional Marxists, they do not reduce the way society defines gender and allocates social positions along gender lines to matters of secondary importance. Nor do they view such matters as deriving from class. Unlike many other Feminists, they refuse to exclude issues of class from the explanation of gender divisions and their social consequences. Finally, their work has helped to put the household high on the agenda for social analysis, taking it out of the shadows to which most Marxist and non-Marxist social theories consign it.[1] However, Marxist-Feminists have not yet been able to integrate well-defined class and gender concepts systematically into a theory which recognizes and incorporates their mutual dependence and transformation. No complex class and gender analysis of the modern household is yet available; hence to begin one is a goal of this book.

We begin with a precise Marxist definition of 'class'; the term refers to the production, appropriation, and distribution of surplus labor (Resnick and Wolff 1987, Chapter 3). It is thus a set of economic processes – processes concerned with the production and distribution of goods and services. Class is not the name for a group of people.[2] Women cannot comprise a class any more than men can; rather, women and men participate in class processes in various ways. It follows that wherever class processes may be shown to occur in society – wherever surplus labor is produced, appropriated, and distributed – that is an appropriate site for class analysis. As we shall show, this includes the household. We must then disagree with such Marxist-Feminists as Heidi Hartmann (1974, 1981a and 1981b), Nancy Folbre (1982 and 1987), Zillah Eisenstein (1979), and others who apply class analysis only outside the boundaries of the household and chiefly to enterprises.[3] All kinds of class process and all sites are grist for our mill, proper objects of Marxist-Feminist analysis.[4]

We also understand gender as a set of processes. Unlike the class processes, which are economic processes, the gender processes are cultural or ideological processes (Barrett 1980, 84–113). That is, they involve the production and distribution of meanings. By gender processes, we mean the processes of defining one specific difference between people – literally what it means to be female or male – and distributing such meanings socially. Just as one's life is shaped by the particular class processes in a society, it is also shaped by the gender processes in that society. Indeed, how people produce, appropriate and distribute surplus labor depends on – and helps to determine – how they produce, distribute and receive definitions of what it means to be male and female.

As Marxist-Feminists, we ask the following questions about any site in a society that we may analyze:

1. Do class processes occur at this site, and if they do, which particular kinds of class process are present?
2. What gender processes occur in this society; that is, what meanings are attached to the concepts of male and female?
3. How do the class and gender processes interact at this site to shape and change it and the broader society?

In this book we address these questions in connection with the household in the contemporary United States.

Our Marxist class analytics (Resnick and Wolff 1987, Chapter 3) distinguish necessary from surplus labor and fundamental from subsumed class processes. By necessary labor, we mean the amount needed to produce the current consumption of the producers themselves. Surplus labor is then the amount they perform beyond what is necessary. This surplus labor (or its products) is received – 'appropriated' in Marxist terms – either by the people who produced it or by others. Those who appropriate the surplus then distribute it to themselves or to others. The organization of the production, appropriation and distribution of surplus labor comprises what we mean by a class structure.

The *fundamental class process* refers to the producing and appropriating of surplus labor. Individuals who participate in fundamental class processes (i.e., occupy fundamental class positions) do so either as producers or appropriators of surplus labor or both. For example, the worker who performs surplus labor in a capitalist commodity-producing enterprise and the capitalist who appropriates that surplus are occupying the two capitalist fundamental class positions. The *subsumed class process* refers to the distribution of the surplus labor (or its products) after it has been appropriated. Individuals can participate in a subsumed class process (i.e., occupy subsumed class positions) either by distributing surplus labor or by receiving a distribution of it. For example, the creditors of a commodity-producing capitalist enterprise and its hired supervisors obtain distributions (in the forms of interest payments and supervisory salaries, respectively) out of the surplus the enterprise appropriates. The distributing capitalist and the recipients of the distributions (creditors and supervisors) are occupying the two subsumed class positions. The subsumed class process aims generally to secure the conditions of existence of the fundamental class process (the two conditions in our example were credit and supervision). The appropriators distribute their surplus so as to continue to be able to appropriate it.

The Marxist tradition has recognized and specified different forms of the fundamental and subsumed class processes: communist, slave, feudal, capitalist, and so forth (Hindess and Hirst 1975). However, while Marx and Marxists named each form in terms of a historical period in which it was prominent, each has been found, in Eric Hobsbawm's words, to 'exist in a variety of periods or socio-economic settings' (Marx 1965, 59). The point for Marxist class analysis is to inquire about which of the known forms of the class processes are present in any particular society or social site chosen for scrutiny. It aims to assess their interactions and impacts upon the societies in which they occur. What we intend here is to focus Marxist class analysis on households within the contemporary United States.

We use the term 'exploitation' in the precise Marxist sense as the appropriation of surplus labor from the direct laborer; it is an economic term referring to the fundamental class process. In contrast, we use 'oppression' to designate the political processes of dominating other persons (directing and controlling their behavior). To exploit persons, then, means to appropriate surplus labor from them, while to oppress them is to dominate them. We separate questions about how individuals understand their situation (i.e., are persons aware of being exploited or oppressed and do these conditions occur against their wills?) from the situation itself. We use the two terms to distinguish certain economic from certain political processes, to explore their interactions, and then to inquire about how they are understood.

We approach gender from one Marxist perspective among Feminist theories. Gender refers to certain ideological processes within a culture. These include the production and distribution of sets of meanings which are attached to primary and secondary sex characteristics. Gender processes usually (but not always) pose differences as binary opposites. Biological differences between the sexes function as signs or markers to which meanings of femininity, as opposed to (as the 'other' of) masculinity, are affixed. Physical differences serve as rationalizations or explanations for differences (oppositions) attributed to males and females across the entire spectrum of life expressions, from sexual preferences to emotional and intellectual qualities to career orientations.[5]

For us, gender exists in the realm of ideology, not biology. Gender processes project particular ideologies of the differences and relationships between female and male. Men and women engage in gender processes (as producers, distributors, and receivers of such ideologies) at all social sites – enterprises, churches, states, households, and so forth. A society produces multiple and often contradictory gender processes since they are shaped by all the other processes of the society. Legal, financial, ethnic, religious and many other pressures combine to shape different gender processes projecting different conceptions of women and men. One pervasive gender process conceives of housework and childrearing as 'natural' or 'preferred' vocations for females, while other kinds of labor performed outside the home are more 'natural' or 'preferred' for males. An alternative gender process rejects such conceptions and argues instead for a notion of innate equality between men and women. Other gender processes offer still other conceptions of male and female. Individuals are pushed and pulled by the contradictory definitions of identities and proper lifestyles that are projected by alternative gender processes.

How individuals understand gendered identities influences what class positions they will accept or seek. Gender processes are conditions of existence for class processes; they participate in determining them. At the same time, gender processes in any society are in part determined by the class processes there. How individuals participate in the production, appropriation, and distribution of surplus labor influences their conceptualization of gender. As we shall argue, households are social sites in which gender and class continuously shape and change one another.

Households and Class Structures

Historically, the term 'household' has carried many different meanings. Sometimes it has referred to the living space occupied by members of a family and sometimes also to the family's working space. However, households have often included persons not considered family members, while family has often included persons not sharing a particular household. Indeed, 'family' has been as variously defined as 'household'. To begin our class analysis of households in the contemporary United States we need first to specify what we mean.

Our analysis focuses initially on households that display certain basic characteristics. They contain an adult male who leaves the household to participate in capitalist class processes (at the social site of the enterprise) to earn cash income. They also contain an adult female, the wife of the male, who remains inside the household. They may also contain children, elderly parents and others, but that is of secondary importance at this initial phase of the analysis. The adult female works inside the household in the tasks of shopping, cleaning, cooking, repairing clothes and furniture, gardening, and so on. While such households do not describe the lives of all residents of the United States in both the past and the present, they do describe a household type generally viewed as quite widespread in the past and still significant in the United States today. In any case, our analysis of this type will then make possible a comparative analysis of other types characterizing contemporary households.

A Marxist analysis asks whether class processes exist inside this household type. There seems to be little dispute among Marxists that class processes exist outside the household in the United States. The male is usually presumed to participate in class processes at the enterprises where he is likely to be employed producing surplus labor for a capitalist. But does the female at home participate in class processes as well, and if so, how?

We believe that she does. She is a direct laborer inside the household. She transforms raw materials (uncooked food, unclean rooms and clothes, broken furniture, etc.) by laboring with produced means of production (stoves, vacuum cleaners, washing machines and detergents, various kinds of household hand tools, etc.). The results are use-values consumed by household members: prepared meals, cleaned rooms and clothes, mended furniture, and so on. Moreover, her labor is not only productive of such use-values, it is also divisible into necessary and surplus components. She does not only produce for her own consumption (necessary labor); she also produces more than that. She performs surplus labor. Her husband appropriates her surplus labor in the form of the household use-values that she produces for him. From a Marxist class analytic standpoint, this wife in this type of household is engaged in a fundamental class process; so too is her husband.

Now this form of the fundamental class process is clearly not capitalist. The husband does not buy the labor power of the wife by paying her wages, no exchange of commodities occurs between them, nor does he sell on the market as commodities the use-values she produces. Since the products of her surplus labor are not sold, her surplus labor has no exchange value as it would have if she were participating in a capitalist fundamental class process. The husband does not engage in the drive to maximize some 'profit' derived from her surplus labor, nor does he compete with others to do so. Therefore, if our class analysis of this household is to proceed, we must inquire as to what other, noncapitalist form of the fundamental class process best captures what is happening.

A consideration of the various noncapitalist forms of the fundamental class process discussed in the Marxist literature readily suggests which form best fits our household. It is the feudal form, that particular kind of fundamental class process which takes its name from medieval Europe, although it has existed at many other times both in Europe and elsewhere across the globe.[6] The feudal form is appropriate because it requires no intermediary role for markets, prices, profits, or wages in the relation between the producer and the appropriator of surplus labor.[7] The producer of surplus on the medieval European manor often delivered his/her surplus labor (or its products) directly to the lord of the manor, much as the wife delivers her surplus to her husband. Ties of religion, fealty, loyalty, obligation, tradition, and force bound serf and lord much as parallel marital oaths, ideology, tradition, religion, and power bind husbands and wives in the sort of household we are analyzing here.

Of course, the presence of the feudal form of the fundamental class process is not the same as the presence of the feudalism that existed in medieval Europe. The feudal form will be different depending upon the social context in which it occurs. Just as feudal class processes in seventeenth-century China differ from those in Latin America in the nineteenth century, so do feudal class processes in contemporary United States households differ from those present on medieval European manors.

An objection might be raised to the designation of this type of household class structure as feudal. Clearly this woman's surplus labor helps to reproduce the labor power that her husband sells to the capitalist. If she raises children, she might also be said to produce future labor power for capitalists to hire. Given such a basic importance to the sustenance of capitalism, one might infer that she occupies a position within the capitalist class structure. While we agree that she provides crucial conditions of existence for the capitalist class structure outside the household, that, *per se*, does not suffice to make her part of it any more than slaves in the southern United States whose cotton production was crucial to British capitalism made them occupants of capitalist class positions.[8] Class refers to particular social processes, and the woman in the household we are examining enters into no class process with capitalists. She does no surplus labor for them, and they distribute no appropriated surplus labor to her. Meanwhile, she does perform surplus labor which her husband appropriates inside the household.

It is conceivable that capitalists, fearing that housewives might not otherwise care for husbands and children, would decide to distribute some of their appropriated surplus directly to women in households. Then, by virtue of receiving such distributions, the women would participate in a capitalist subsumed class process. This conceivable but rarely evident situation should not be confused with notions such as the 'family wage.'

That males demand and sometimes obtain wages which are defined as partly for them and partly for their families is not equivalent to capitalists distributing directly appropriated surplus to women in households. The capitalist appropriator may distribute surplus to the male laborer or to the

woman in the household or to neither. Only if the appropriator distributes
to the woman is she involved in a capitalist subsumed class process. If the
capitalist distributes to the male laborer, then only the latter occupies the
subsumed class position. To collapse a distribution to the male as if it automatically passes to the female is to overlook precisely the sort of analysis
of the household we intend.

The capitalist class processes centered in enterprises are distinct from the
feudal class processes centered in the laborers' households, however much
the two class structures may reinforce each other in particular historical circumstances. Wages are value flows within a capitalist class structure. They
are conceptually distinct from the surplus labor flows within feudal class
structures. Keeping them distinct is the logical prerequisite here for exploring
the social relationship between them in the contemporary United States.

Capitalist and feudal class structures do not exhaust the possibilities
within households. One can imagine (and there is historical evidence to
suggest) that household members can be involved in slave class processes.
Likewise, what Marx called the 'ancient' fundamental class process, where
direct laborers produce and appropriate their own surplus labor individually, and the communist class process, where direct laborers do the same,
but do so collectively, could characterize households (Hindess and Hirst
1975; Gabriel 1989; Resnick and Wolff 1988; Amariglio 1984; and Jensen
1981). We will return to these latter two class structures to argue that there
is now a rapid transition to them in households in the United States.

In the feudal households we have described, the labor performed by
women (necessary plus surplus) can be conceptualized quantitatively.
Women spend blocks of hours shopping, preparing food, cleaning, repairing,
serving, counseling, and so forth. An extensive literature has established
that the American woman who is a full-time homemaker spends an average
of over eight hours per day (roughly 60 hours per week) cooking, cleaning,
preparing food, and so on.[9] We may suppose that three hours per day are
necessary labor, the quantity needed to reproduce the housewife's own
existence as a performer of household feudal labor. Then the other five
hours would be the surplus labor she performs for her husband.

The woman uses household means of production to provide surplus to
the man in the form of services, products, or cash. In the case of services,
for example, she cleans the man's living space in addition to her own. In
the case of products, she transforms raw foods into prepared meals for the
man as well as for herself. If she sells the products of her surplus labor –
sweaters, pies, childcare – she may deliver the cash receipts to the man.

For the feudal (rather than another) fundamental class process to exist
in such a household and for women (rather than men) to occupy the class
position of household serfs, the conditions of existence for this situation
must be in place. That is, there must exist other nonclass processes, the

combined effects of which produce such gender-divided feudal class processes in households.[10] We group these conditions of existence into three kinds of social process: the cultural, the political, and the economic.

By cultural processes, we mean the processes of producing and disseminating meanings in society. For example, a woman's performance of feudal surplus labor results partly from explanations in churches and schools that proper womanhood means caring for a home and the people within it while adopting a subordinate position in relationship to the 'master of the house.' Such explanations also typically deny, explicitly or implicitly, that exploitation or oppression exists in households.

By political conditions of existence, we mean processes of establishing and enforcing rules of household behavior and adjudicating disputes over those rules. Thus, for example, the fact that laws punish physical or sexual assault outside the home while treating such assault within marriage more leniently or not at all, helps to condition household feudalism and women's position as household serfs. The political processes of establishing and differentially enforcing such laws help to define the feudal sphere of the household in which the rights of women in the home are different from the rights of citizens outside of the household. The political power of the lord of the feudal manor similarly facilitated his extraction of surplus labor.

By economic conditions of existence, we mean the processes of producing and distributing goods and services. Thus, for example, the economic processes of paying wages and salaries for female labor power that average 70 per cent of that paid for male labor power pressure women into feudal households to achieve desired living standards. The commodity exchange processes outside the household then promote a different kind of exchange inside the household – women's indirect benefits from higher male paychecks in exchange for their production of household surplus labor for men.

Surplus labor appropriated by the husband is distributed by him (in labor service, product, or money forms) to accomplish a number of nonclass processes needed to secure the reproduction of the household's feudal class structure (assuming such reproduction is his goal). The recipients of these subsumed class distributions are expected to make sure that such nonclass processes occur. These occupants of subsumed class positions include individuals both within and without the household.

To ensure that the woman spends time producing surplus labor for the husband, feudal subsumed classes must, for example, secure processes of planning and organizing surplus labor tasks, directing and managing the surplus labor performed, replacing depleted feudal means of production, and increasing such feudal means. These form a subset of the nonclass processes of household life that must occur for the woman's feudal class position to exist and be reproduced.

One of the many possible divisions of labor within a feudal household might involve the woman performing most of these nonclass processes by herself, her husband only keeping records, while both share the bill-paying. The husband distributes portions of the surplus appropriated from his wife to defray the costs of securing these nonclass processes from those who actually perform them. He distributes a part of his wife's surplus labor time (in labor, product, or cash forms) directly to her performance of particular nonclass processes. He distributes another part to himself to enable him to perform particular nonclass processes.[11]

Of course, what subsumed class distributions aim to accomplish need not result. There is no guarantee that the needed nonclass processes will be performed properly or at all. For example, in the feudal household we have been considering, the wife may demand and receive a portion of her husband's appropriated surplus (as, say, a household budget) to sustain processes of household management. Suppose that she decided one day not to perform them, not to work beyond securing her own needs. She now cooks meals only for herself and cleans only her own space and clothing. Her husband arrives home to discover that his feudal existence as a surplus appropriator is in jeopardy. His wife is not running an efficient, well-managed, surplus labor operation within the household despite his satisfying her demand for a subsumed class distribution to do so.

His response might be to devote time to disciplining his wife to ensure her performance of surplus labor. He may supervise her directly. If he distributes a share of his appropriated surplus to himself to achieve either of these responses, he would then occupy a subsumed class management position within the household alongside any other class positions he may occupy.

Alternatively, gender processes may push her to discipline herself. She may need little if any motivation from her husband to do so. Such self-motivation can lead her both to produce a surplus and to manage its production efficiently. Gender processes may affirm that the household is the essential support of our society and that the essence of the household is its wife and mother. This might well instill in the woman the idea that her role in life as wife and mother is to shop, cook, clean, and so on, for her family while simultaneously becoming a super manager of all its activities. In such a cultural climate, she may well replicate the highly motivated managers of an industrial corporation.[12]

Men and women may then occupy different class positions within the feudal household – fundamental class positions as producers or appropriators of surplus labor and subsumed class positions as providers of this surplus labor's conditions of existence. To the degree that women occupy feudal subsumed class positions, they act to ensure their own continued exploitation. Men and women may share supervisory power in the household, just as they may share property ownership or anything else. The sharing of power or property does not necessarily lead to a rejection or even a questioning of the continued existence of feudal exploitation in households. Whether or not it does depends on the entire social context in which the power or property ownership occurs.

The male also distributes portions of feudal surplus appropriated from the woman to people outside the household. Such subsumed class distributions secure other conditions of existence of feudal households. To take one kind of example, consider certain fundamentalist Protestant churches, conservative Roman Catholic churches, and orthodox Jewish synagogues. Feudal households may distribute surplus labor to such institutions in the form of cash, contributions in kind, or women's auxiliary services of all kinds. A nonclass process that all these institutions perform is the preaching of doctrines that prohibit or discourage birth control and abortion. Two effects of these doctrines are unplanned and often unwanted children. The care for such children, urged on women by all manner of other preachings and teachings in those religious institutions and at many other sites in society, ties women to their feudal household roles.

Consider, as one of several possible examples from the religious institutions cited, the orthodox Roman Catholic churches in the United States. They receive distributions of women's household surplus labor in several forms – as services in, for example, fund-raising, cleaning, and teaching; as products in meals offered to clerics and crafts given for the church to sell; and as cash in donations. Feudal husbands have appropriated surplus labor from their wives and distributed a portion of it to secure particular cultural (e.g., religious and gender) processes.[13] The churches in question preach doctrines prohibiting divorce, birth control, and abortion. They affirm that women are not created in God's image and should be kept from the priesthood and other authority positions within the hierarchy (O'Faolin and Martines 1973, 128–33; Rich 1976, 134–7; Reuther 1974, 41–116, 150–291; Adams and Briscoe 1971, 10–14).[14] Women's true vocation is maternal service as well as service to the husband. Such views are not limited to Catholic churches but exist comparably in fundamentalist Protestant churches and orthodox Jewish synagogues (Rich 1976, 135; O'Faolin and Martines 1973, 196–203; Delaney, Lupton and Toth 1976, 10). The doctrines propounding these views are cultural conditions of existence for female feudal surplus labor in households.[15] The religious institutions promoting such misogynistic attitudes often count women as the overwhelming majority of their active members.

We may now summarize our discussion to this point of the feudal household's complex class structure. First there are the fundamental class performers of feudal surplus labor – in our example, the women. Opposite them are the fundamental class appropriators of that surplus, the men. To secure certain conditions of existence of the household feudal fundamental class process, the surplus is distributed to persons who will engage in the nonclass processes that provide those conditions. Inside the feudal household, both men and women may provide some of these conditions and thus obtain distributions of surplus to enable them to do so. To the extent that men and women provide such conditions and receive such distributions, they occupy complex combinations of fundamental and subsumed class positions. Feudal surplus may also flow outside the household of its origins when other social sites (churches, schools, the state, etc.) provide its conditions of existence and receive, therefore, subsumed class distributions. Then a class linkage connects households to other sites.

All sorts of contradictions and changes are occurring inside feudal households and in their relations to other social sites. They contribute to basic changes in the United States where enterprises are predominantly capitalist rather than feudal in their class structure. Before examining the class contradictions and changes, however, we will consider the gender processes conditioning feudal households.

Gender Processes and the Feudal Household

Gender processes determine class processes and vice versa. Sustaining feudal household class structures requires that some people be exploited and that they somehow understand their situation to be desirable or the best available or else unavoidable. Gender processes, among others in the United States, have long inculcated in many women some or all of such understandings. In this way, gender processes have helped to fashion the feudal class structures inside households. Feudal class processes inside households have also contributed to prevalent gender processes in the United States. The exploited situation of women in feudal households has played its role in generating or supporting particular images of women and their proper roles in society. These gender processes have left deep impressions, even on women who have escaped from or altogether avoided feudal class positions.

One especially relevant set of gender processes concerns a particular concept or ideology of love. This concept of love is distributed through romance novels, magazines, legal principles, television and films, sermons, advertising, fairy tales, political speeches, and so forth. It holds that when a woman loves a man, a 'natural form' for that love is the desire to take care of that man by marriage, preparing his meals, and cleaning up after him. Men's love for women does not 'naturally' take this form. Instead it is said that males want love and sex from females but are rather more ambivalent about lifetime commitment, via marriage, to financial support for the family (Ehrenreich 1983, 42–51).

Within this ideology of love, particular definitions of male and female are elaborated. Men fear the loss of their freedom, while women strive to ensnare them into marriage. Females want marriage with its assumed home maintenance tasks, childbearing, and childrearing. Males relinquish their freedom somewhat begrudgingly or, in intense love, freely relinquish it. Females seemingly have no freedom to relinquish. This ideology of love affirms that such marriages represent the best possible relationship for men, women, and children from their individual points of view (it secures 'fulfilment' and 'happiness'). It is also posited as the best in terms of society's well-being.

In the context of such gender processes, feudal surplus labor production appears as a 'natural' outgrowth of female love. It is thus not considered to be 'labor' but rather has the meaning of 'nest-making,' a biological metaphor signaling the 'naturalness' of this way of expressing love. This ideology helps to impose on women their servile status and on men their lordly position within the household. Through this ideology, the love of one human being for another becomes a means to facilitate class exploitation between them. Even today, when women's exclusive *performance* of most housework is beginning to be questioned, the reality of women's special *responsibility* for household maintenance remains unchanged (Hartmann 1981a, 366–94; Blumstein and Schwartz 1983, 143–8; Pleck 1982, 251–333; Hayden 1984, 81–4; and Hewlett 1986, 88–90).

A second set of gender processes that helps to reproduce feudal households involves the production and spread of biologically essentialist theories in forms that range from scholarly treatises to casual conversations. The gender ideology of biological essentialism has several faces. 'Scientific' biological essentialism is represented by, for example, those theories that conceive feudal surplus labor in the household as an outgrowth of genetically programmed female passivity and male aggression (Ardrey 1961; Washburn and Lancaster 1968; Morris 1968 and 1969; Tiger 1969; Wilson 1976 and 1978; Lumsden and Wilson 1981; Barash 1982; Dawkins 1976). Females need a protected place to rear children. Males' superior aggression somehow facilitates their roles as protectors of females, whose passivity 'naturally' suits them for a private household situated outside of the aggression-ridden male spheres of industry and government. Women are, therefore, genetically suited to childbearing and household maintenance.

Biological essentialism can also appear with a religious face. God created women and men to be biologically different because he intended women to remain in the household rearing children while he intended men to function in the outside world. Such biological essentialism characterizes, for example, many anti-abortion movements: God intends women to bear children and people should not interfere with God's plans. Defining women in this way consigns them to home and housework and can serve to validate a feudal situation. Biological essentialism sometimes wears a psychoanalytic face. In some psychoanalytic schools, women are viewed as naturally passive and masochistic, willing to serve a cause or human being with love and selflessness, while men are naturally active and aggressive (Deutsch 1944, 219–324 and especially 273; Abraham 1920; Bonaparte 1934; Freud 1925). A feudal class position for women in the household would accord well with such views of women's nature. A variation on this theme emphasizes the physical appearance of female genitals as automatically generating the perception of them as castrated, lacking in comparison to male genitals. Females are, therefore, seen to be inferior; females disparage themselves and are disparaged by males. What can compensate females for their castrated anatomy is the ability to give birth, especially to sons (Erickson 1964, 582–606). To have babies and care for them in the household often follows as the social role for women warranted by their natural endowments.[16]

Gender processes affirming biological essentialism also surface within arguments about sexual activity. Males' aggressive sexual drives are contrasted to females' presumed lesser sexuality. Sex is described as something men want and women withhold or else they are thought to be suspect, tainted, and evil (Hays 1965; Prusack 1974, 89–116). Such gender processes impart a meaning to sexuality which implies that 'good' women (i.e., those not sexually active) need protection from men's rapacious desires. They need one man to protect them from all the others. Women who are sexually active outside the household are in dangerous territory, fair game for the others. In the feudal households, they are ostensibly protected in return for delivering their surplus labor.[17]

Still other gender processes mix biological essentialism with different notions of how or why women belong in households doing surplus labor for men. There is the view that women are irrational and morally weaker as well as physically weaker than men. Freud attributes women's inferior judgement to what he calls a lesser female super-ego (Freud 1977). Some writers cite women's menstrual cycles or childbearing as placing them closer to nature and further from culture (Ortner 1974, 67–88; for a criticism of such views see Coontz and Henderson 1986). In such meaning systems, women belong in the home doing housework and need the supervision of superior males. If they work outside the home, the appropriate circumstances will be household-like situations such as waitressing and nursing within male-supervised institutions.

Gender processes affirming women's inferiority do not necessarily or automatically relegate women to the household and to housework. The latter must themselves comprise a socially devalued sphere for the woman, as gender devalued, to be assigned to them.[18] Other cultural processes must rank household production and childcare as less important, less prestigious, and less productive. Then the conditions are in place for the feudal fundamental class process to combine with the inferiority status attributed to women to consign them to the role of feudal surplus labor performers.

The gender processes discussed here influence the experiences of women in households and in the class processes occurring there. They contribute to the shaping of women's conscious and unconscious ideas about themselves and their possibilities as female people. Many women today identify with their mothers who were usually feudal household serfs. They often feel intense pressure to validate their mothers' lives by following in their footsteps to become future feudal housewives and mothers (Chodorow 1978; Dinnerstein 1976; and Fraad 1985).[19]

While our focus here is the interplay of class and gender processes, they are only two kinds of the many processes that shape the feudal household we have been analyzing. We turn next to certain political and economic processes that are conditions of existence for feudal households and for the particular gender divisions of class positions that they exhibit.

Political and Economic Conditions of Existence

Political processes that formally or informally induce women to stay in feudal households performing surplus labor include a variety of laws and regulations. So-called 'protective' legislation for women (and not for men) often eliminates women from work assignments necessary for job and income advancement. Many state laws and regulations require men only nominally to support their children financially, while they actually require women to care for children physically. Laws and informal practices blocking women's access to birth control and abortion keep women at home caring for unplanned or unwanted children.

Many nonlegal regulations and conventions diminish women's options and so reinforce their feudal position in households. Sex discrimination in hiring and work assignment tends to keep women in lower-paid jobs. Corporate career advancement commonly requires adjusting one's life to weekend or evening meetings, unexpected overtime, and after-work socializing. Since such adjustments are difficult or impossible for women with primary childcare and household responsibilities, career advancement is all the more problematic. Sexual harassment can keep women out of the paid labor force altogether (Bergmann 1986, 308). Such conditions keep women dependent on the higher wage and salary incomes of men to raise children and secure desired living standards. That dependence translates into feudal household surplus labor production.

The absence of laws, or the failure to enforce laws, can also push women to 'prefer' household to extra-household labor. For example, failure to enforce equal rights on the job can keep women in the household. Without laws requiring job return after paid maternity and paternity leaves and low-cost childcare centers, women are left with the domestic burdens of infant care. The absence of laws providing free healthcare for the elderly and handicapped prevents women with such responsibilities at home from competing as equals in the labor markets.[20] A remarkable political condition of existence of the feudal household in the United States is the fact that its housewives are workers for whom virtually no legal protection exists – no minimum compensation, no limit on hours, no requirement for health or pension benefits, no mandatory vacations, and so on (Hayden 1984, 65).

Political processes also include domestic violence, the threat of the use of physical force inside the household to control the behavior of its members. These are the household equivalents of police and military forces in the wider society. The syndrome of the battered wife is now well documented (Chapman and Gates 1978; Dobash and Dobash 1979; McNulty 1980; Pagelow 1981; Roy 1982; and Stacey and Shupe 1983). The class and gender positions of the women within traditional households are effects, in part, of potential and actual physical force used against them there.

Governments in the United States tolerate a degree of violence in the household not tolerated elsewhere in the society.[21] A male spouse often has state-tolerated, if not officially sanctioned, freedom to dominate his wife physically. If and when the state intervenes in extreme cases, the abuser is often referred by the court to religious officials, psychiatrists, or marriage counselors, rather than being legally tried (Lerman 1981; United States Commission on Civil Rights 1982). Household violence is treated as fundamentally different from violence outside the household. The formal equality of all before the law, long seen as a political condition of existence of capitalism, is not in fact practiced inside the household. This is, perhaps, not surprising since it is feudalism and not capitalism that reigns there.

Indeed, there are arresting parallels between the political power of the man in the feudal household – whether or not exerted through physical force – and that of the medieval lords of feudal manors. The lords often vested this power, including force, in manorial officials whom they maintained for that purpose (important subsumed classes of that time) (Duby 1968, 228–31; Bennett 1971, 151–92). In the United States today, male spouses may themselves occupy similar subsumed class positions within their households, controlling and perhaps forcing their wives to occupy feudal class positions.

The feudal position of women in feudal households is conditioned by economic processes in the United States as well as by political and cultural processes. The economic processes generating levels and changes in wages and salaries, job benefits, pensions, and social security benefits influence the quality of the feudal housewife's life and her rationale for remaining in such a life. Now that most American women are employed outside the home in addition to their work inside it, these economic processes condition household feudal class processes through their direct impact on wives in paid employment. Since women earn 70 per cent of what men earn, and many millions of women hold part-time jobs with few or no benefits, they tend to remain financially dependent on men (Beechey and Perkins 1987; Beechey 1987). In this way, women's economic situations outside the household serve to reinforce their feudal positions within it.

Since infant and childcare are often private enterprises in the United States, their profit-driven prices keep many women at home or induce them to interrupt career progress to care for young children (Hewlett 1986, 82–8). Women stay home since their husbands can usually earn more in paid employment. Further, when women interrupt their careers, they earn even less over their working lifetimes and so heighten their reliance on the male's superior income and benefits. Moreover, evidence suggests that housework among couples is allocated in part on the basis of career success: the partner who has the more successful career does less or no housework (Blumstein and Schwartz 1983, 151–3). Such situations are conducive to feudal household class structures.

The pricing of commodities is another economic process that conditions the feudal household. High prices for meals (restaurants or 'take out'), home maintenance services, healthcare, transportation, and care for the elderly or disabled pressure women into the feudal household production of these goods and services in noncommodity form. To take another example, the economic process of lending money is often constrained by criteria, such as job histories and salary levels, that discriminate against women. Without access to credit, women lose another means of moving out of a feudal household class structure.

Property Ownership and Feudal Households

Surplus labor appropriation by males in feudal households may depend in part on differential access to property in the means of household production. There may be laws or customs in society established, adjudicated, and enforced which empower males rather than females to acquire and hold such property. If, in various ways, women are denied access to such property, much as serfs were denied it in medieval Europe, their propertylessness may push them into feudal household class positions. If, however, women stop being so denied because laws, customs, and economic conditions change, they may acquire and hold property in houses, appliances, and so on. If women also own household property, they need no longer depend on men for the means to enable them to perform necessary and surplus household labor. They might, for example, appropriate their own surplus while working with their own property in their own households. In this case, ancient class processes would replace feudal class processes in households.

This is by no means necessarily the case. Women's ownership and access to property is a change in only one condition of existence of household feudal class structures. Only the political process of ownership (political because it concerns control of behavior, namely people's access to objects) has changed. Since the existence of feudal households cannot be reduced to merely one of the many conditions of their existence, it follows that women's access to property may, but need not, undermine feudal households. Whether and to what extent it does so depends on all the other social processes that produce such households. Since each of these other social processes is continually changing, so too are their influences on the presence or absence of feudal households.

Suppose, for example, that women's ownership of household property coincides with gender processes stressing the propriety of women being mothers and obedient wives. Women may then perform more feudal surplus labor without even imagining the possibility of using their power over property to resist their husbands' demands. If gender definitions stress pride in expertise and dedication to housework, as well as pride in ownership, the female may work extra hard to clean the feudal household of which she is the co-owner. Her co-ownership might then be a condition of existence of more rather than less exploitation by her husband. Similarly, gender processes which affirm that males should be in charge of all financial and property matters may well convince women to relinquish in marriage all control over what they own to their feudal husbands. It may well not occur to a feudal wife to demand any subsumed class payment from her husband for his access to her property. Indeed, women who accept the gender notion of their own incapacity for financial management may willingly and freely convey control over their property to males. The feudal housewife might also fear psychological or physical retaliation from her husband should she protest or struggle against his use of her property, without payment, to exploit her feudally.[22]

All the other processes in society, including the conscious and unconscious processes within the family, combine to create gender processes specifying how individuals within households are to relate to, love, and mutually support one another. Within such relationships, joint husband and wife property ownership may be recognized as a progressive form of mutual sharing of material objects complementing the proper social role of each partner in his or her work. Gender processes may define the role of the male as the protector and supporter of the female by means of the sale of his labor power outside the household. The role for the female may be to do the same for the male by means of freely contributing her property and performing feudal surplus labor in the household.

The fact that women acquire property and the 'right' to demand payments for making its use available to feudal males will not undermine feudal household class structures if women readily perform surplus labor for their husbands because it is thought to be a 'natural' outgrowth of love. Within the ideology of love, it becomes unthinkable for women to use their political power to withhold property or to demand subsumed class payments for access to it. It is unthinkable, in part, because a woman can expect to get no support from others (courts, friends, etc.) if she does this.[23] The same ideology constrains the male appropriator of feudal surplus from making payments. Such actions would threaten and undermine the very social roles each has come to accept as a combination of nature, love, and socially acceptable behavior. These considerations may help to explain why joint property ownership between husbands and wives has not altered the feudal households of many Americans.

On the other hand, women's ownership of property may become a change of importance to the feudal household. Political power over property has enabled some women to alter the terms of their marriages or to resist them altogether. For example, women's threat to withhold their property may lead males to reduce their demands for surplus labor from their wives. The portion of the day that the female works for herself may expand at the expense of the portion of the day that she does surplus labor for the male in the feudal household. Then the feudal rate of exploitation has been altered in her favor. To take a second example, women property owners may demand increased subsumed class payments from their feudal husbands (e.g., larger household budgets) for making their property available to them: a greater distribution of the surplus labor they produce for their husbands. In both examples, the household's *feudal* class structure would not have changed. The quantitative dimensions of the housewife's feudal exploitation in the first example, and her receipt of subsumed class distributions in the second, would have changed.

We might expect such developments if the change in property ownership happened within a social context where, for example, women's liberation movements actively sought to alter the predominant concept of women as best suited to be society's homemakers and childbearers. To the extent that their efforts changed the prevalent gender processes and generated laws to reduce sexual harassment, sexual discrimination, and barriers to employment, women might be decreasingly inclined to accept their feudal positions in the household. Were women's acquisitions of property to provoke or at least to coincide with sufficiently changed gender processes that stress female independence and equality, and with complementary changes in other social processes, then it might become possible for women to force a fundamental change in the class structures of households. They might demand the dismantling of feudal households and their replacement, for example, by households in which men and women both perform necessary and surplus labor collectively, then also collectively appropriate their surplus and decide how to use it for their mutual benefit – Marx's idea of a communist class structure. As we shall argue, in some households this has happened and is happening.

The point is that change in the political process of property ownership enabling women to own property does not either weaken or strengthen feudal class processes in the traditional home. It does both. It grants a new degree of freedom to women: it opens possible options. Yet, it also confronts them with the need to make decisions about how to use that property, to whom to entrust its management (themselves, husbands, others). It may threaten husbands who retaliate in various ways to pressure women more heavily into feudal subservience. In short, the impact of property ownership on class is contradictory.

There is no way *a priori* to assess the effects of this change in one political process on the class and gender processes inside households. Those effects depend on the influences of all the other social processes which have an impact on the household. We cannot reduce a change in household class and gender processes *merely* to the effects of property ownership (or any other single phenomenon).

Contradictions and Changes

Our discussion of gender and class processes in feudal households in the United States cannot explore all the other economic, political, and cultural processes that condition those households. Our goal has been rather to launch the Marxist-Feminist analysis which we think is needed and then to focus illustratively on some processes that strike us as particularly worthy of attention. However, we wish to stress that our analysis is not functionalist; the conditioning of the feudal household is contradictory. In our view, the selfsame social processes that in some ways promote women's class positions in feudal households can also be shown to undermine it in other ways. While feudal households have been and remain widespread in the United States, they have been full of shifting contradictions and tensions and, consequently, always changing. The contradictions and changes emerge from the multiple, different, and often inconsistent influences exerted upon feudal households by all the social processes that produce them.

The contradictions within the feudal household appear to have intensified in recent decades. The tensions and changes in feudal households threaten the conditions of their existence and may transform both their class and gender structures. New ways of thinking emerged in part from these tensions and changes, and in part from a broader questioning and examination of women's social situation generally. The notion of the 'naturalness' of women's traditional position has been exploded. One result has been a rich, new literature of social analysis to which we are indebted. The connecting of parts of that literature to Marxian class analysis generates new questions. In the remainder of this book, we apply our Marxist-Feminist approach to obtain answers to some of these questions: Do the contradictions and changes in feudal households suggest that a crisis point has been reached? Are gender processes and female/male social divisions being fundamentally altered? Is feudalism in the household being displaced by radically different class structures? Are we witnessing a revolution in a Marxist-Feminist sense in American households?

Women today live a virtually infinite array of contradictions both inside and outside feudal households. On the one hand, they confront the biologically determinist notions that God or nature created women to remain in such households because they are unfit physically and psychologically for the outside world of compensated labor and must be protected from its burdens. On the other hand is the reality that the majority of women work outside the home.[24] The gender processes that define women as the 'weaker' sex needing protection thus contradict the economic processes putting double or triple work burdens (housework and childcare in addition to paid employment) on such 'weak' shoulders.[25]

Gender processes holding that females are intellectually and morally inferior to males contradict the practice of giving females the nearly exclusive role of moral and intellectual guides for young people as mothers, daycare staff, and elementary school teachers. Similarly, the idea that organically passive, nurturing women need male protection because they cannot manage in the world conflicts with giving women custody of children to manage alone while working outside the home. It conflicts also with the fact that alimony payments are no longer routinely granted.[26] Finally, it conflicts with the reality that it is statistically rare for women actually to receive the largely inadequate child support payments granted to them by divorce courts.[27] There is a legal contradiction between compelling women to care for their children while only nominally requiring financial support from fathers and historically condoning fathers' evasion of such minimal responsibility.[28]

Laws and regulations that oppose birth control and abortion, such as the recent decisions of several states to deny government funds for abortions, coexist in contradiction with government refusal to support the resulting, often unwanted, and hence at risk, children. Another contradiction finds opposition to abortion as an immoral violence to an innocent child's life coexisting with opposition to systematic protection of that child through free healthcare, daycare, education, housing, and so on. Protective legislation is supposed to free women by limiting their lifting of heavy objects and working overtime, by requiring female rest areas, and so forth. Yet in practice, these regulations are widely and safely ignored, especially in the so-called 'female professions' of nursing, childcare, house cleaning, and industrial and office cleaning. Nurses and aides routinely move and lift heavy adult patients and often must work overtime. Housemaids and industrial office cleaning women routinely lift heavy furniture, industrial vacuum cleaners, and other things. Housewives lift children, furniture, heavy bags of groceries, and work 'overtime.'

The gender process that depicts males as sexually aggressive contradicts the weak protections for women against sexual harassment. Ostensibly aggressors against women, men are nonetheless supposed to protect them in traditional marriages while genuine support and financial alternatives for battered wives are nowhere systematically available. The ideological representation of women as passive and less sexual than men contradicts the media's pervasive presentation of them as infinitely sexual.

Women are pressed simultaneously to stay at home to care for families and to earn funds outside to sustain proper family life. On the one hand, gender ideologies and laws and regulations block birth control and abortion for women. They marry into and remain in feudal households because they cannot otherwise financially support the children. Yet in recent years, the lowering of real wages and the reduction of public services push housewives into the wage labor force.

Change emerges in feudal households through the contradictory interactions of their class processes, the gender processes in society, and the distribution of power within contemporary marriages. Marriage is a particular form of social contract between men and women, in which each is recognized to have responsibilities to the other. Mutual obligations are sanctified by religions, celebrated by the mass media, and enforced by laws. Each spouse becomes inscribed in a complex set of socially recognized and enforced rules, attitudes, and desires. Interwoven with the conscious ideologies of marriage that influence behavior are the unconscious meanings that people associate with marriage and that shape their behavior as well. A relationship in which the marriage contract is present gives each spouse specific powers over the other. Yet these specific powers are also constrained by the social construction of the marriage contract.

The male's recognized right and obligation to work hard outside the household to support his family and protect it from economic suffering is complemented by the female's understood right and obligation to work hard inside the household to support and protect her family. However, each spouse may respond to the contradictions we have noted in the feudal household by using marriage rights and obligations to improve his or her situation at the expense of the other spouse's authority, self-image, or class position.

These exercises of power can take many forms. They may include a woman's assumption of the design and decoration of the household to her tastes, not the male's. A wife may attempt to reduce the amount of surplus labor she performs or change the form in which she delivers surplus labor by arguing that marriage empowers her to order her own and others' behaviors inside the household. The exercise of power over children may be used by women to forge familial alliances of themselves and children against their husbands. This may exclude husbands from intimacy with children by presenting the father as someone to avoid and fear while presenting the mother as the channel for all personal information and contact.

The wife may perform her household labor with demonstrative suffering to generate guilt and exact penance from her husband. Sexual processes between men and women will not remain unaffected by such power struggles. When women plan their household labor, they may define that labor to exclude or minimize tasks they dislike and maximize those they enjoy. For example, a feudal housewife may define her primary task as child-rearing and education and so neglect household maintenance, including the surplus labor and products destined for her husband.

The male, as receiver of his spouse's surplus labor, may have his feudal household life threatened by this type of behavior. He may be unable to get to work on time, and thereby jeopardize his job, because his clothes are not clean and ready, or because there is no food in the house. If he begins to undertake household tasks, he may be unable to arrive at work rested, to function productively, to work overtime, and to advance his career. He may be forced to purchase commercial laundry and food services which erode his financial base as a feudal lord and also erode, as we shall see, his capitalist role as a seller of labor power outside the home. Similarly, the power structure of marriage may translate a wife's illnesses, alcoholism, or other incapacitating conditions into demands upon the male for household labor and expenditures that effectively undermine his feudal and capitalist class positions. Illnesses and plagues likewise brought crisis to medieval feudalism and contributed in places to its disappearance.

On the other hand, the male's responsibilities and obligations to support and protect his family may be exercized inside the household in ways that maximize the female burden of performing feudal surplus labor. He may dictate that, as the 'master' of the house, his tastes and preference must prevail regardless of their impacts on 'his' wife and children. The man may decide not to spend on such labor-saving machinery as a microwave oven. He may decide that daycare or nursing help for elderly relatives are unnecessary expenditures, and instead pressure his wife into caring for them through more surplus labor exacted as her wifely duty. He, too, may be an alcoholic or ill and unable to hold the kind of job allowing him to provide means of production for his wife's labor in the household yet pressuring her to compensate through more surplus labor. He may be unemployed for any reason and do the same.

The rights and obligations of partners in marriage – the political processes within the relationship between them – are pushed and pulled in all manner of contradictory directions by all the other processes of the society in which the marriage exists. Marriage rights and obligations, and even the marriages themselves, become objects of conflicts and struggles. These struggles over power within the household are also complex causes and effects of struggles there over class and gender processes. On the one hand, resignation, depression, compromise, stalemate, separation or violence may follow. On the other, crises in marriages and feudal households may also lead to transitions to new households and new marriages, to nonfeudal class structures there, and to new gender and political processes comprising new interpersonal relationships.

Among the possible results of such interconnected struggles is violence by one spouse, usually the male, against the other.[29] Many of the same institutions which help to create the conditions for marriage have increasingly had to support or create new mechanisms – religious family counseling, state social agencies, battered women's shelters – to address the tensions, struggles, despair, and often violence besetting American households. The marriage contract and joint property ownership mean that the male in a feudal household cannot easily replace a recalcitrant spouse with a more docile surplus labor provider. Females cannot legally be thrown out of such households or separated from their marriages and property without formal settlements and compensation. Similarly, a married female surplus labor producer, especially one with children, cannot easily escape a particularly hostile household.

Thus, the marriage contract serves in some ways to support the feudal class structure of traditional households and yet, in other ways, to undermine it. In part, it drives the female to provide surplus labor for the male, while it also stimulates and enables her to push in the opposite direction. The resulting contradictions, in which female surplus labor producers and male appropriators are pulled in different directions, help to generate the dynamic of the feudal household. It may continue to exist, although with continually changing class and nonclass processes. Alternatively, the feudal household may reach a crisis point where its contradictions explode.

One result of crisis may be the destruction of the feudal household through divorce.[30] Another result may be the construction of entirely different, nonfeudal class processes within households. Divorces may be painful adjustments followed by remarriages in which new partners readily re-establish households with feudal class structures and traditional gender divisions. Or divorce may be a first step in establishing households with different class structures of the ancient and communist sort and different gender divisions. In any case, we may speak of the crisis of the feudal household as a moment when the survival of the feudal household is in jeopardy, and a social transition to radically different households is possible. Such a moment may be at hand in the United States today. However, to explore this possibility further, we need to consider the impact of capitalism on feudal households – how its particular influences contribute to crisis and change in those households.

Capitalist and Feudal Class Interactions

Our thesis is that the United States has long included many feudal households of the sort we have been discussing.[31] If we are right, it follows that any class analysis of the United States requires examination of the usually neglected interactions between capitalist class processes outside the household and the existence and possible crisis of feudal class processes within it. Women in the United States have often, and increasingly in recent decades, added to their feudal household surplus labor the sale of their labor power to capitalist enterprises. This addition has created the 'double shift' in the household and the enterprise.[32] These women move, on a daily basis, between two dissimilar class structures making dissimilar claims upon their time, energy, thoughts, and feelings.

To the contradictions we have noted within the feudal class structure of the household must be added those within the capitalist class structures of enterprises and those that arise between the two different social sites. A crisis of feudal households in the United States may be one result of the interactions between capitalist and feudal class structures. Such a crisis would represent a possibly transitional conjuncture – to nonfeudal households – the ramifications of which could transform the entire society, including its gender processes and the class processes at all other sites. The possible presence and qualities of a crisis in feudal households is thus an urgent problem and object for Marxist and Marxist-Feminist theory. After all, concern with historical transitions and class transformations such as Europe's 'passage from feudalism to capitalism,' current shifts from noncapitalist to capitalist class structures in the Third World, and socialist revolutions have long been central foci of Marxist analyses. Is it possible that revolutionary transformations are underway in an unexpected site, the household?

To assess the possibilities of a revolutionary transformation arising out of the interactions between the two sites, we will examine how the existence of feudal class processes within households affects capitalist wage exploitation and how the existence of capitalist class processes within enterprises affects the exploitation of women within feudal households. Our goal is to clarify when and how the relationship between capitalist enterprises and feudal households could reinforce or destroy one or both of them.

The different class processes at the two sites depend upon and affect each other. However, their interactions are mediated by all the other processes in the society. No one particular outcome of their interaction is necessary or inevitable. For example, the existence of female surplus labor in feudal households may coincide with either high or low, rising or falling, wages. In our approach, capitalist and feudal class structures at different social sites are not necessarily either compatible with or hostile to each other. We must therefore disagree with other participants in current debates on the household who see a constant, predictable relationship between females' unpaid household labor and men's capitalist wages.[33]

Let us consider first the example of a male occupying two dramatically different class positions. In the household, he appropriates 'his' woman's feudal surplus labor; at the workplace, he performs surplus labor for his capitalist employer. On the job, he is exploited; at home, he exploits. The woman in this simplified example occupies only one class position, that of feudal serf. Let us locate this man and woman in the United States of the 1980s. There has been a war on taxes and the governmental services and service jobs they provide. Unions are increasingly under attack by state officials and capitalists. They have serious internal problems and declining memberships. They are losing strikes, credibility, and the initiative in industrial disputes.[34] Unemployment, by historical standards, has remained high across the decade. Low-wage service sector jobs partially replace high-wage jobs lost in manufacturing. Women, especially, enter the low-wage sectors as both an effect and cause of falling wages. One result of these and other conditions is a falling real wage for men selling their labor power.

To offset the impact of a falling real wage, this man may push this woman to increase her household surplus labor to maintain the standard of living that he derives from his two class positions. He may insist on more homecooked meals, more cleaning, and more care of relatives to replace costly conveniences such as dry cleaning, restaurants, nursing-home care, purchased entertainments, and so on. In this case, the feudal household functions to sustain lower wages and thereby higher enterprise profits. It enhances capitalist development. Looking at the situation from the vantage point of the household, enterprise capitalism can contribute to an increased rate of women's feudal exploitation in the household. Feudal households can help to make possible lower wages that might not have been tolerated otherwise.

The particular relationship between feudal households and capitalist enterprises depicted in our example has been recognized by other analysts of the household (although in different theoretical terms). However, they tend to treat this one of many possible relationships as the *necessary* relationship. For them, the household labor of women is a straightforward, predictable affair that always benefits capitalists at women's expense (Hartmann 1981b; Delphy 1984; Fox 1980; Folbre 1987; Dalla Costa and James 1980; Eisenstein 1979; Coulson, Magav and Wainwright 1980; Gardiner 1979; Seecombe 1980; and Sokoloff 1981). We disagree. Under alternative conditions, feudal households (with or without increasing feudal exploitation) can contribute to rising wages. There are still other conditions in which capitalist class processes in enterprises (with or without increasing wages) help to reduce feudal exploitation in households, benefiting women at the expense of men.

We may illustrate the range of possibilities with a second example. In the United States in the late 1960s, the labor market was relatively tight. The Vietnam War had absorbed many workers while an inflated economy absorbed many others. President Johnson's 'Great Society' drew many workers away from private employment and into government social services. Workers were able to use their then still effective unions to push up wages. At the same time, a militant and rapidly growing women's liberation movement made women's oppression its target. We may suppose that this movement decreased women's surplus labor production in at least some feudal households. Where men could obtain higher wages, they could thereby compensate for reduced feudal surplus labor from their wives at home.

Such male workers were both provoked by their wives and enabled by market conditions to charge their capitalist employers a premium over their previous wages. In this example, specific social processes shaped the interaction between feudal households and capitalist enterprises such that feudal exploitation was reduced at capitalists' expense.[35] The premiums paid to workers reduced the amount of surplus value available to capitalists to secure such other conditions of existence as management, research, and capital accumulation (Resnick and Wolff 1987, 109–230). Changes in the class structure of the household here contributed to a weakening of capitalist enterprises. Stated conversely, the capitalist enterprises had compensated for weakened household feudalism, but in ways that made their own reproduction more difficult. In contrast to our first example and to other theories of the household, this second example shows how the feudal household can function as a barrier to capitalist development.

To take a third example, we may return our attention to the falling wage situation of the 1980s. We have seen, in our first example, how this situation could contribute, in some households, to greater feudal exploitation of women. In other households, however, the lower wages could contribute rather to a lesser rate of feudal exploitation or even to a displacement of feudal class processes from households altogether. During the last decade, many more American women entered part-time and full-time employment. They have often been motivated by desires to maintain family living standards when faced with their husbands' declining real wages. They have also been influenced by those voices within the women's movement that extolled wage labor over unpaid labor in the household. Many were driven by the financial consequences of divorce, then and now occurring at a rate of 50 per cent among newly married people and at an even higher rate for those in second marriages (Blumstein and Schwartz 1983, 34).

Women who sell their labor power often have to reduce their performance of feudal surplus labor at home. Double shifts take their toll. Opting for capitalist exploitation in the enterprise, they may no longer tolerate feudal exploitation at home. Divorced women often break with feudal traditions and establish single adult households without lords or serfs – the ancient class structure cited above. Some women establish still another kind of nonfeudal household in which the production, appropriation, and distribution of surplus labor is accomplished collectively – the communist class structure mentioned earlier. In these circumstances, falling real wages in the capitalist sector contribute to the transition of some households out of feudal class structures altogether.

Capitalist enterprises do not always profit from the feudal class structure of households, nor do the latter always flourish alongside capitalist enterprises. They may strengthen, weaken, or destroy one another. Gender processes will both influence and be influenced by the interactions between the different class processes at the two sites. Marxist-Feminists need constantly to reassess the varying interactions between the two sites and the two kinds of process to adjust accordingly their revolutionary strategies. An alliance of Marxists and Feminists will be more flexible, more durable, and more effective if it is aware of the range of possible interactions between feudal households and capitalist enterprises. Different interactions generate different relationships, thoughts, and feelings among household members – matters of importance to advocates and strategists of social change.

Changes in the amount of surplus labor produced and appropriated within feudal households do not occur without tensions, if not also struggles, between men and women. In our first example, where men compensated for reduced wages by exacting more feudal surplus from women at home, we implicitly presumed that women offered no effective resistance to those exactions. In the second example, where feudal wives produced less surplus for their men, the latter were compensated by obtaining higher wages;

here we implicitly presumed that employers did not resist. Yet we need to question these presumptions.

For example, changes in the capitalist existences of males can produce contradictions and tensions in feudal households. If wages fall, and men pressure their wives for more feudal surplus labor, the women may resist and tensions may mount. To take another example, if women reduce their household feudal exploitation, contradictions and tensions may intensify, especially if the husbands' wages cannot then be raised. Such contradictions and tensions can have far-reaching social significance.

Contradictions and Tensions in the Household

To the degree that women resist pressures to increase feudal surplus labor to offset men's falling wages, the men's living standards may fall. This may exacerbate contradictions and produce tensions inside and outside the household. If women do not prevent an increase in their feudal exploitation while men's wages rise simultaneously, men's living standards may rise sharply. Still other contradictions and tensions will then arise.

Tensions in households will depend on and shape how men seek greater flows of goods and services within feudal households. Their options are: (1) increasing the rate of feudal exploitation by having wives work fewer hours for themselves and more for their husbands; (2) increasing the number of individuals who do surplus labor in the household; and (3) increasing the productivity of household labor so that more goods and services are produced in the same time. The first option directly pits man against woman and increases tensions between them accordingly (Rubin 1976; Westwood 1985). In terms of the second option, men can enhance the flow of surplus labor in feudal households by adding laborers such as children, relatives, or live-in servants. Where this option is pursued, another set of contradictions and tensions will arise in feudal households.

The third option involves increasing the productivity of household labor by improving the management and organization of housework tasks or by using more and improved means of production (Hartmann 1974; Vanek 1980). By these means, a feudal wife's surplus labor time can remain unchanged, while a larger quantity of goods and services are produced for the husband in that time. However, since these improved means of household production are usually capitalist commodities, the male would have to allocate portions of his wages to buy them. To afford them, he would have to reduce the purchase of wage goods for himself. Tensions can arise between men and women in feudal households over the quantity, quality, and timing of purchases of such means of production. Men may also press for increased rates of feudal exploitation to offset at least the initial impacts on their living standards of such purchases. In any case, the contradictions and tensions in households will influence the mix of options males pursue, and vice versa.

The money problems faced by husbands in feudal households are not limited to shifting from the purchase of required wage commodities to the purchase of household means of production. They must also pay taxes, donate to churches, and purchase commodities needed as inputs into household production (raw food, soaps, etc.). Where feudal households have been established on the basis of credit (home mortgages, automobile loans, credit card debt, etc.), husbands face large interest payments.[36]

To secure his feudal class position, the husband must distribute household feudal surplus labor in all these *cash* forms. Yet that surplus is rarely supplied to him in cash; it is usually in the form of his wife's services or products. Thus, the husband uses his cash wages not only to buy means of consumption, to reproduce the labor power he sells to capitalists. He also transfers some of his wages to make the cash feudal subsumed class payments needed to reproduce his feudal household.

Spending a portion of wage revenues to maintain the male's feudal household class position raises another possibility of a clash between the feudal household and enterprise capitalism. What is left of his wages to buy goods and services may not be enough to reproduce the labor power he sells every day. He may then try to divert some of his wife's surplus labor or products away from securing the household's feudal class structure and to the securing instead of his own capitalist class position (i.e., to his own consumption). If he fails to do this, perhaps because of his wife's resistance, his health may deteriorate and his productivity in the enterprise suffer. If he takes a second job, as so many Americans now do, he may maintain his consumption of goods, but at the cost of exhaustion and ill health. Were these conditions to impair productivity generally, feudal households would become obstacles to capitalist production and development.[37]

There may be struggles in the household over how much of the male's wage revenues is to be used to secure the needs of the feudal household.[38] Men would be better off individually if they could receive more feudal surplus with a smaller transfer of their wages to feudal household outlays. Women would be better off individually if they could produce less feudal surplus and receive more transfers of wage income to pay for more feudal household outlays. Men are driven to give less of their wages to wives for household means of production, donations to church, consumer debt repayment, childrearing expenses, and so on, in order to maintain their capitalist position as wage-earners. Yet, they are also driven to give more of their wages to their wives to secure the requirements of their position as feudal lords. They are, of course, also motivated by their complex thoughts and feelings about other household members.

Feudal wives are also torn. On the one hand, they need to press their demands for the money with which to maintain the feudal household. On the other hand, they cannot push the feudal lords too far. Many fear violence. Most fear the loss of security of a feudal household and the males on which it, and hence they, are financially dependent.[39] Yet, women may rebel when husbands do not maintain their feudal obligations, particularly their financing of feudal means of production. In these circumstances, increased feudal surplus labor for the man may mean reduced necessary labor for the woman. Her standard of living will fall, and she may rebel. These rebellions are expressed in both open and subtle forms (Westwood 1985, 177–83; Rubin 1976, 69–81).[40] Rebellion threatens violence and the end of the feudal household. It is tempered by concern for the husband, the children, and the marriage. Women may want to compensate their husbands for financial difficulties and resulting emotional depressions. They may agree with the husband's view that it is the woman's task to make everyone happy, to hold the family together. That, after all, is their traditional role, the effect in part of the powerful gender processes that mold them.

Women are caught in a particular dilemma. To resist openly the demands of their men and their feudal position undermines their own understanding of their role in the household and in society at large. It can challenge certain prevailing gender processes. Women's identities are at stake. Yet, to yield to the demand for more feudal surplus labor, especially at a time when real wages are falling, also creates a difficult situation for them. Women could reduce their surplus labor within feudal households and compel children to become surplus labor producers alongside their mothers. Or, where children already perform feudal surplus labor, women could increase their rates of exploitation.[41] Many women both decrease the necessary labor for themselves and increase their total household labor hours: they quite literally work themselves to death (Delphy 1984, 50–3).

Others may resist such demands and 'escape' their feudal household existence through separation or divorce. However, since divorced and separated women are often plunged into poverty, the most common choice for women is to seek new income-generating positions outside of the household, while usually remaining in feudal bondage. They may supplement their husbands' wages with their own while still performing feudal surplus labor at home.

We do not want to suggest that unemployment, falling real wages, rising prices for household means of production or increased demands for household surplus labor are the only reasons for women to enter paid employment. Even in prosperous times, women may seek such employment because of their preferences for capitalist over feudal exploitation, given that the former was so often closed to them. At times (e.g., during the Second

World War), the state has directly encouraged women to enter the wage labor force (Milkman 1987). In any case, just as the contradictions within and between feudal households and capitalist enterprises influence many women to enter paid employment, so such employment introduces its set of new contradictions and tensions into the household. The forces undermining the feudal household can be brought to crisis intensity when feudal wives move massively into wage employment.

Women, Wages, and Class Struggles

When wives, as well as husbands, from feudal households sell their labor power for wages, both will need to make consumption expenditures to secure the conditions of existence of their wage labor positions. However, to understand the complex consequences of women's wage labor, we must look beyond aggregate family incomes and expenditures to the many changes and perhaps even class transformations occurring in feudal households and to the changes in capitalist enterprises. Women's wage labor may have changed the feudal class structure of the household, changed gender processes inside and outside the home, and changed the interaction between feudal households and capitalist enterprises.

In recent US history, women who have entered the paid labor force increased their total work week by 14 to 25 hours.[42] The average non-employed wife spends 56 hours per week on housework, while the average employed wife spends 30 hours per week on housework, in addition to 40 hours in paid employment plus travel time to and from paid employment. The higher family income costs women an increased work week, as well as capitalist exploitation added to feudal exploitation.[43] When women do full-time wage labor, the evidence suggests that their husbands do not appreciably increase their participation in domestic work.[44] Instead, the burden on them more likely takes the form of reduced domestic services as their wives do less surplus labor (Strober 1980, 386–400). This adds strains to the feudal household as men and women struggle over the allocation of women's wage revenues between household costs and their personal wage-earning needs (comparable to the tensions noted earlier over men's allocations of their wages). There may also be problems of guilt and anger about reduced female surplus labor.

Women's participation in paid employment can provide both financial and emotional support for women to make demands for change within the household.[45] Women on the job gain comfort and strength from the support of female co-workers.[46] They gain some measure of financial independence. Thus, two of the conditions of existence of feudal class processes in the household, women's nearly total financial and emotional dependence on husbands, may be eroded with their entry into paid employment. Women as wage laborers often develop new needs with respect to their home lives or are driven to express needs they felt earlier but repressed. The former acceptability of a steady, financially dependable husband gives way to demands that husbands value and provide supportive companionship, emotional sharing, and intimacy, in addition to equal sharing of the household labor tasks. With new personal support systems and new financial resources, women may challenge men's feudal lordship position or decrease their feudal production of domestic use-values or both. Men, in turn, may feel their feudal position to be threatened and may reinforce it by heightened demands for surplus labor.

These contradictory pressures can precipitate serious tensions and conflicts inside feudal households – more or less intense struggles over any aspect of relations between husband and wife, between parents and children or other household members. Shifting alliances among male and female adults and children can coalesce around the varying objects of struggle – child-rearing practices, major commodity purchases, drinking habits, sexual behavior, and styles of dress, among other things. Under certain social conditions, they can become class struggles – struggles over the quantitative or qualitative dimensions of the feudal class processes themselves.

These are class struggles because their objects are class processes. Parents, children, relatives, and friends in varying combinations or alliances can take opposing positions on change versus stasis in the household's class structure. One side, perhaps led by the male appropriator, may seek to retain the feudal form of the class process and to increase the rate of feudal exploitation of women. The other side, led typically but not necessarily by the female surplus labor producer, aims at least to reduce feudal exploitation or sometimes even to change the household class structure to a nonfeudal form.

These class struggles become revolutionary if they move households toward a transition from feudal to nonfeudal class structures. Instead of women performing feudal surplus labor for their husbands, they can demand changes that involve an equal sharing of household tasks. If men and women together (collectively) perform both necessary and surplus labor, collectively appropriate their surplus, and collectively decide the distribution of that surplus, the households have accomplished a transition to a communist class structure (Resnick and Wolff 1988). Household class struggles can become revolutionary in other ways – if people leave feudal households (via divorce or separation) and establish new communist households (both gay and heterosexual), or if they establish one-adult households in which they perform and appropriate their own surplus labor individually.

The changed gender processes defining maleness and femaleness that are necessary for revolutionary changes in household class structures are themselves revolutionary alterations in the culture. Moreover, such changes in class and gender processes are also revolutionary in emotional terms. Relatively few contemporary women or men have had familial models of shared intimacy, shared decision-making, shared housework, and shared, mutually supportive companionship or models of one-adult households. Yet, many are now caught up in struggles and transitions for which they have been emotionally as well as theoretically ill-prepared.

The conditions of existence of such revolutionary changes evolved historically with much difficulty, pain, and danger. Statistics about domestic violence, alienation of children from parents, sexual activity, separation, and divorce are so many indices of this. We are struck by one other index. By the 1970s married women in the United States had become the prime users of psychotropic drugs and psychotherapy. Married women are the social group now considered to be most at risk for mental breakdown, while the second and third riskiest groups are single men and married men respectively. Single women have the lowest risk of mental breakdown (Showalter 1985, 195–250; Chesler 1972; Rapping 1987, 18; and Berch 1982, 199–200). Although risk is overdetermined by many interacting causes, these rankings do suggest the pressures on married women.

The tensions and strains inside traditional households may drive women sooner or later to leave paid employment and resign themselves to lives within feudal households. There are certainly political, cultural, and economic processes pushing for that historical 'solution' to the current crisis in the household. Political conservatism, gender processes resisting changes in the conception of woman, economic processes consigning women to poorly paid employment – these and other processes reinforce the feudal option for households. Yet, there are also processes supporting other options such as communist or ancient households. Political radicalism, new concepts of gender, and improving economic possibilities for women are among the processes making possible and favoring radically different 'solutions' to households in crisis.

The struggles in feudal households may react upon the other sites in society in ways which deepen the crisis. For example, the religious ideologies that have long sanctified feudal households (as 'the family') are increasingly arenas of struggles over those ideologies and the personnel who articulate them. The burning questions include abortion, birth control, homosexuality, and the roles of women in church leadership. The churches have become social sites of struggle among individuals over the cultural, political, and economic processes that together comprise modern religion. These struggles, and their effects upon religion, can deepen the crisis of the feudal household by questioning and sometimes removing certain of its religious, gender, and other conditions of existence.

The federal, state, and local levels of government have also become sites at which conditions of existence of the feudal household are being contested.

Literature produced and distributed by state agencies, curricula for all levels of schools, regulations, and laws are now objects of struggle. Groups with very different definitions of gender and very different preferences for and participation in particular household class structures confront the state. Their concerns include policies, regulations, and laws such as those governing abortion and birth control rights, gay rights, adoption procedures, domestic violence, spousal rape, child support by divorced parents, protected maternity and paternity leaves from employment, rights to guaranteed childcare, and social security provisions for the elderly and disabled. As with struggles to change religion, campaigns to alter state policies can also question or remove conditions of existence of household feudalism.

Despite crisis conditions in feudal households, men and women may hold on to them to avoid the threat and the consequences of their disruption. The feudal class structure and traditional gender divisions may then continue, although often leaving couples with feelings of alienation and loneliness, expressed as psychological depression, alcoholism, and extra-marital sexual activity among other ways.[47] Although millions of American couples remain in feudal households, we believe that they do so with ever greater difficulty. The mounting intensity of nonclass struggles over gender processes and other cultural, political, and economic processes, inside and outside the household, is taking a heavy toll on the stability, tranquility, and viability of those households. In recent years, the addition of class struggles over reducing wives' feudal surplus labor and over the transition to nonfeudal class-structured households has brought millions of households to a crisis state.

Beyond the pain and suffering this has meant for most Americans, an increasing number have reacted by establishing nontraditional households in which both feudal class processes and traditional gender divisions are absent. They thereby testify to the profundity of the social contradictions and tensions that have brought crisis to so many feudal households. Since we can show that the numerical growth of nonfeudal households has been significant in recent US history, and since this marks a revolutionary class transformation in households with far-reaching social consequences, we need to consider the two major forms of nonfeudal household.

The 'Ancient' Alternative

We use the term 'ancient' to acknowledge the formulation of the concept by Marxist writers to designate a form of producing, appropriating, and distributing surplus labor that was particularly significant in ancient Rome and also during the European transition from feudalism to capitalism.[48] In the ancient form of class structure, the performer and appropriator of surplus labor is the same individual. S/he does necessary labor to reproduce her/himself and also performs surplus labor which is individually self-appropriated. S/he then decides to whom to distribute that surplus to secure the conditions of existence of this form of the class process. Common examples include peasants and craftspersons individually producing and distributing goods and services, possibly as commodities through market exchanges. There is an affinity between Marx's ancient class structure and what is loosely called 'self-employment' in non-Marxian terminologies. There is also a direct link between ancient class processes and one-adult households.

One-adult households dramatically increased both absolutely and relatively in comparison to all households from 1960 to 1987 (US Bureau of the Census 1987, 43). While total households in the United States rose from 53 to 89 million, the one-adult households rose from 13 to 34 million. By 1987, one-adult households accounted for over 38 per cent of all US households. Moreover, the growth in such households cannot be explained by the changing age distribution of the US population – such households are increasingly being established by all age groups (Waldrop 1989). Most of the people in one-adult households individually appropriate their own surplus labor; they participate in ancient class processes there. These individuals neither establish feudal households nor move into the feudal households of relatives, typical strategies in previous eras when feudal household structures were virtually unchallenged socially.

People may accept or choose to live in households with ancient class structures for many different reasons. Among some groups in the United States, one-adult households have been common for many decades. However, certain recently changed social conditions have made their number proliferate rapidly. The ideology of female independence is one such changed condition. For over two decades the women's liberation movement in the United States has exposed and opposed sexist ideas of all kinds and sexual discrimination in all areas, including inside marriages and households. It has denounced the gender processes which are among the conditions of existence of women's class positions in feudal households. It has celebrated alternatives to the feudal household and female dependence. One of these has been and continues to be a 'single lifestyle' in what amounts to an ancient household.[49]

Dissatisfaction with the traditional feudal household and advocacy of the ancient alternative are not restricted to women. Since the 1950s, American males have increasingly spoken out against marriage and the feudal household as an oppression of men because of the onerous obligations of their provider roles (Ehrenreich 1983, 42–87, 99–116; Adams and Briscoe 1971, 38–9). A diffuse movement for a kind of male liberation has emerged. Through the gender processes that it has advanced, this movement has provided conditions of existence for men to opt for ancient instead of feudal households.[50] Ideas communicated by magazines such as *Playboy, Hustler,* and *Penthouse* express one of the central themes of these gender processes. The sexual dependence of men on women and the economic dependence of women on men which traditional marriages and households impose are seen as obstacles to self-fulfilment, both occupationally and personally. Sexual need and sexual dependence become symbolic of the neediness trap which can enslave men in feudal domesticity.[51]

The crisis of the feudal household and the proliferation of the ancient household have, of course, many other conditions of existence in addition to the movements for women's liberation and for male disentanglement from marriage. The weakening of orthodox religions amid the celebration of many kinds of individualism facilitates ancient households. The media, especially television, function as a powerful force combining programs with advertisements to promote commodities as the chief means to self-realization. They increasingly portray the single, sexy male or female as the *sine qua non* of adventure. They rarely depict the serious struggles of couples of all kinds for honesty, friendship, and intimacy. They also rarely treat the complex difficulties of being single.

A pervasive ideological condition of existence for ancient class households is the US cult of the individual from the 'self-made man' to the 'Lone Ranger' to the 'Equalizer.'[52] Particularly after the Second World War, the intensified individualizing of all problems and their solutions has made it very difficult for couples to imagine jointly analyzing and solving their problems. Individuals rather fear group life, including family life, as conformity to another's needs. Single lifestyles are often romanticized as a necessary individual rebellion against that conformity. Few seem able to imagine, and still less to insist upon, the joint exploration of their respective needs and the solutions to them.

Finally, the intensifying contradictions and tensions of feudal households in the United States have apparently convinced many of their children not to replicate them in their own lives. Ancient households are not, however, the only alternative to the feudal households that significant numbers of Americans are exploring. The social processes that have brought crisis to the feudal household and the rise of the ancient household have also prompted the formation of communist class structures in some households.

The 'Communist' Alternative

Communist class structures in households are now widely regarded as components of the definition of successful modern family life. Of course, what our analysis sees as a class structure is not understood as such by those for whom notions of class apply only outside the household, if they apply to society at all. For example, couples therapies increasingly encourage the equal sharing of the performance, management, and fruits of domestic labor and all household decision-making. The broad goal is to share wealth, work, power, and emotional intimacy, substituting what, in our terms, approaches communism for the relations of economic exploitation and sexual and emotional subordination that characterize feudal households.

Although the family ideal in principle has long been close to the communist slogan, 'from each according to her/his ability and to each according to his/her needs,' women's abilities and needs were defined by gender processes consistent with feudal households. Changed gender processes redefined women and men as having corespective needs for independence as well as dependence, for mutual friendship and mutual protection, and for generalized equality. Newly redefined in these ways, the old family ideal is now consistent with and a condition of existence for communist class processes in households.

Approximately 20 per cent of two-adult households in the United States may be characterized now as comprising communist class processes.[53] Yet in spite of the widely acclaimed virtues and successes of the modern communist family, the recognition and examination of its particular class structure have been virtually nonexistent.

Our general notion of the communist class structure of the household is based on previous work in the Marxian tradition seeking to clarify and extend Marx's few and fragmentary discussions of communism (Resnick and Wolff 1988). Communist class processes differ from feudal class processes since communist performers of surplus labor are also its appropriators, and they also differ from ancient class processes since the production, appropriation, and distribution of surplus labor are accomplished collectively rather than individually. Within a communist household, then, all adult members (whether married or not, heterosexual or gay, two persons or more) do necessary and surplus labor collectively and collectively appropriate their surplus. All decide together as a collective household how (to whom) to distribute this surplus so as to secure the conditions of existence of such a communist household.[54] Examples range from communes and group homes of many kinds to heterosexual and gay couples who organize the class structures of their households in this communist way.

Communist households have their distinctive contradictions and tensions. The point is that they differ from the contradictions of noncommunist households and so impart correspondingly different qualities to them. For example, collective decisions about surplus distribution invite all sorts of disputes that are quite different from a class structure in which one person – the feudal or ancient appropriator – makes such decisions individually. Meetings and discussions among household members about all aspects of household life will often distinctively characterize communist households.

To take another example, some members of communist households will occupy subsumed class positions inside the household such as household record keeping, managing housework, and so on. However, unlike feudal households, communist households may want to avoid inequalities and disputes that may arise if some members of the decision-making collective were consistently to hold different class positions from others. In short, a policy of regular, systematic rotation of persons across all the class positions in the household might well be deemed a condition of existence of household communism. This, too, would distinguish communist households from feudal and ancient households.

The transition from traditional feudal households to this communist alternative is, like all class transitions, complex. Since we have already discussed many of the conditions producing a crisis in feudal households and making possible the transition to ancient households, and since these served also to produce transitions to household communism, we need not re-examine them here. The processes that had fostered the feudal household changed in some ways that encouraged ancient households and in other ways that encouraged communist households. Those who reject feudal households, but do not want one-adult households, may find their solution in communist households. Those who seek independence alongside, rather than instead of, dependence may do likewise. Buffeted by all the social processes that make them refugees from feudal households, the communist and ancient seem to be the major alternatives chosen in the United States today.

The substantial growth of communist and ancient households alongside feudal households adds new contradictions and tensions to society. Their different class structures will generate conflicts between them. They will struggle over the class and other processes at other social sites – state, enterprises, churches – since developments at those sites will influence household class structures in different ways. For example, communist households pay taxes out of their surpluses much as feudal and ancient households do. What distinguishes the subsumed class payments made by the differently class-structured households is the precise nature of the conditions of existence they seek to secure in return for these payments.

Feudal households will pressure the state to enact laws and regulations that support their class structures. Ancient and communist households will exert pressures for different and often opposing laws supporting their respective class structures.[55] While all the other social processes shaping state activities will determine which pressures predominate, two recent examples can illustrate the problem and what is at stake. First, between 1984 and 1987, eight states passed legislation outlawing spousal rape.[56] Secondly, in 1987, intense debates occurred in the US Senate over expansion of government-funded childcare facilities. Both of these developments may be dangerous for feudal households, as they contribute to changing power relations between women and men inside the household and to expanding women's economic opportunities outside the home. Those in ancient and communist households have little to fear from these developments and much to applaud.

Religious institutions have also recently been the sites of battle affecting the conditions of existence that they do or do not provide to religious households of differing class structures.[57] We may consider the case of the Roman Catholic Church (although similar conflicts agitate many other religious institutions).[58] During the Pope's 1987 visit to the United States, Catholic priests requested a reconsideration of the Church's bans on birth control and women's ordination into the priesthood. Mass protests in 1987 opposed papal efforts to oust Catholic University professor Charles Curran and Seattle Bishop Hunthausen for their generally 'liberal' attitudes and teachings on birth control and abortion. There has been open, public controversy among Catholic bishops on the issue of AIDS prevention through the use of condoms. A Catholic homosexual group, Dignity, mounts regular public protests seeking to change the official attitude toward homosexuality and homosexual households.

These changes would not be likely to strengthen feudal families and would at least implicitly encourage ancient and communist households. Not only competing theologies, economic pressures on Church finances, and power struggles within the hierarchy, but also pressures from Catholic households of different class structures are combining to shape the movements for and against doctrinal change within Roman Catholicism in the United States.

The growth of communist households raises a special kind of problem for capitalist enterprises. Men and women from such households may become increasingly accustomed to collective power processes (decision-making), communist class processes, and gender processes stressing sexual equality. Many of them will leave such communist households daily to earn wages and salaries in capitalist enterprises with very different class, gender, and power processes. How will they experience, understand, and react to their daily occupation of such different and opposing class, gender, and power positions? More precisely, how will the interactions between capitalist enterprises and communist or ancient households differ from the interactions between those enterprises and feudal households?

Will capitalist employees coming from communist households recognize the different class processes at both sites as such? Will they apply such class consciousness to the definitions of their problems and their searches for solutions? Will they seek to extend the communist revolution in the household to one at the workplace? Will gender processes stressing sexual equality and political processes stressing collective decision-making, fostered in and by communist households, become parallel issues for struggles at worksites? For example, will the struggles for 'comparable worth' (equal pay for equal work) evolve into struggles for equality and collectivity in all aspects of enterprises, including the production, appropriation, and distribution of surplus labor?

The class and gender revolution underway in households is profoundly changing the United States. How the causes, components, and possibilities of that revolution are understood will itself play a significant role in transforming our society. This implies a specific agenda for Marxist-Feminists: (1) to develop and apply a theory focused on the particular roles played by class, gender and power processes in contemporary life; and (2) to intervene in social struggles by utilizing that theory and its findings.

Conclusion: A Marxist-Feminist Agenda

By integrating Marxist and Feminist theories in a particular way, we can offer the beginnings of a new analysis of the class structures and class dynamics inside US households today. Presuming the interdependence and mutual transformation of gender and class and power processes, we can show how changing conceptions of woman and man have functioned as complex causes and effects of changing household class structures. The analysis has produced some preliminary hypotheses. Basic class, gender and power struggles are underway in American households today. Revolutionary changes in class structures, gender definitions and power allocations have occurred in millions of those households with profound social consequences. Specifically, communist class structures are developing where few had even thought to look for them, let alone to chart their actual and potential social impacts.

Marxists and Feminists need to remedy the neglect of the complex interdependence of class, gender and power processes in general, and in households in particular. That neglect characterizes not only many other approaches to social science, but also the practical political activities of many Feminists and Marxists. Marxist-Feminists need to stress that class processes and struggles occur in different ways at different social sites. Any *a priori* presumption that they occur only at some privileged sites, such as enterprises and states, is unwarranted. This is as true for gender and power processes and struggles as for their class counterparts.

The agenda of Marxist-Feminists must discard such *a priori* notions and replace them with a commitment to identify the class, gender and power processes that may exist and interact at all social sites. On that basis, we can proceed to understand the ongoing contradictions, tensions, and changes within the societies whose class exploitation, gender oppression, and general social injustice we seek to abolish. In that way, Marxist-Feminists can contribute significantly to the efforts of all those seeking social transformations toward a communist, egalitarian, democratic system of economic, political, and cultural processes.

CHAPTER 2

Debating the Marxist–Feminist Interpretation of the Household

A Response by Julie Matthaei:
Surplus Labor, the Household, and Gender Oppression

One of the most perplexing questions facing progressive economists in the 1980s and 1990s is the relationship between gender, class, and race inequality in modern capitalism. Traditional Marxists, focused almost entirely on the capitalist/worker relation, have been unable to shed much light on gender or race inequality. Feminists who continue to value Marx's insights have, for the most part, moved towards a conceptualization of capitalism and patriarchy as separate, if intertwined, systems; many of these analyses portray patriarchy and capitalism as centered in household and workplace, or reproduction and production, respectively.[1]

In 'For Every Knight in Shining Armor, There's a Castle Waiting To Be Cleaned: A Marxist-Feminist Analysis of the Household,' Harriet Fraad, Stephen Resnick, and Richard Wolff develop a theoretical formulation of the relationship between gender and class oppression which is similar to the Marxist-Feminist dual systems theory. They conceptualize our economy as characterized by distinct modes of production, feudal and capitalist, centered in the household and the enterprise, respectively. In essence, the approach taken allows the authors to identify exploitation, not just oppression, in both the household and in the firm, in the form of class relations where surplus labor is extracted. Thus, just as the capitalist extracts surplus labor from the worker by making the latter work longer than necessary to produce his/her means of subsistence, with the capitalist pocketing the extra labor, so the husband in the feudal household makes his wife work longer than the hours necessary for her own reproduction, with the husband consuming the surplus labor in the form of her caring for, cleaning for, and feeding him, and so on. While I find this analysis full of insights, I also find it flawed in serious ways.

This approach has major benefits. First, it recognizes that the activity of the housewife is indeed work, important to the production and reproduction of social life, but at the same time, work which is distinct from wage labor. As such, the approach integrates the insights of the domestic labor debate (the insistence that the activity of housewives is productive) without falling into the trap of equating housework with wage labor. Efforts to do the latter, as in the domestic labor debate, had the effect of emptying each kind of work of any qualitative content; housework and wage labor could only be viewed as the same if viewed as time spent or energy expended, that is, if voided of the social relations which organize them and give them meaning. Viewing each type of work as taking place within a distinct mode of production finesses this problem nicely and allows the authors to explore the distinctiveness of each type of activity.

Second, the feudal mode approach highlights the inequality and conflicts of interest present in husband-wage-earner/wife-homemaker households. It posits the husband/wife relationship as exploitative, in that the husband extracts surplus labor from his wife. On this theoretical basis, the authors are able to make sense of many present-day struggles within marriages, such as struggles over how much household labor is done, by whom, for whom, and according to whose tastes. The sections 'Contradictions and Changes,' 'Contradictions and Tensions within the Household,' and 'Women, Wages, and Class Struggle' all present rich and perceptive analyses of such struggles, using the feudal household framework.

Third, because the approach conceptualizes traditional marriages as class relations, it elevates relations within the household to a level equal in theoretical and political importance to those within the capitalist enterprise. For years, Marxist-Feminists have been struggling to force Marxists to recognize that gender oppression is not simply a 'secondary contradiction' within capitalism, best relegated to 'after the (socialist) revolution.' Part of this struggle has been with Marxists' insistence that class and class struggle are primary. Conceptualizing housework as domestic labor and looking at the household as a mode of reproduction (à la Engels's view of a society as a mode of production and reproduction) are two ways in which Marxist-Feminists have tried to integrate gender oppression into core Marxist theory. Conceptualizing gender relationships within marriage as a class relation, as the authors do, automatically gives these relations a position of theoretical and political importance within Marxism. Indeed, if convinced of this approach, Marxists (not just Feminist Marxists) would view gender oppression within the household as a central economic process, and the struggles of women against it as revolutionary.

Fourth, this approach both allows for and develops other conceptions of household organization – ancient and communist – rather than proclaiming unequal relations within the household as universal or trans-historical.

Contradictions and struggles within the feudal household give rise to these other family forms. This typology helps to make sense of the efforts of some couples, gay and straight, to construct democratic, nonexploitative familial relationships. One of the most thought-provoking parts of Chapter 1, indeed, was the analysis of twentieth-century history as generating growing contradictions in the feudal household and the rise of communist households, and the discussions of the potential challenges these contradictions might pose to capitalist class relationships within enterprises.

Fifth, I applaud the authors for their 'nonreductionist' stance. Rather than positing a particular relationship between capitalist and feudal modes, they allow their interactions to take different forms. Also, there is a clear understanding of marital relations as not simply a manner of extracting surplus labor; the authors discuss love and gender identities as aspects of these household relations, including their role in binding women and men into feudal relations.

Along with these strengths, I find a number of drawbacks; what follows is an interconnected listing of points of contention. In essence, I find problematic the view of the household and the capitalist economy as separate modes of production; the view of gender oppression within marriage as surplus labor extraction; and the downplaying of class differences among households and of the role of households, feudal or otherwise, in reproducing capitalist class relations.

Can we really view the household and the capitalist firm as distinct and separate modes of production? In fact, the feudal household described arose simultaneously with what the authors call capitalist class relationships, as commodity production left households and slave plantations and became organized by capitalist firms. Gender difference and inequality pervade both household and firm, and not by accident; capitalist development built on and transformed the precapitalist sexual division of labor into one between household and labor market, as well as one within the labor market.[2] With the husband focused on labor market activity and the wife on unpaid work in the home, the 'feudal' household is more of a marriage between the two spheres, rather than a distinct sphere. Indeed, using the terminology 'feudal' to refer to a household form particular to capitalism, and which has little in common with feudal relations other than the performance of unpaid labor, seems very inappropriate.

Also, while this dual mode of production formulation appears to give gender importance by spotlighting women's unpaid work in the household, the view of this work as essentially organized by a class relation (in which gender plays a large role), similar to class relations in the labor market, in fact downplays the importance of gender. Construing relations in the feudal household as class relations has its benefits: for example, the authors do not make the common mistake of locating all gender oppression within the household and hence of ignoring gender oppression in the labor market. And, indeed, in their concrete discussions of the operation of the feudal household, gender is always present. However, because this approach focuses on class and surplus labor extraction, gender (particularly the interconnections between gender relations in the household and in the labor market and polity) tends to fall between the cracks. The fact that husbands have power in the household precisely because they participate more in the capitalist sphere and because both economy and polity are male-dominated receives little attention. The fact that men earn higher wages than women in segmented labor markets receives short shrift; indeed, the authors appear to refer to unequal wages for equal work as 'subsumed class payments,' implying that they are not gender related. So, although the authors do discuss in detail the ways in which household and enterprise class relations support and undermine one another, their conceptualization of these as *class* relations seems to prevent them from focusing on the ways in which gender difference and inequality in the home and economy support or undermine one another. Indeed, in their section 'Women, Wages, and Class Struggle,' the authors discuss women's efforts to change extra-household supports of the feudal household, such as religion, the state, the content of teaching, and abortion laws, but do not mention at this point women's struggle in the labor market for higher wages and for access to men's jobs. In this way, gender differences among workers, and struggles of women versus men in the labor market, tend to disappear.

The separation of society into separate modes of production is central to the authors' analysis of household labor as exploitative. For the analysis of these relations focuses exclusively on the work within the household and the fact that this work is unequally distributed. What the authors ignore, or downplay, is the fact that usually the husband is also involved in long hours of work, but in this case, work for pay for the capitalist enterprise (or as a self-employed worker). But if we recognize (as the authors do in many parts of Chapter 1) that the 'feudal' marriage involves reciprocal obligations between the spouses – for the wife, doing the unpaid work in the home and the childcare, and, for the husband, earning family wages in the labor market – what happens to the notion of exploitation? The authors are silent on the fact that, while the husband is living on some of the unpaid labor of the wife, so is she living on his paid labor, which is used to purchase commodities to fill the family's needs. At one point, they seem to conceptualize his or her spending of his earnings on household consumption as his provision of the means of production, parallel to a capitalist's provision of means of production to the workers. But in the case of the capitalist, the means of production are procured through ownership of and access to capital, while in the case of the husband, the means of production are procured through labor. Indeed, in terms of overall hours of work (both paid and unpaid), it is not always or even necessarily the case that the wife works longer hours than the husband; indeed, recent studies show that, in husband-wage-worker/wife-full-time homemaker marriages, the husbands tend to work more total hours (paid plus unpaid labor) than the wives.[3] What sense can this feudal mode framework make of these data? Does exploitation exist here?

And how can the feudal household approach make sense of the hiring of domestic servants, a practice common at the turn of the century, if less so in the present? In this case, the wife may do little or no work, using the husband's income to pay the servant to do the work of maintaining the household, even to cater to her every personal need. Would the authors argue that the homemaker's time spent overseeing the servants is either necessary or surplus labor? Exploitation of the housewife, again, appears to be absent (although the domestic servant, whom the authors appear to situate in the 'ancient' mode of production is, in fact, the exploited one), and again, perhaps in terms of total hours of work, the husband works more and is hence exploited by his wife.

These examples point out the problems in understanding the essence of gender oppression within marriage as an issue of surplus labor extraction. Yes, we have seen above that construing gender relations in this way has its advantages. But perhaps these are outweighed by the disadvantages. A formulation which denies or ignores the fact that in many white, middle-class households, the majority of the domestic work has been done by poor women, disproportionately women of color, is very problematic. The focus on labor extraction further ignores another essential aspect of traditional family life which is central to the reproduction of those hierarchical and undemocratic relations in family, economy, and polity which concern the authors: authoritarian parenting.[4]

In my mind, for all its benefits, the conceptualization of traditional marital relations as surplus labor extraction is incorrect. To me, the essence of gender oppression in the household lies not in unequal labors performed but in the fact that the wife has specialized in unpaid labor in the household and the husband in income-producing activity, paid labor for the capitalist enterprise (or in self-employment or in being a capitalist). This kind of sexual division of labor, allied as it is with men's domination of the political and legislative arena, gives husbands power over their wives in many ways. Any individual husband, earning a family wage, is less dependent upon his wife than she on him. If they separate, he can purchase commodities to substitute for her labors; gender roles have already engendered in him a lack of interest in his children. She, on the other hand, would be unable to continue as before without his income to support herself and their children, for whom she has inherited responsibility according to the sexual division of labor. She cannot, for example, pay the rent or medical bills with her unpaid domestic labor. If she tries to earn income in the labor market, the jobs available to her make her survival and that of her children precarious. Add to this the fact that the economic and political spheres are organized to express and defend the gender interests of her husband. Laws and their enforcement are from the masculine point of view (as the authors point out, for example, condoning male violence against women, or failing to enforce child support laws); the capitalists who dominate the economy are almost all men, as are most employers; women, when in the labor market, have earned much less than men, even for jobs requiring comparable skills and experience. All of these factors – products of the sexual division of labor and male dominance not only in the home but in the economy and polity – work together to make traditional marital relationships oppressive to women, whether or not women work more total hours. The husband's power over his wife, secured in the other spheres, does allow him in some instances to extract extra work from her or, if he so chooses, to keep her out of the labor force like a protected lap dog. Thus the full-time homemaker married to a high-paid manager, who may do little or no 'labor' for him because of household servants, is at the same time totally financially dependent upon him, and may be psychologically subordinate as well. He may batter her or threaten her with divorce when she attempts to assert her opinions and needs within their relationship or when she tries to get a job to increase her independence. The 'ancient' household type – or single-mother family – is not simply an alternative possibility for such women, but a threatened outcome for many women and children if their husbands divorce or desert them.

Another problem with the feudal household analysis is the downplaying of class and race differences among households and of households' role in reproducing class and race inequality (indeed, race is not mentioned at all in the article). Situating gender/class relations in the household and capitalist class relations in the enterprise downplays the existence and importance of class differences between households and of race in both spheres. As I have noted, women from poor households have been forced to do the domestic labor of women living in wealthy ones. Up to half of all employed women worked as hired domestic servants through 1900; up through the Second World War the majority of employed black women worked as domestic laborers for white women. So the household is a site of class and race oppression as well as gender oppression. Economic inequality, including racial inequality, is reproduced generationally by the household's distribution of its income and wealth (or lack of it) to its children. What the authors might see as a communist household, in which the members democratically share decision-making, may be a household that exploits and oppresses domestic servants, who may be undocumented female workers of color, and one which derives considerable income and power from ownership of wealth, which it guards jealously for its children.

While I was contemplating the authors' analysis of the feudal household, I was struck by a counterexample. Two of my close friends are in a lesbian relationship and have a daughter. Both are trained as lawyers and have practiced as such. When their daughter was born, both took time off; the biological mother (whom I'll call Sue) took six months off and her lover and co-parent (whom I'll call Amy), one month. When the first month was over, it was with great sadness that Amy returned to her job; she had loved full-time parenting and missed their child tremendously, but the couple needed income to pay the bills. In the next few months, Amy's dissatisfaction with her job and her strong desire to be at home, plus a new job offer to Sue, then brought this joint decision: Amy would quit her job to stay at home full-time with their child, while Sue took the new full-time job offered to her. According to the authors' analysis, this is a feudal couple who have switched roles: first Sue was exploited, and then Amy. In actuality, both Sue and Amy appear to have preferred their period as full-time parents (false consciousness perhaps?); at this time, two months into the new arrangement, Sue is feeling particularly exploited.

How can we make sense of this example? First, each very much enjoys the work of caring for their child and the associated housework (although cleaning is not either's favorite). Second, the partner who specializes in unpaid work in the home is not at a gender disadvantage relative to her partner in the labor market: both have similar skills and can and have earned similar salaries in the labor market. Thus the wage-earning partner has no real long-term economic power over the other, in terms of a threat of withdrawing support; each member of the couple could financially support herself within a few months. Third, since both are women, ideological, political, and economic relations (other than the actual paycheck) do not in any way empower the wage-earner over the homemaker. In the sense of making joint and democratic decisions, then, this couple would fit in the communist household type; however, the specialization of one in household labor, doing more than half of it, places them in the exploitative, feudal mode. In my mind, this example shows both that: (1) we cannot understand the household, consistently, in terms of surplus labor extraction; and (2) we cannot separate oppression/exploitation in the household from relations in the capitalist economy. It is precisely the traditional man's specialization in paid work, and his privileged position in the economic and political spheres, which make his relationship to his wife an oppressive (but, I would argue, not necessarily exploitative) one; while gender relations oppress both Sue and Amy, they do not give Sue special powers over Amy, or vice versa.

In sum, while I am taken with many of the particulars of the authors' analysis of US households, I am not ready to adopt a feudal mode of production approach to the household. What then do I see as our options for understanding gender, class, and race? First, as the authors have done, we must avoid simple generalizations about the nature of gender, class, *and race* oppression/exploitation. Second, we must understand that these systems of differentiation and inequality are not simply interdependent and inter-connected, but also simultaneously determined and, in many ways, inseparable; each individual is, at once and inseparably, raced, classed, and gendered. Hence, gender has a different meaning for a black professional woman than for a white upper-class housewife or a Chicana domestic servant. Similarly, class, in the sense of one's relationship to the capitalist production process, is not separable from gender; jobs, for example, are race- and gender-typed, and the labor market systematically privileges men over women and whites over people of color. Third, we must recognize that there is no trans-historical content to any of these categories; they only have meaning in a particular time and place, in a particular society.[5] What the authors describe as a 'feudal household' did not exist in the colonial US economy, and may soon be relegated to the past. Fourth, I challenge the practice of giving primacy to issues of surplus labor extraction, as the authors do; as I have suggested, this may not in fact be the best way to understand gender inequality in the home or in the labor market, or to understand the process of racial oppression.

A Response by Zillah Eisenstein: Rejecting 'Precise' Marxism for Feminism

Let me just begin – in midstream thought – because I do not know how else to start a response to the Fraad, Resnick, and Wolff argument. I wonder why this argument has been written in this way at this particular time. After all, there are hardly any 'knights' or 'castles' in our discourse *or* our practice in the 1990s. There are just a very few 'feudal' households remaining in terms of the particular definition used. Households exist within the significant transformations of both gender and state relations as they play back on one another. If one agrees that this is the case, viewing the household as a 'precise' economic unit unto itself is at best problem-atic. So what is it these authors are thinking about?

Clearly they are thinking about Marxism – what they term 'precise' Marxism – but they are not *really* rethinking what it means. I do not think that one can creatively theorize about gender within the constraints of 'precise' Marxism. There is a problem here because it is not enough just to *rethink* Marxism. This is what many Feminists were doing through the 1970s but not what many of us who identify ourselves in part as Marxists are doing now. Our starting point is different today. It is not precise

Marxism. It is a Marxism that has been transformed by Feminism. It no longer stands alone, independent, as a guide in and of itself for analysis. In the past decade Feminists have revised Marxist analysis for our own purposes: I no longer am interested in precise Marxism.

The problem here is that Marxism is being re-*used,* not rethought. In contrast to Fraad, Resnick, and Wolff, I have no similar starting points for evaluating the household. Why? Because gender is not merely an ideological or a cultural construction as the authors state. Nor is gender devoid of biology. There is a complicated mixture of processes here which does not leave economics and its independent meanings intact. In a similar way, the household cannot be thought of as an economic construct without completely interweaving it with transformations of state relations (welfare, for instance) which are hardly solely economic. Gender weaves its way economically, politically, and culturally through the state and the family, the family and the household, the household and the market. I do not think that the place to focus is the household as a unit unto itself, much less as the unexpected site (in and of itself?) of revolutionary transformations (p. 41).

The authors cite me as someone who sees household labor as a straightforward affair: the capitalist always benefits at the woman's expense (p. 27). This may have been true in my 1979 writing, but clearly has not been true since then. I argue in *The Radical Future of Liberal Feminism* that the struggle which emerges from the conflicting relations between family and market, and between family and state, lays the basis for progressive and radically Feminist transformations. It is the politically engendered relations which are key here, not the economic household *per se.*

But to recognize this is to recognize the sexual class structuring of the state, the family, and the economy. I have written at great length on this issue in *Feminism and Sexual Equality* and *The Female Body and the Law.* The authors merely write off the possibility that women constitute a class as impossible: 'Women cannot comprise a class any more than men can' (p. 2). Obviously, the authors mean economic class here: they define class as any site wherever surplus labor is produced, appropriated and distributed.

But I do not mean that women are an economic class. Nor are we merely a biological class. Rather, we are a political class with a potential for consciousness as such. Women's 'engendered' bodies make us a class. It is a biological and political construction that is formulated through history. As a gendered class we enter the household after a day of work, and very often there is no man present, let alone a knight. There are just a very few women who work only in the household. Very many women today are poor. Quite a few of us are on welfare.

I'm sorry, neither the feudal nor the communist model helps me sort this out. Actually, the feudal model (silently) assumes the stance that all women are similar; exactly the view that is attributed to the notion that women are a class. My point, however, is that women constitute a political class, and we do this through very different economic and racial forms of household and family life. Why focus on the feudal model? I am lost.

I do not want to sound mean-spirited. But I am bothered by an argument which seems to make Marxism irrelevant to contemporary Feminist analysis by making it relevant to Marxists. There was a period in the mid 1970s, when Marxist-Feminists tirelessly addressed the issue of domestic labor and/or the household through a Marxist lens. I thought most of us were tired of trying to push and squeeze engendered labor into precise economic categories derivative of surplus value. We need instead to encompass the changing relations between state and family(ies) and between gender and economic class relations, to account for transformations of the market, like fast food restaurants, *into* family life and to acknowledge the effects of race and class on household and market relations.

I use the term 'socialist Feminist' to identify myself much less frequently than I did. It isn't because I am not still committed to a very similar politics. Rather the context has changed, and it almost takes too much time to try to explain what it does not mean than what it does. Instead, I try to talk and write about the ideas of racial and sexual egalitarianism in other ways. Until Marxists *really* rethink Marx this will continue to be the case.

A Response by Kim Lane Scheppele: Constructive Marxian Theory

American intellectuals and academics live in an age of theory. In the post-modernist, poststructuralist, discourse-driven, image-ridden, text-constituted culture of much of the humanities and some parts of the social sciences or the mathematically modeled, rational-choice, fully abstracted, history-indifferent, context-transcendent alternative which has gripped most of economics and many other parts of the social sciences, it's quite easy to forget that there's a world out there. And it's quite easy to imagine that theory actually makes a difference in the worlds about which academics and intellectuals write, though such is rarely the case. To those who are suffering, many of today's writers might as well be saying, 'Let them eat theory.'

And yet, theory matters. If there's one thing of which the new philosophy of science and the explosion of interpretive methods in the last decade should have convinced us, it's that there cannot be perception without theory and that everyone, whether professional theorist or not, acts in the world on the basis of systems of perceptions and beliefs that are inevitably organized around concepts and categories, rules and principles, that indicate what is important to notice and that provide a scheme for making sense of what happens. We are all theorists at some level or another. And it matters what theories we have.

Harriet Fraad, Stephen Resnick, and Richard Wolff have written a powerful chapter that expands and extends a particularly robust version of Marxian theory to an analysis of the traditional American family. By using concepts and categories from the analysis of more traditional economic sites to analyze family structures, Fraad, Resnick, and Wolff allow readers to *see households differently*. And those changed perceptions have obvious implications for action. This is not unworldly, 'academic' (meaning 'irrelevant'), theory-for-theory's-sake scholarship. This is theory that matters in the lives of people.

In my comments, I would like to take up two points. First, I will explore what is distinctive about Fraad, Resnick, and Wolff's method of theory-making and show its connections to another tradition of social analysis, one forwarded by Georg Simmel. Then I will show how the extension of this form of Marxian analysis to the family can help us think about the class dynamics of other social sites.

Marxian Theory as a Theory of Forms

The most striking thing about Fraad, Resnick, and Wolff's analysis is that class is primarily an adjective and not a noun. No, this is not a point about grammar. It is a point about the structure of thought. In much Marxian analysis, class is used primarily as a noun, where the classification of people into various categories and the description of what these various classes do is the main focus of research. In Fraad, Resnick, Wolff's analysis, however, how people are classified is secondary to another concern, the importance of *class processes*. Moving class into the adjectival position in this phrase has the effect of making the dynamic in which classes are produced central and the particular content of the various classes less crucial. Once that happens, it becomes possible to think about the 'process' as a fundamental social strategy that can have widely varying social content and can occur in a wide variety of social situations.

This is what Fraad, Resnick, and Wolff have done. Taking a process – the production, appropriation, and distribution of surplus labor – and abstracting it from its usual context (the workplace), Fraad, Resnick, and Wolff see what sense it makes in a different sphere of life, the household. There, the labor involved is of a very different sort (cooking, shopping, and cleaning rather than producing durable goods, for example). But it is labor nonetheless, and produced in surplus besides, since the individual household worker does more than provide for her own needs. From this similarity in basic structure of the workplace and the household, some unusual

observations can be generated. Fraad, Resnick, and Wolff are able to see
that the structure of the traditional American family is very much like the
structure of feudal workplaces. And the woman in the traditional American
household has much the same place as the serfs in the manor-based system
of medieval Europe.

Now this similarity has its limits. For one thing, women who are wives
in traditional American families are not treated in law the same way that
serfs were treated in medieval Europe, since among other things, women
can inherit property. For another, women and men share in joint projects
like the raising of children in which they both have an important stake
(though the sorts of sacrifices that each makes may differ enormously), and
this sort of joint project with obligations and benefits for both has no easy
parallel to the feudal context. Still, there is a surprising number of similarities. And that's where this analysis turns up much that is valuable.

Let us look more closely at just how this analysis is done. Fraad, Resnick,
and Wolff take a view that has been highly elaborated in the setting of the
workplace and abstract from this nuanced and detailed description a
particular fundamental social process – the production, appropriation, and
distribution of surplus labor. What Marxian theory has provided here is a
sense of what is important to examine and a way of making sense of social
processes in which this particular set of relations is judged to be most crucial
for an understanding of the whole context. Marxian theory is, as it were,
a sort of filter, admitting particular aspects of the description and screening
out other aspects. Marxian theory gives the analyst something in particular
to look for and a particular set of concepts and categories into which he
or she can assimilate new knowledge. Prepared with a conceptual scheme
and a sense of what to look for, the Marxian analyst can come into a new
social context and frame observations in useful, new ways.

But if analysis were simply a matter of sticking old labels on new things,
there wouldn't be much to say here. That is not what Fraad, Resnick, and
Wolff do, however. Once in this new setting, they unpack their conceptual
apparatus, and reveal just how powerful their framework is in redescrib-
ing familiar phenomena in new terms, terms that allow us to see the
interrelations and tensions in a setting which we might have thought we
already understood. Their extended description of the feudal household,
using what they know about the structure of feudal Europe to organize
observations about the traditional American household, enables the rest of
us to see important features of the social organization of the household that
would otherwise be missed.

Much, too, is revealed about the potential flexibility of Marxian theory.
In traditional form, Marxian theory has been applied chiefly to that sector
of human activity thought to be strictly economic, showing how that sector
is more basic and fundamental than others. Though, of course, other

sectors of life have been examined by Marxists, it has generally been to show that economic processes have consequences that go well beyond the boundaries of the economic sphere. But Fraad, Resnick, and Wolff's analysis does something else. It shows that class processes operate *within* other sectors and that those processes may take a form that is very different from the class processes of the larger economy. The prevailing economic form in the American economy may be capitalistic, but the form of class relations in the traditional American household is feudal. And there are strong interdependencies between these two forms; one does not displace the other. The conditions of existence of the feudal family may well include capitalist class processes in the larger economy. And capitalist class processes may come to depend, at least in part, on feudal households to produce and socialize new workers and to provide goods and services for those who spend most of their waking hours working for someone else.

How is it that this sort of analysis has escaped Marxians until now? My guess is that most Marxians have been focusing on the *content* of the class analysis rather than on the *form* of the arguments. This may seem too facile a distinction. Let me explain. By *content,* I mean that aspect of Marx's thought that emphasizes the specific locations of participants in traditional economic environments. As Marxism has grown and splintered, various theorists have come to disagree about the ways in which workplaces and economic processes ought to be examined but have not disagreed about the centrality of conventionally conceived economic sites in the analysis. A content-based Marxism sees economic sites and class relations in those sites as crucial to Marxian explanation, both for the analysis of economic relations and for the analysis of other social sites. A focus on *form,* on the other hand, allows analysts to see Marxian theory as a unique style of explanation, one that puts at center stage a person's relation to the production, appropriation, and distribution of whatever goods matter in a setting regardless of the specific site in which this happens. This detaches Marxian analysis from the traditional contexts and allows it to be applied to more and varied social settings. The study of form opens up a new range of potential subjects for Marxians. By moving from Marxian content to Marxian form, Fraad, Resnick, and Wolff have transcended the usual limitations on Marxian analysis.

In some ways, their method borrows more from Georg Simmel than it does from Marx himself. Simmel was a German social theorist, writing in the second half of the nineteenth century, who emphasized the study of social forms. Though Simmel never explained exactly what he meant by social forms, his writings emphasized social processes that could be found in many settings, and Simmel focused on those aspects of a social process that proved to be similar across social sites. For example, in one of his most famous essays, 'The Triad,' Simmel described how the entry of a third party into a dyad completely changes the dynamics of a social grouping (Simmel

1950, 145–69). With the presence of a third party, coalitions may form, the third party may mediate between the other two, or the third party may try to derive advantage from playing the other two against each other. Exactly which of these options occurs depends on the specifics of the circumstances, but these various new potentials are there regardless of whether the triad occurs in law (with the entry of a judge into a fray between two disputants), in marriage (with the entry of a child – or even a lover to one of the spouses – into the formerly exclusive pairing), or in any other social settings where dyads and triads can be found. By extracting the basic social process underlying the specific manifestation in any individual instance, Simmel was able to provide substantial insight into many different substantive areas.

Fraad, Resnick, and Wolff do this also. By emphasizing the basic social form of a *class process* (rather than a class with specific content that cannot be generalized across settings), they transcend the site-specific analyses that have characterized much of Marxian theory. And they open up a new range of possibilities for Marxian thought. The study of the household is an important beginning, but their method should allow them to perform equally insightful analyses in other spheres as well.

Rethinking Marxian Concepts

Fraad, Resnick, and Wolff's analysis not only performs the valuable service of giving us a new framework within which to think about and analyze households, but it also has the potential to be even more helpful than that. If there are similarities between forms of economic organization and forms of household, as their analysis certainly demonstrates, then perhaps we can work from the study of household forms to refine our understanding of economic organization, just as Fraad, Resnick, and Wolff work from explication of the forms of economic organization in order to analyze the forms of households.

Theories act as filters, screening out those observations and elements that distract from the central business at hand, and the specific research sites that are used to refine and elaborate theories have properties that tend to focus theoretical development in particular ways. But when a theory developed for one purpose is transferred to a new site, as is the case in the Fraad, Resnick, and Wolff piece, the opportunity arises to see what features of the new site might usefully be brought back into the study of the site from which the theory originally came. The study of households allows for more fruitful development of the original theory.

For example, one persistent feature of most of the workplaces which Marxians study is the imbalance in numbers between those whose labor is appropriated and those who appropriate the labor of others. In most work sites, there are almost always more workers than appropriators. But in the feudal household, the reverse is usually the case. Often a wife and mother will find her labor appropriated not only by her husband, but also by her children, leaving her in the apparently anomalous position (from a traditional Marxian point of view) of being a single person providing surplus labor for multiple appropriators, each of whom may have different needs and demands. But perhaps this situation is not as unique to households as it may appear. Perhaps there are classes of workers who have that pattern of demands in their work setting, even in capitalist economies. Service workers may come closest, particularly teachers, nurses, and other not-so-incidentally female-dominated occupations. And perhaps this Marxian-Feminist analysis of the household could be extended and borrowed in such a way that it encourages new insights in analyzing the more traditionally conceived work sites. The presence of demands from several different directions may encourage such workers to do what housewives often do, to turn structural problems into psychological problems[6] and internalize the conflicting expectations as a personal failure, thus limiting the potential for seeing the class processes as changeable.

Take, for example, the isolation that many traditional housewives feel. One characteristic of the feudal household is that each woman has her own 'castle' to clean – and group organizing and group projects are not encouraged. There is a duplication of effort and labor in many different isolated households, and generally one and only one serf per site. Now this is quite different from feudal organization as it was practiced in medieval Europe, where there were typically multiple serfs per manor, but perhaps this new adaptation tells us something important. Perhaps there are work sites in the contemporary United States that share this feature of the household, where workers are isolated from others similarly situated and where close ties to those in different class positions are a more prominent feature of daily life than ties to those who share one's own class position. Again, female-dominated occupations strike me as some of the most prominent examples: secretaries who work in isolated offices for single bosses may feel this way just as teachers who work alone in a classroom might. (Traveling salesmen may also have this sort of social organization, though most traveling salesmen are not women.) Perhaps the class processes in these sites operate differently from the class processes in sites where workers share a common bond with others similarly situated. For one thing, there are much higher barriers to the development of class consciousness where those whose labor is appropriated are systematically isolated from others who share a common fate.

Fraad, Resnick, and Wolff's analysis of the ideology of love also illustrates something useful that might be taken back into work settings for further refinement. Women learn that being in love with a man has its appropriate expression in cooking, cleaning, and shopping for him, though there are many other forms that feeling could take. Similarly, workers learn that being dedicated to a job means working longer hours, with strong commitment and substantial neglect of other aspects of their lives – even though they don't get all the benefits from such effort. Salaried professionals may find themselves in this situation, where dedication to 'the profession' finds its expression in self-sacrifice not for other persons or even for a particular firm, but rather for the profession as a whole. The ideology of professional communities may be to economic organization what the ideology of love is to households. In both cases, the ideology generates sustained pressures that produce benefits for concrete individuals who themselves never have to get mixed up in the nasty business of coercing someone else to work. The work is done from ideology, not from explicit force or pressure, and that makes the cost of maintaining particular class processes much smaller. Seeing the process at work in the ideology of love ought to make our analysis of the ideologies of work more sophisticated.

This Marxian–Feminist analysis of the household, then, provides an occasion for rethinking the traditional subject matter of Marxian theory. And it provides new tools for Feminists as well. Once we realize that individuals are engaged in multiple class processes simultaneously, and that these class processes are importantly conditioned by gender processes which provide some conditions of existence for the class processes, Marxians and Feminists should find that there is a common analysis that recognizes the complexity of human existence for both men and women who might struggle to do things differently.

A Response by Nancy Folbre and Heidi Hartmann: The Persistence of Patriarchal Capitalism

We commend Fraad, Resnick, and Wolff for their detailed analysis of the household as a site of production and distribution. We agree with their basic argument that gender inequality is analogous to class inequality and that no particular social site should be privileged in theory or practice. We disagree, however, with many of their specific arguments, including their characterization of our work.

It is a pleasure openly to debate a theoretical interface that most economists have ignored. The authors locate their analysis within the Marxist–Feminist problematic and waste little ink on criticisms of economists who reject this problematic. But it is important to note that – unlike Fraad, Resnick, and Wolff – many contemporary neo-Marxists who pride themselves on their

departure from traditional orthodoxies along some dimensions utterly fail
to recognize the significance of gender inequalities. Although practitioners of what has come to be known as 'analytical Marxism' occasionally deign
to use Feminine pronouns, they seldom if ever cite Feminist theory or
research. For such practitioners, economism and androcentrism go hand
in hand – all the more reason to appreciate the critique of economism that
informs this contribution.

This common ground notwithstanding, we challenge the authors' interpretation of Marxist and socialist Feminist theories, their general theoretical
perspective, and their optimism regarding the rise of 'communist,' or egalitarian households. Fraad, Resnick, and Wolff overstate the uniqueness of
their substantive claims. Many Feminists have described the revolutionary
changes taking place in US households, including the trend towards more
egalitarian marriages and more nonmarriage (Hartmann 1987; McCrate 1987;
Bergmann 1986). Many Feminists have emphasized that men, as well as
capitalists, benefit from control over women's labor power (Hartmann 1981
and 1979; Delphy 1984; Gardiner 1979). Others have described these
benefits in terms of the expropriation of surplus (Folbre 1982; Harrison
1973). Others have used feudalism as an analogy to describe the traditional
household, with the husband-master appropriating the surplus labor of the
wife-serf (Benston 1969; Middleton 1983). And still others have emphasized
the importance of considering gender relations at all sites, not only within
the family (Hartmann 1979 and 1981; Sokoloff 1981; Eisenstein 1979).

We disagree with their characterization of our work. They include
Hartmann and Folbre in a long list of Marxist-Feminists 'who apply class
analysis only outside the boundaries of the household and chiefly to enterprises', and later they write, 'for them the household labor of women is a
straightforward, predictable affair that always benefits capitalists at women's
expense'. In note 33, they attribute the 'notion that women's unpaid
household labor is universally supportive of and positive for the capitalist
system in general' to Hartmann, among others. How disturbing to be listed
as perpetrators of the very arguments we have actively criticized! We have
explicitly contrasted these traditional Marxist-Feminist arguments with
our own emphasis on the changing interactions between patriarchy and
capitalism.

Heidi Hartmann was one of the first to call attention to the economic
dimensions of inequality between men and women within the household
and to insist that capitalists were not the primary beneficiaries. In (1979)
'The Unhappy Marriage of Marxism and Feminism,' she wrote, 'men and
capitalists often have conflicting interests, particularly over the use of
women's labor power ... men [seek] to control women's labor power ...
for the purpose of serving men in many personal and sexual ways' (1979,
11, 14). Two other articles stress that women and men have vastly different

economic interests within the family household and that men's control over women's labor power occurs outside as well as inside the household (Hartmann 1976, 1981). Nancy Folbre's (1982) article 'Exploitation Comes Home' develops the same point in more formal terms, explicitly defining the rates of exploitation of individual family members in terms of necessary and surplus labor.

These inaccuracies in the characterization of Marxist Feminist literature in general, and of our work in particular, distract from the more important aspects of the essay. Its most important contribution lies not in any new emphasis on what goes on within the household, but rather in its narrative of the complex interrelationships (or should we say overdeterminations?) between cultural, psychological, religious, political, and economic 'conditions of existence' of inequality. Fraad, Resnick, and Wolff argue convincingly that we need to move beyond the household to a consideration of 'the class and gender processes that may exist and interact at all social sites' (p. 41).

While we agree with this general argument, we are not convinced that a formulaic set of class processes, including ancient, communist, feudal, and capitalist, provides the best set of conceptual tools for analyzing class and gender processes and their interaction at all sites. This terminology calls attention to the ways surplus is appropriated rather than to who extracts it and benefits from it. Sometimes these two aspects of surplus appropriation overlap, as in 'capitalist class process' which effectively conveys both a process and an outcome. But sometimes they are at odds, as when the term 'feudal class process' is used to describe the appropriation of surplus by men for men, not by or for feudal lords. Fraad, Resnick, and Wolff occasionally lose sight of the men who control this class process. For instance, we learn that 'a married female surplus labor producer, especially one with children, cannot easily escape a particularly hostile household' (p. 24). Surely they mean 'husband,' rather than household.

We call attention to these seemingly minor issues of terminology because they convey a reluctance to deal with patriarchy as a social system that perpetuates male power over women. Aside from a brief reference in the opening quote from Simone de Beauvoir, Fraad, Resnick, and Wolff ignore both the concept of patriarchy and efforts to conceptualize it in Marxian terms. Many socialist Feminists, like ourselves, describe the appropriation of surplus by men as 'patriarchal' exploitation in order to emphasize the ways men can benefit economically from their traditional authority as fathers and as husbands and, in an era when the roles of husbands and fathers are changing, from their position as men. Why should we describe this process as 'feudal' when the appropriation of surplus by men from both women and children long preceded and probably provided a model for the appropriation of surplus by feudal lords, not vice versa (Lerner 1986; Folbre 1987)?

The 'gender processes' which the authors use to describe the non-economic (i.e., cultural, political, and psychological) dynamics of inequality between men and women also require elaboration. Unlike economic class processes, these do not seem to come in different historical forms. Are they constant over time? Do they vary by the class, race or ethnicity of the householders being discussed? We are troubled by this stark dichotomy between economic and noneconomic, which equates 'gender processes' to noneconomic processes. What about the many cultural, political, and psychological dynamics of inequality between capitalists and wageworkers? These are apparently neither gender processes nor class processes.

Although we admire the authors' account of the importance of noneconomic processes, we believe that many aspects of the capitalist economic system reinforce patriarchy, including sex segregation in the labor market, women's lower wages, and the devalorization of nonmarket work. From our point of view, these are more than conditions of existence. They are examples of a basic economic complementarity between patriarchy and capitalism that has made patriarchy quite resistant to change.

Our theoretical perspective acknowledges the importance of what Fraad, Resnick, and Wolff term class and gender processes, but we place these within the larger context of systems of inequality. We believe that class and gender and ethnicity and race identify collective interests as well as social processes, and these collective interests shape cultural and psychological as well as economic dynamics. Men are at odds with but also dependent upon women and children, just as European-Americans are at odds with (but also dependent upon) other racial and ethnic groups and capitalists are at odds with (but also dependent upon) wage earners.

These dimensions of conflict define different systems of inequality that complement and contradict, stabilize and destabilize each other in fairly contingent and unpredictable ways. Their coevolution has a historical logic far more complex than the 'laws of motion' of a single mode of production known as capitalism. But we can discern possibilities and probabilities that go beyond the simple observation that everything is a condition of existence for everything else. People develop collective identities based on class, gender, ethnicity, and race and consciously choose to participate in the shifting coalitions that shape political struggle.

Finally, we believe that Fraad, Resnick, and Wolff's optimism about the imminence of the communist household can not withstand a deeper understanding of the systemic nature of patriarchy. Their descriptive narrative of women's rebellion against the traditional feudal (cum patriarchal) household is complex and subtle, but the underlying plot closely resembles Friedrich Engels's old line that women's participation in wage labor would increase their bargaining power and empower them to end patriarchal oppression. The authors paint a rosy picture of contemporary households, with many women living separately from other adults and engaging in ancient class processes (control over their own surplus) and as many as 20 per cent of all women in couples enjoying communist class processes (collective control over surplus).

From our point of view, patriarchal inequalities have proved far more persistent. Increases in women's bargaining power in the household have been counterbalanced, in part, by men's increased freedom to avoid household responsibilities. Yes, many women living in households without adult men have control over their own earnings, but those earnings are far lower than those that men enjoy. More importantly, many mothers are raising children on their own with virtually no financial assistance from fathers and very little assistance from the state. Far from controlling their own surplus in an ancient class process, many of these women are being exploited by men who are not even present in the household, indeed by all those who benefit from the work of mothering but avoid paying for it. They are being exploited not by a feudal class process, but by a publicly sanctioned patriarchy enforced by the state, one that is barely preferable to the private patriarchal household (Folbre 1985; Brown 1981).

Perhaps Fraad, Resnick, and Wolff's optimism about the prevalence of communist households stems from a vague analysis of the politics of the household. The authors write that 'in a communist household, all adult members ... do necessary and surplus labor and collectively appropriate their surplus'. How is collective appropriation defined? Are decisions made by consensus, or by majority rule? Do children get a vote? Later they suggest that 'regular, systematic variation of persons across all the class positions in the household might well be deemed a condition of existence of household communism,' but they seem to ignore this strict criterion when they assert that 'approximately 20 per cent of two-adult households in the US may be characterized now as comprising communist class processes'.

That 20 per cent of American two-adult households are egalitarian, let alone communist, is surely news to Betty Friedan, Molly Yard, and the FBI, let alone to the 10 million women supposedly in such households. No statistical data on time spent on housework by men – or on equal earnings by women – supports Fraad, Resnick, and Wolff's optimistic view that women and men can freely adopt all class positions in the household.

We share Fraad, Resnick, and Wolff's enthusiasm for many of the changes they describe. We join in celebrating the important gains that women have made, gains that redound – in the long run – to the benefit of men and children as well. We recognize that many men and women value the ideal of the communist household, an ideal that can inform and sustain the struggle against capitalist class processes. But we do not think that patriarchy is so easily vanquished. All the more reason to work together to develop a better theory and a better practice, one that places relations between women and men – not the household or any other specific site – at the center of economic analysis.

A Response by Stephanie Coontz:
History and Family Theory

Too many Marxist discussions of household or family have treated reproduction and gender either as relatively changeless and natural or as mechanical 'reflections' of the larger mode of production. Emphasis on exploitation in the paid workforce has led Marxists consistently to underestimate or downplay the intractability of male domination and the extent of violence against women, which often takes place in a household setting; male workers' interests as a gender have been ignored and their prejudices against women or active attempts to sabotage women's organization dismissed as 'false consciousness.' A focus on rational economic behavior and abstract 'class interests' in the marketplace has led to predictions that have time and again proved false: that the entry of women into the work world would dissolve sex role distinctions and the bourgeois family; or that employers would substitute cheap female labor for male labor instead of perpetuating sex segregation; or that a strong labor movement would facilitate the full integration of women.

In welcome opposition to such approaches, the authors urge Marxist economists to accept a point long made by radical Feminists and too long ignored in other circles: women's labor is appropriated in families as well as factories. Women's household work is controlled and unevenly divided by their husbands or fathers rather than by a capitalist; the household is a fundamental unit for economic as well as historical and sociological analysis.

At the same time, the authors want us to look beyond the immediate economic dynamics of household production and distribution so that we can understand the ideological role of gender in society at large. 'Gender processes are conditions of existence for class processes,' yet gender processes are also determined by class processes. Asserting the 'complex interdependence of class and gender,' the authors ask us to consider not only the production and distribution of 'surplus labor' in the household, but also the production and distribution of meanings in both the family and the larger social formation. They label this a 'gender process,' as distinct from the 'class process' of producing, appropriating, and distributing surplus labor.

The last distinction, however, reveals that, despite its merits, the essay has not fully broken with the problems that plague much Marxist economic writing: its lack of historical specificity and the reduction of complex social relations to formalistic categories. In some places, the essay sounds as if the authors mean to apply 'precise' economic measures of surplus labor to the household. But when they begin to do so, they reduce the complex meaning of family life for the working class into an economic model of men expropriating all of a woman's labor beyond that required to reproduce her existence. While such a theoretical construct correctly highlights women's subordination within the family, it is too simplistic in describing male relations to the family and it fails to grapple with the complexities of defining 'surplus labor,' especially in households with children.

Men do gain material benefits from women's domestic labor, but calling this the production and appropriation of 'surplus labor' does not avoid the problems the authors correctly identify in earlier Marxist arguments that women produce surplus value. An economic model of the household that does not incorporate the special social relations involved in childrearing, or reduces them to neoclassical cost-benefit equations, misses some vital dynamic in gender and age inequalities.

Male dominance and privilege within the family are real, but most men neither make a profit on them nor enjoy unlimited seigniorial rights. Men do support women and children at a level beyond which the latter could reproduce themselves in this society (as postdivorce statistics on poverty show) *at the same time as they appropriate work and deference from them.* Are children extracting their parents' surplus labor? Are leisured middle- or upper-class women surplus-takers from their husbands?

An adequate theoretical account of the family not only has to strip away the myth that it is an organic unit with an equal distribution of power and resources, but it *also* has to show how gender and age hierarchies confer familial, sexual, and enhanced consumption privileges on working-class men at the cost of binding them more firmly to their class position. It must show how middle- and upper-class women are subordinated as part of the same processes that strengthen their class privileges. Such an account must also explore the ways in which these processes backfire.

Family theory must address the tension between the family's role in maximizing the use of material and emotional resources for all its members, at least vis-à-vis other units in society, *and* in legitimizing the unequal distribution of power and rewards, both internally and externally. It must, in other words, explain the dualities of family life in working-class survival and resistance as well as encompass the variations in family form and function among different classes and ethnic groups.

I do not think such a theoretical model can be centered on surplus labor. I would reserve that concept for specific cases in which male control over women (and children) intersects with or paves the way for control of wealth-producing property. In some patrilocal kinship societies, for example, male household heads built on age and gender inequalities to extract household surpluses from wives and children. They then used these surpluses in feasting, gift-giving, and bridewealth exchanges outside the household, thereby accumulating new labor, obligations, and clients from outside the family. The work of wives and children allowed certain chiefs to become 'big men' and to parlay their rank and status into regular entitlements to labor from *other* households. During this process, as Engels recognized more than a century ago, wives can be said to occupy a class relationship to their husbands. Similarly, in twentieth-century rural Turkey, landowning household heads have used traditional prerogatives of age and gender to extract their relatives' labor in carpet-weaving workshops with the emergence of capitalist relations of production (Berik 1989).

It is important to distinguish between such cases and other kinds of oppression of women, else we miss some of the complexities of gender and class interactions. Typically, once a group of men does parlay the expropriation of their wives' labor into more regular methods of labor extraction beyond the household, pressures for intensified household production subside and the direct extraction of surplus product from wives and children declines. This may mean, however, that a wife's isolation and dependence increase at the same time as her exploitation decreases. Domesticity, for example, tends to emerge only in family systems where gender relations have been separated from the mechanisms for consolidating property or extracting surplus products and/or labor. In these circumstances gender relations within the family begin to play quite a different role, one closer to the authors' discussion of the production and distribution of meanings.

Of course, both the extraction of household labor from women and the ways in which women's work is organized and appropriated in the larger class system are intimately connected to the production and distribution of sexual meanings. Conversely, the production of gender inequalities inevitably means that women have diminished control over their labor and a smaller call on resources than their husbands, even when they are not producing 'surplus labor' for their husbands. I am not sure that it makes sense at any time to separate the production and distribution of meanings from 'class processes' and to define class processes solely in terms of surplus labor; I wonder if this is a way of sidestepping a base/superstructure argument. I would like to see a fuller integration of the 'economic' and the ideological elements of the family: on the one hand, emphasis on the way that work and resources are organized and distributed within the household; on the other, recognition of the household's role in reproducing cultural meanings and power relations that organize the entire social division of labor. Such an integration will require much more specific historical and empirical analysis of the 'complex interdependence of class and gender.' Let us turn, then, to the authors' analysis of modern American households.

Fraad, Resnick, and Wolff recognize that 'traditional' households in capitalist America – by which they seem to mean the nuclear family with breadwinning husband and domestic wife – do not operate on capitalist or liberal principles but incorporate some social relations usually associated with tributary or feudal systems. They label such households 'feudal,' arguing that the wife's role cannot be understood in terms of capitalist economic processes, and they make a vigorous case against the notion that there is some invariant or necessary relation, either positive or negative, between women's 'noncapitalist' labor in such households and men's wage labor in the economy. They point not only to the ways that 'feudal' households sustain capitalism but also to the conflicts between such household relations and those of capitalism. These conflicts have accelerated in recent years, they argue, breaching old walls between 'private' and 'public' spheres and opening new political possibilities for anticapitalist struggle.

Yet these points should lead toward a much more geographically and historically specific discussion of class, gender, and household relations than is found here. The description of the 'traditional' household, for example, never explains when and where the 'feudal' household and gender system arose or how it interacted with early capitalist development. There is no analysis of how the household relations and gender roles which the authors describe vary by class, race, period, or nationality. Indeed, the model conflates some elements that were historical *alternatives* in successive family systems even within the same social stratum. What the authors call the 'feudal' household is what historians usually term the domestic or Victorian family: this family ideal severely condemned and endeavored to end legally and socially sanctioned male violence in the home, substituting an ideology of romance and separate spheres for an earlier type of male dominance based on force and patriarchal authority. (To be sure, this ideology did not end male violence but merely privatized it; yet it also gave women much more moral and legal leverage to struggle collectively against such violence.)

The designation of the white, Victorian, Anglo-American nuclear family as 'feudal' rests on some rather dubious historical analogies. Most European historians would not agree that feudal societies require 'no intermediary role' for markets or prices 'in the relation between the producer and the appropriator of surplus labor,' and few demographers would accept a quantification of a woman's labor which assumes that the hours above those necessary to reproduce her own existence constitute surplus labor for a husband/feudal lord. Analogies between wives and serfs are surely rather impressionistic. The ideology that justified European serfdom as well as the sites of both the most intense exploitation and most successful resistance of serfs were qualitatively different than the ideology of domesticity and the sources of coercion and resistance for wives in the nuclear family.

Dynamics of social control are also not comparable. The political alliances and overlapping powers that allowed feudal lords to extract surplus from their serfs were qualitatively different from the web of emotion, dependence, and carefully separated spheres that bound nineteenth-century women to their husbands despite a legal revolution in the rights of wives. The modern battered wife syndrome has little in common with a feudal military foray or police action, and may indeed be associated with the breakdown of older patriarchal structures.

The authors never clarify the origins or physical location of the 'feudal household,' but it seems clear that this household did not exist in European feudalism. Wealthy medieval households were centers of production and distribution, involving many people beyond the family and operating on very different dependencies from those centered on female domesticity. The households of the poor were often truncated, since children left home to work in the homes of richer neighbors; both husband and wife engaged in work that generated goods or wages. Only among the emerging middle class, and only slowly, did a sexual division of labor become a defining household characteristic, and it did not originally denigrate household production but glorified it.

Most of the gender processes which the authors describe as conditioning the 'feudal household' are very specific to western capitalism, especially democratic capitalism. The example of how romantic love is used to generate 'feudal' households illustrates this point, since the ideology of romantic love developed in close association with wage labor and the modern petit bourgeoisie. Earlier ideals of romance, such as medieval courtly love, were very limited in scope, and they specifically undermined the relations necessary for the 'feudal' household described in Chapter 1 by denigrating married love and sanctioning adultery. While Chaucer provides one early literary example of the bourgeois ideal of married love, he significantly situates it in the relatively new middle class exemplified by the Franklin who marries above his station, and he bases it on values of honor and rationality that were left out of the later evolution of romantic love.

Gender processes in the nineteenth-century 'feudal' household in America, moreover, were quite different from those in the earlier colonial one. Colonial households had no concept of 'breadwinning' husbands and 'dependent' wives, nor did they justify male dominance on the basis of separate spheres and different male and female natures. Men were clearly in charge of religion and carried out most religious duties, at home and in the larger community.

The ideology of romantic love and separate spheres was a nineteenth-century alternative to an earlier notion that women were simply bound by God and law to subordinate themselves to their husbands. So was the 'Feminization of American religion.' The authors' explanation of women's religious activities as resulting from a man's distribution of his feudal surplus is clearly inadequate here. Such a formula does scant justice to the American phenomenon of evangelical revivals where wives and daughters led the congregation in prayers for the sinner who headed the household, besieged him with tracts, and eventually listened to his emotional confession at 'the anxious bench.' Nor does this formula explain the leading role of women in constructing new forms of social control and social welfare in America. The authors do note that in some cases women freely donate their labor to religious groups, but they remark that in such cases 'no class process ... at all' is involved. Surely this is too stark a pair of alternatives, even by their narrow definition of what constitutes a class process. The immersion of nineteenth-century women in religious activities has to be seen as part of a major sea change in both class and gender relations.

Theories of biological essentialism, similarly, which the authors consider to be a prime mechanism for reproducing 'feudal' households, arose in reaction to the contradictions between democratic ideology and the inequalities of gender and race in developing capitalism. They are surprisingly absent from earlier defenses of male dominance. Indeed, one recent comparative study of the United States, Italy, Russia, and Sweden found that the ideology of women's separate sphere and biologically ordained differences in behavior developed only in America.

It appears that the growth of democracy, wage labor, and racism worked together in the eighteenth- and nineteenth-century Anglo-American milieu, and to a lesser extent in France after the French Revolution, to create a hitherto unknown model of the family, based on an ideology of separate spheres, romantic love, and female domesticity and morality. At the beginning of the twentieth century, this family ideal began to be undermined by a new culture of consumption, a more democratic but also more passive notion of individual rights, and a transformation in work patterns and political discourse. These came into conflict with many earlier bourgeois family forms and ideologies, although they reinforced others, leading to a recurring twentieth-century sense of crisis in the family.

We need a theory of the western household that explains the precise historical relation between the emergence of capitalism, the rise of liberal theory, and the creation or re-creation of 'noncapitalist,' antiliberal behaviors and values in familial or gender roles. Labeling these behaviors 'feudal' or even noncapitalist seems questionable because it fails to capture the dialectical relationship and mutual reconstitution of phenomena such as contract law and romantic love, the 'rights of man' and the biological definition of woman. Our theoretical model of capitalism must encompass its characteristic use, revival, and reworking of many coercive behaviors and values that violate its liberal theory.

In correctly rejecting a functionalist model of how the male-dominant, 'feudal' household is linked to capitalist production, the authors fail to develop an alternative, more nuanced account of the articulation, interaction, and conflicts between the two. We need a theory that explains the mutual reinforcement of 'noncapitalist' household processes and capitalist worksite processes. Such a theory must then explain how, where, and why those nonliberal household values began to be undermined by or came into conflict with the economic, political, and cultural processes of maturing capitalist nations. Generalizations about 'the feudal household' in an abstract capitalist economy, by contrast, invite the same objection Marx raised against attempts 'to metamorphose my historical sketch of the genesis of capitalism *in Western Europe* into a historical-philosophic theory of the *"marche generale"'* (letter to the editor of *Otyecestvenniye Zapisky,* late 1877, emphasis added).

The authors never give us concrete examples of where communist households have arisen and precisely how they function, but I suspect that a more historically grounded discussion of the origins and nature of 'feudal' households would modify the authors' contention that an egalitarian, or even a collective, household marks a new 'communist' alternative to feudal traditions. The ideology of bourgeois domesticity never sanctioned male violence within the household, and most early theorists of the 'traditional' household – especially female ones – advocated many of the so-called communist features of the modern model: an absence of force, even against children; joint decision-making; unselfish commitment; sharing of resources, and so on. Childcare and housework were certainly not shared equally, but the middle-class household relieved women of their formerly most onerous aspects by hiring servants and buying new labor-saving devices. I am not suggesting that traditional households were not male dominant, merely that they introduced qualitatively new ideals of reciprocity and opened the door to calls for new kinds of equality.

But the egalitarian innovations of the domestic family were not only compatible with, they were often *supportive of* exploitative economic relations at a level *above* the family, much as many modern egalitarian households could not exist without their members' class and race privileges – for example, the ability to hire household help. Indeed, nineteenth-century bourgeois ideology advocated a kind of socialism *within* the family as an antidote to agitation for reform *beyond* the family. The family was to be a site of social cooperation and resource pooling, where competition and the cash nexus were banished. Investment in such a family was explicitly put forward as an alternative to wider schemes for economic cooperation. Many modern families, especially those that avail themselves of 'couples therapy,' likewise serve to cover their members' retreat from wider social concerns: what Yuppies call 'cocooning' is not what most of us would call communism.

(Like their nineteenth-century counterparts, moreover, most such families' rhetoric about shared work and equality disguises continued gender inequalities. Arlie Hochschild's (1989) *The Second Shift* documents the immense gap between rhetoric and reality in families that claim to subscribe to the 'full partnership' ideal.)

Even if one were to accept the characterization of the nineteenth-century domestic family as a household with feudal relations and to agree that a revolution is currently occurring in many such homes, one might more plausibly argue that the revolution taking place is a bourgeois one, with all the contradictions of the same. Historically, bourgeois revolutions have simultaneously fostered radical new ideas about equality, liberty, and fraternity, *and* accelerated the gap between haves and have-nots. Bourgeois freedom meant new liberation for the lucky, new isolation for the unlucky. The 'ancient' and the 'communist' household types described by the authors might simply be two sides of the same bourgeois revolution in the family.

To appreciate fully the 'complex interdependence of class and gender' we need to explain how the evolution of democratic capitalism simultaneously reinforced and undermined 'noncapitalist,' noncontractual values within the household, as well as how gender relations and family forms have both resisted and facilitated the spread of wage labor. Only such an explanation will pave the way for a grasp of the complex and contradictory processes that comprise the current 'family crisis' in America.

Finally, in addition to the problems associated with the ahistorical nature of this discussion, I am bothered by the narrow definition of class relations that is used. Many of the authors' insights into the complexity and mutual determination of class and gender relations seem to me to point toward an understanding that class is far more than the economic process of production, appropriation, and distribution of surplus labor. After all, surplus labor was and will be produced, appropriated, and distributed in nonclass societies as well. Class is a system of symbiotic but opposed power relations and interests involved in both organizing and contesting the process of defining, producing, appropriating, and distributing surplus labor. One of those power relations is gender.

In prehistoric and ancient societies, the use of gender relations to extract household surpluses was critical in the development of ranked clans from communal kinship societies and in the transformation of leading clans' redistribution functions into class privileges. Racial or chauvinistic categories were also central to the development of early class societies: patron-client relations between different kin groups, tributary exchanges, and outright conquest established a lower class of 'strangers,' who were permanent juniors in relation to the ruling elite. The production and distribution of such hierarchies has helped constitute the class relationships of all new modes of production.

Marxist theory needs to develop a way of conceptualizing gender, race, and chauvinism as part of the class process. These are not subsumed by class but they are also not separate systems; gender, race, and chauvinism are vital components of the development and dynamics of class. No society has constructed class relations without the aid of specific gender and ethnic dynamics. It is not just a question of adding gender and race analysis to class analysis and bringing them all into interaction, but of expanding our definition of class processes to include gender and race relations.

In *The German Ideology*, Marx suggests that the 'mode of cooperation' is inseparable from the productive forces: 'a certain mode of production, or industrial stage, is always combined with a certain mode of co-operation, or social stage, and this mode of co-operation is itself a "productive force."' Modes of cooperation – or coercion – are critical in defining class, which is, after all, a relationship rather than a quantity of labor. Race, gender, and family are central methods of organizing cooperation and coercion, of defining what is surplus labor and ordering its appropriation or distribution. They are also sites of contradiction in the Marxist sense – places where built-in oppositions occur that are both necessary to perpetuate a particular process or social system and yet are also destructive of that process or social system.

I look forward to the authors' further research on the relation between the process of organizing and distributing labor in the household and in the larger society, and I hope for an integration of the currently disconnected 'economic' and 'political' analyses of that process. A satisfactory Marxist account of the household must achieve such an integration. It must also be historically and geographically grounded, for different societies have built gender and race into very different class relations. No analysis of the contradictions of class and gender or the political prospects of utilizing such contradictions for progressive social change can afford to neglect concrete historical and empirical study; no concrete historical and empirical study, however, is useful if it fails to address the definitional and theoretical questions raised in arguments such as those in Chapter 1.

The Authors Reply:
Class, Patriarchy, and Power

The commentaries on our argument range from the appreciative to the dismissive, from welcoming a different kind of Marxism into the domain of household analysis to exuding a cold hostility to its presence there.[7] The 'unhappy marriage' of Marxism and Feminism has, not surprisingly, convinced at least one of our commentators that divorce is the only, necessary and sufficient, response. Others share with us the sense that both partners need and complement each other. Our common goal is to make the basic changes on both sides that can enable a new, different, and more effective partnership to be built.

The commentators raised important issues about the relation between Marxism and Feminism and the project of analyzing household transformations in the contemporary United States. The serious disagreements among us suggest the need for some sharp confrontations between the Marxist-Feminist position we advance and the different positions of some of our commentators. In this reply, our chief aim is to clarify the alternative kinds of thinking available to those Feminists and Marxists who are genuinely interested in each other's work.

We see three basic areas of disagreement. The first concerns our view of the relevance and role of Marxist class analysis for Feminism in general and for understanding households in particular. Here much attention was focused on our designation of contemporary household class structures as 'feudal.' The second issue concerns class, gender, and power – what these concepts mean, how they connect, their priorities in social analysis, and their respective roles within the theoretical projects of Marxism and Feminism. The third issue is epistemological; it turns on how to understand theoretical disagreements – as matters of right or wrong theory versus the idea that theories are different, alternative ways of making sense of social life.

Before replying to our commentators, we want to reiterate what our argument did *not* intend. We have no interest in supplanting a Feminist perspective with a Marxist one; we aim to integrate the two. The focus on class is not aimed at rendering gender (or patriarchy) secondary in any sense; rather our approach emphasizes how gender and class (and gender, class, and patriarchy) mutually constitute each other. In this sense, we separated our kind of Marxist theory (stressing 'overdetermination') from the economic determinist orientation of other theories within the Marxist tradition. Likewise, we separated our concept of class (as a *process* of surplus labor production and distribution) from the traditional Marxist concepts of class (as distinct groups of people owning property and/or wielding power).

The Marxist-Feminism of Chapter 1 is, for better or worse, unique. It proposes to apply an integration of Feminist literature and a new kind of Marxian theory to the analysis of United States households today. Unfortunately, many of our commentators attacked kinds of Marxist theories that we do not use. The attacks reflect and re-engage old battles with those theories that have left suspicions, resentments, and hostilities. They do not pertain to what Chapter 1 actually does. They do get in the way of the kind of critical dialogue with other Feminists and other Marxists that we seek.

Kim Lane Scheppele

Kim Lane Scheppele begins her response by formulating an epistemological position that is, as she notes, quite close to our own. By her standard, our theoretical framework succeeds because it allows readers to survey a terrain – the household – in new ways, seeing things not seen before by people perceiving and conceiving via different theories. She recognizes in particular our focus on class as a kind of social process, the production and distribution of surplus labor. It is thus fundamentally different from the traditional Marxist and non-Marxist notions of class as a noun designating groups of people. Indeed, she suggests that we may be borrowing more from Georg Simmel than from Marx in our stress on class as process and different class structures as different forms of this class process.

We appreciate and will follow her suggestion to consider Simmel's relevance. As to whether we borrow more from him than from Marx, our prime concern is with effective social analysis, not with loyalty to this or that among the many influences upon us. We acknowledge our substantial debt to Marx for two reasons. First, our reading of his work provided us with centrally valuable conceptual tools. Second, we have no wish to join the now fashionable chorus of denial of Marx's importance.

The meaning of a debt to Marx is as variable as the many different interpretations of Marx now available. What we read in Marx is not what many others, both admirers and critics, find there. We would thus recast Scheppele's comment as follows: we borrow more from certain unorthodox readings of Marx in defining our terms and our analytical project than from the mainline, official Marxism. In short, ours is a particular kind of Marxism, especially suited, in our view, for Marxist-Feminist social analysis.

Stephanie Coontz

Stephanie Coontz approves our contribution and then remarks that it was 'long made by radical Feminists and too long ignored in other circles' (p. 62). Our point, she thinks, is that 'women's labor is appropriated in families as well as factories; women's household work is controlled and unevenly divided by their husbands or fathers rather than by a capitalist; the household is a fundamental unit for economic as well as historical and sociological analysis' (p. 62). Now, we cannot take credit for this point because we did not make it, although we agree with her that it has indeed been made by many Feminists. Attributing it to us offers a glimpse into how she, and not we, theorizes both the relationship between men and women in households (issues of class, gender and power) and between history and historical analysis

(epistemology). By examining her interpretation, we can clarify our differences not only from her position on these issues but also from those of other
Feminists including Matthaei, Folbre, Hartmann, and Eisenstein.

First, however, let us take Coontz to task for some extraordinary
statements. Marxists, to whom she refers in a wholesale fashion, 'consistently underestimate or downplay the intractability of male domination and
the extent of violence against women ... male workers' interests as a
gender have been ignored and their prejudices against women ... dismissed
as false consciousness' (p. 62). While Chapter 1 tries to recognize and draw
upon the rich and diverse tendencies within Feminism, unfortunately
Coontz does not do likewise for Marxism. While we cannot here detail
the long, complex struggles for and against Feminism within the Marxist
tradition, we suggest to Coontz that she consider the works of Alexandra
Kollontai, the first woman on the executive committee of the soviet
government (1971, 1972, 1975, 1977a, 1977b, 1981). Her discussions
ranged, in varying prose forms, from the struggles for intimate personal
recognition in sexual relationships with male revolutionaries to the
profoundly critical dissection of the forces in soviet society that pushed
women into personal domestic drudgery, prostitution, marital misery, and
economic and emotional dependency on individual men.

Coontz might also ponder the content and context of Lenin's statements
on these topics, such as the following:

> Not withstanding all the liberating laws that have been passed, woman
> continues to be a *domestic slave,* because *petty housework* crushes, strangles,
> stultifies and degrades her, chains her to the kitchen and the nursery,
> and wastes her labor on barbarously unproductive, petty, nerve-wracking
> stultifying, and crushing drudgery [original italics] (Lenin 1919, 14).

To mention an example from our own country, in 1949 the Communist
Party, USA (not the most progressive organization in these matters),
debated the revolutionary Feminist positions of Mary Inman (1946, 1949)
whose targets included chauvinist practices within the party. Especially from
a historian, we are very uncomfortable with what seems to us a breezy
disregard and dismissal of all manner of Feminist positions and struggles
inside the Marxist tradition. This does no service to the dialogue of
Feminism and Marxism.

To write, as Coontz does, of men appropriating women's labor, rather
than their surplus labor, is to ignore the Marxist distinction between
necessary and surplus labor. The definitions of the class process – as the
appropriation (and distribution) of surplus labor – and its different feudal,
ancient, and communist forms are a focus of our work on the household.
She apparently missed the uniqueness and specificity of this definition and
so could not explore our analysis's dependence on it. Nor did she pay

attention to our specific theory of gender as a cultural process and our notion
of overdetermination as the linkage between class and gender.

Rather than criticizing our approach, focused on class and gender
processes inside households, she instead proffers and elaborates her completely
different approach. Her focus is on the power men wield over women –
the ordering of women's behaviors. It is, for her, *the* necessary analytical
basis for understanding relationships between men and women. As we shall
see, Coontz is not alone in focusing on power as the necessary theoretical
point of entry into and essence of explanation. This power essentialism is
a tradition of analysis that is far different from what we think a Marxist-
Feminist class and gender analysis is all about.

Consider how power is used in her argument. She does not think a
theoretical model 'can be centered on surplus labor,' because that applies
only where 'male control over women (and children) intersects with or
paves the way for control of wealth-producing property.' Once men have
secured the latter, 'pressures for intensified household production subside
and the direct extraction of surplus product from wives and children
declines' (p. 64). Since relatively few males control wealth-producing
property outside households in our society, this would hardly seem to
invalidate a surplus labor approach. Yet it does for Coontz.

More important in the logic of her argument is its traditional power determinism: control (i.e., power over women's and children's behaviors)
generates surplus labor in households. When that power-caused surplus leads
to control of property outside the household, it reduces the need for a
household surplus. Here the concept of control (over people in, and then
property outside, households) serves as the essential causal explanation of
both the presence and absence of surplus labor. She does not merely prefer
power to class (as we define it); she argues that class *cannot* be the basis for
household analysis. That basis must rather be power (which she then quite
consistently makes the essential determinant of class as well).

Toward the end of her commentary, Coontz indicates her problem with
how we define class – it is too narrow – and again proffers her alternative.
Her worry is that we have somehow turned nonclass processes – gender,
race, power – into secondary influences by excluding them from our
definition of class. In her view, we 'reduce the complex meaning of family
life for the working class into an economic model of men expropriating
all of a woman's labor beyond that required to reproduce her existence'
(p. 63). We nowhere argue anything of the kind.[8] The very term 'working
class' does not appear in our work precisely because we do not reduce
individuals to the class processes in which they participate (Scheppele
notes this in terms of the significance of making class an adjective). Nonetheless, Coontz reads into our argument, despite the strict antireductionism

of its emphasis on overdetermination, the view that class is the ultimate determinant of everything in social life that is not class.

The tendency to read this into our approach – and indeed into all Marxist theories without qualification – indicates at best a seriously incomplete notion of the range of differences within the Marxist tradition. The Marxist theory we use contains neither a hidden agenda nor any statement making class somehow more important than gender and power. Ranking these different processes in terms of their importance in shaping history is incompatible with overdetermination.

Nonetheless, Coontz responds critically to what she presumes is our effort to make class 'most' important by demanding the broadening of the definition of class to include gender, race, and power. This response appears also in the commentaries by Matthaei, Folbre, Hartmann, and Eisenstein. A narrow definition of class necessarily signals to them a position affirming that the narrow concept dominates and functions as the essential cause of all else socially. That is not our position. Coontz cannot imagine that a narrow definition is intended to disaggregate complexities (for example, household relationships) for the purpose of analyzing the interconnections among their elements (class, power, and gender processes) *without essentializing any of them.*

Her broadened, composite definition of class leads into a discussion that is predictably murky. She also demotes class only to pave the way for power eventually to shine through as most important, that to which all else, especially class, should be reduced: 'Class is a system of symbiotic but opposed power relations and interests involved in both organizing and contesting the process of defining, producing, appropriating, and distributing surplus labor. One of those power relations is gender' (p. 69). She simply ignores the import of overdetermination: since every social process is simultaneously one of the causes and an effect of all the other social processes, none is ever solely determinant of another.

Coontz attributes a class essentialism to us, opposes it, and concludes by counterposing her power essentialism: processes of power (including gender understood as power) serve as basic causal determinants of household structures and dynamics. Unfortunately, political rather than economic determinism is still determinism. It reintroduces the very kind of reductionist thinking from which many Feminists, including Coontz, have elsewhere tried to distance themselves.

Reductionist reasoning need not be limited to theorizing relationships between men and women in households. It also may occur in one's thinking about theorizing itself. Unfortunately, Coontz falls into this other kind of essentialism – the epistemological argument for a single, essential truth – when she argues that our designation of the feudal household rests on 'dubious historical analogies' (p. 65). Implicit here are two particular epistemological assumptions: (1) that a real History exists 'out there,' in the past, and (2) that we can know its truth (singular) independently of the particular theories we use to reach it. Coontz's argument amounts to the following: (a) feudalism is a fact discovered by historians; (b) our designation of the household as feudal does not correspond to this discovery; and (c) therefore, our use of the term 'feudal' to describe the household is unacceptable.

The problem with such reasoning is that it proceeds in absolute fashion as if one feudalism existed, the one construed by the theorists she favors, rather than the alternative conceptions produced by various other theorists across the years. From our epistemological standpoint, there is no one essential truth. Historians, theologians, economists, Feminists, sociologists, Marxists, and others continue to construct alternative notions of what feudal means and to apply those notions to their objects of analysis. We offer one approach, drawn from the Marxist tradition of distinguishing different kinds of surplus labor performance and distribution.

Coontz is surely free to prefer a different approach and elaborate it for analytical purposes. However, we do not claim that our approach has captured the essence, the truth of feudalism, now and forever, here and everywhere. She has likewise no warrant to do so for her alternative approach, but her claim that our approach is historically dubious implies such a warrant. It is as if a Feminist discussion of patriarchy in the home were to be dismissed on the grounds of inconsistency with, say, some historians' depiction of patriarchy in another context. This is an episte-mological essentialism – an absolutism – totally at variance with the sort of Marxist-Feminist theory we advance.

As Chapter 1 states (p. 7), the feudal kind of class structure has existed in many different forms, not only across the eighth to nineteenth centuries in Europe, but also from Scandinavia to Sicily and from Ireland to Russia. Marxists have debated its presence in yet other forms at various times and places in all the other continents, thereby generating new and useful insights into their histories. Our innovations are to identify households in the United States as yet another form – another particular time and place – of the feudal kind of class structure and to begin to elaborate the impli-cations of such an identification.

We reject any attempt to make Coontz's alternative approach into some sort of absolute standard and hence imperative for all theorists. Consider a few of her phrases (our italics) about how to proceed theoretically: 'the immersion of nineteenth-century women in religious activities *has to be seen* as' (p. 67); '*only such an explanation* will pave the way for a grasp of' (p. 69); 'the production of gender inequalities *inevitably means*' (p. 64). We do not think History makes itself known to resolve the debates among those trying to make sense of history through their varying theoretical perspec-tives. There is no one right or wrong way to proceed. The past is produced for us only through the variously constructed histories composed by means of alternative theories. There just are different ways of thinking about households, history, and everything else. Ours is an overdeterminist, class way to think about US households and their history. It has some particular insights to offer, and they are its justification. Coontz does not merely ignore or dispute our way of proceeding; by falling into an epistemological absolutism, she questions our right to proceed in this way at all.

We are, in a sense, prisoners of a Marxist discourse but, in our view, so are we all prisoners of discourses. The interesting theoretical and political questions concern the differences between them. Coontz's view of twentieth-century households differs from ours because she deploys concepts of class and causation very differently from the way we do. The essentialized politics of power and the dichotomy of theory and history inform her discourse on the household, but not ours.

Julie Matthaei

Julie Matthaei's differences with us crowd on to the first page of her commentary: 'one of the most perplexing questions facing progressive economists' is 'gender, class, and race inequality in modern capitalism' (p. 42). She claims that we develop a 'relationship between gender and class oppression' that is 'similar to the Marxist-Feminist dual systems theory' and that we 'conceptualize our economy as characterized by distinct modes of production.' We disagree.

Chapter 1 does not focus on 'inequality' as the object of analysis. Contrary to her claim, dual systems theory is radically different from what we do. We carefully and explicitly set out why we do not use 'oppression' to refer to class but rather to power. Finally, we never use the term 'mode of production.' So extensive a problem of communication leaves us perplexed. In any case, in replying to her comments we may extract a hypothesis to help explain the communication problem.

Matthaei writes that 'I challenge the practice of giving primacy to issues of surplus labor extraction, as the authors do' (p. 49).[9] She thus echoes Coontz's attributing to us the idea that class is the most important factor in explaining social phenomena, despite our elaborations of overdetermination as an alternative to all such determinisms. Matthaei also displaces what she rejects as a class essentialism by counterposing her power essentialism. Inequality in general, and unequal power relations in particular, are the dominant themes throughout her commentary. Committed to power as entry point and to essentialism as the necessary mode of analysis, she produces a very different reading of household relationships. As inequality is not only Matthaei's entry point, but also an essence for her,

differences of gender, race, class, and labor become, in the last analysis, the
phenomenal forms of unequal power relations. It is, as Engels once said,
a 'force theory' of society (1962, 219–54).

Matthaei's commentary switches from our definition of class in terms of
necessary and surplus labor to the very different idea that class has to do
with comparing the total numbers of hours worked by two people in a
household (p. 46). She does not see this difference and so challenges our
designation of households as feudal by noting that many husbands work
more total hours – inside and outside such households – than their wives
do. This prompts her to demand, 'Does exploitation exist here?' (p. 46).
For Matthaei, unequal power – and hence class and exploitation – are
reflected and measured in the different number of hours that the two partners
in a household have to work. By counting total hours worked by both
partners and from this deducing class, she abstracts from the necessary/surplus
distinction and from its different forms inside and outside the household.
This we did not and could not do, given our Marxist framework.

Matthaei substitutes her own power/inequality-based notion for our
necessary/surplus labor concept. Yet she seems unaware of the substitution, since she chastises us for finding exploitation (via our theory) where
there is none (via hers). For her, there is no issue of different theories constructing different analyses. Rather, our conclusions have to measure up
to her theory's standards as if they were our own. Thus she negates our
concept of class, replaces it with her power-based concept, and then rejects
those of our conclusions that do not conform to her concept. This is not
quite kosher.[10]

Matthaei is concerned with the example of households hiring servants
(p. 46). If this occurs, she wonders whether feudal exploitation can exist
there. Although we focus here only on the class position of the wife when
a servant is hired, 'servant' deserves a class analysis comparable to that of
'housewife.' There is nothing obvious or given in either category. If a servant
is hired for a wage, different results are possible. The wife may continue
to perform necessary and surplus labor as before, with the servant's labor
simply yielding the feudal husband its use-values alongside the wife's
exploitation. Alternatively, the servant's labor may substitute for the wife's
necessary and surplus labor, thereby ending her class exploitation inside the
household. There are additional possibilities. While the presence or absence
of a servant will influence a household, there is no logical warrant for
deducing as necessary any one particular consequence for the quality and
quantity of a feudal wife's exploitation. The consequences will depend on
all the many factors – economic, cultural, and political – that combine to
overdetermine the household's class structure. However, if one's essentialized
entry point is an inequality of labor effort, then the presence of servants
can become a basic index of radical change in the household.

Our approach and the 'dual-systems' theory of other Feminists are not, as Matthaei suggests, similar. Dual systems theory posits separate spheres of production and reproduction (or 'sex-affective production') such that Marxist class analysis applies to one whereas other analyses apply to the other.[11] In sharp contrast, we stress how social processes such as class and gender overdetermine one another and interpersonal relations *differently* at all social sites. Our Marxism analyzes how class processes occur, albeit in different forms, in both enterprises and households. Our Feminism analyzes how gender processes occur, albeit in different forms, at both sites. Our Marxist-Feminism explores the mutual constitution of distinct class and gender processes at all those sites where they occur in any society.

Matthaei's commentary targets what she sees as our analytical neglect of gender, power, and race when we elaborate our alternative entry point of class as surplus labor production and appropriation. On one hand, her criticism has a point. The way any theory enters into its explanation of events – its entry point – aims to bring an order to the chaos of the many interacting processes shaping and comprising those events. Our class entry point brings a distinctive discursive order, and Matthaei's alternative of inequality and oppression brings a different kind of order. In that sense, we neglect hers by beginning with ours, and vice versa. That is an unavoidable implication of difference in theoretical orientation. However, we reject the other sense of neglect in her critique – that we demote the inequality and oppression of women as important causes of social life. We fear that she misses the point of overdetermination as the logic we use to connect social processes to one another.

One of the central problems Marxist-Feminists confront is how class, race, gender, and power can be linked together without making *any* one of them the essence of the others. For us, the notion of overdetermination enables just such a linkage. It insists that each social process – for example, gender – participates in constituting *every* other social process.[12] It avoids class reductionism; class is not the essential cause of anything. It precludes counterposing to class reductionism some other reductionism (power, race, gender, etc.). Finally, it avoids the response to reductionisms that broadens and blurs the definitions of basic concepts such as class. Then basic concepts become great aggregations of components such as 'the relations of production' or conflationary terms like 'gender and class oppression.'

Within an overdeterminist framework, analysis first aims to distinguish the oppressive or power/inequality aspects (processes) of social life from the exploitation that results from the class aspects (processes).[13] Secondly, overdeterminist analyses explore the particular relations among the different components (processes) that comprise social sites. Thus, within our overdeterminist analysis of the household, we separate power processes, class processes, and gender processes and construct their interactions and mutual

constitutivity. Overdetermination banishes all efforts at determinist, reductionist theory while it redirects the discussion toward analyzing the different
ways in which different social processes – power, gender, class, race,
ethnicity, nationality, religion, and so forth – constitute and shape one
another.

Matthaei's interesting discussion of the couple, Amy and Sue, exempli-
fies our disagreements with her. She focuses on the power either may or
may not have over the other as compared with couples including a man.
She also stresses the feelings of the women toward their household activities.
Together, her interpretation of the women's power relations and feelings
leads Matthaei to find our discussion of feudal class relations in such
households incapable of understanding them.[14] Our reply begins by noting
that, while power and feelings are interesting and important components
of relationships, our Marxist-Feminist focus is rather on the class and
gender processes in those relationships. Matthaei's question is, What power
processes or feelings exist between Amy and Sue? Two of our questions
are, Are there class and gender processes between them, and if so, what
forms do they take and what consequences do they have?

Matthaei's work answers the question posed by her theory; ours answers
the different questions posed by our theory. A feudal class relation can exist
if the serf loves the lord, if they have a sexual relationship, straight or gay,
and if they have changing power relations between them. All those
dimensions have every bit as much to do with the relationship as a whole
as do its class and gender dimensions. Our point is to inquire particularly
about the interaction between the class and gender processes (dimensions)
of the relationship. This is partly because, as Marxist-Feminists, we want
to remedy the minimal recognition and analysis of that interaction in the
Marxist and Feminist literatures we encounter.

We might put the point this way: any relationship, such as that between
Amy and Sue, may include class and gender processes that its participants
neither wish nor see but that can undermine its future. Our analysis aims
to reveal and examine the existence of class and gender processes and their
linkages to other aspects of any relationship. We thereby enable related
persons to understand their relationship in a new way and, if they wish,
to transform it.

Nancy Folbre and Heidi Hartmann

Power essentialism comes home in the comments by Folbre and Hartmann.
As Matthaei, they too begin by underscoring the importance and similarity
of class and gender inequalities. When they write that 'we agree with their
basic argument that gender inequality is analogous to class inequality'

(p. 57), we find ourselves again protesting that we make no such argument. On the contrary, our aim is rather to stress the differences among class, gender, and power processes as the basis for investigating their complex interdependencies and overdeterminations.

Folbre and Hartmann make inequality the key causal determinant of household life: 'Our theoretical perspective acknowledges the importance of what Fraad, Resnick, Wolff term class and gender processes, but we place these within the larger context of systems of inequality.' The inequality that Folbre and Hartmann have in mind is clarified by the expanded terms 'patriarchal inequalities' and 'patriarchal exploitation' (pp. 59–60). In short, their commentary's logic projects the power or control men wield over women as the central tenet and causal determinant within the social totality they call patriarchy. Class relations themselves flow from and depend finally upon control or power, as in 'men who control this class process' (p. 59).

Given their focus, it is not surprising that their criticism, like Matthaei's, turns on a view that our focus on class means that we 'lose sight of' the issues of control and patriarchy, namely the power wielded by men over women. Our reply to Folbre and Hartmann mirrors that to Matthaei. Different entry points (our class and gender versus their power and gender processes) lead to different analyses, but our strong commitment to overdetermination precludes any ranking of class as one whit more socially significant or determinant than gender, power, or any other process.

We need to restate the view presented in Chapter 1. Class processes are those in which surplus labor is performed, appropriated, and distributed among people. In addition to the different positions individuals may occupy within class processes (as performers, appropriators, distributors, etc. of surplus labor), those same individuals occupy various positions within all the other, nonclass processes of social life. They are wielders of power over certain others and have power wielded over them; they participate in creating and spreading concepts of gender, and so forth. No one of the positions any individual occupies in any of the myriad processes that constitute her or his life is more or less important than the others in shaping that life. Rather, overdetermination means precisely that each participation has its distinctive, *incommensurable* role to play in constituting who that individual is and what s/he does.

Thus, one aspect of a woman's life in a household may be her participation in the feudal kind of class process and/or other class processes. Another aspect will likely be her participation in power processes: having various kinds of power or control exerted over her behavior by her father and/or husband and exerting other kinds of control over children or others. Still another aspect will be her participation in the creation and dissemination of particular concepts of what male and female mean (what we called gender processes). We stress that none of these processes or aspects dominates, outranks, or is secondary to any other. Our point is to articulate their mutual constitution and transformation of one another with particular focus on the class and gender processes as befits our Marxist-Feminist orientation. Indeed, we adopt that label and that approach because of our commitment to the creation of households that are classless, egalitarian, and nonsexist institutions. We want a revolutionary transformation of personal life and see Marxist-Feminism as a way to achieve that transformation.

We need also to confront Folbre and Hartmann's issue of choosing the 'best set of conceptual tools' (p. 59) – their notion of patriarchy versus our gender and class/overdeterminist approach. We need to repeat our epistemological objection to any claim that there is a 'best set' of tools (versus different sets), as we did in regard to Coontz's parallel claims.

Let us address patriarchy from our viewpoint. The Feminist movement has created patriarchal analyses of the United States that are powerful, insightful descriptions and indictments of the subordination of women inside and outside households. Together these comprise patriarchy, an encompassing term that conveys the totality of women's unacceptable social situation but that often obscures its different and contradictory components. We are among those Feminists who disaggregate the totality to explore its components and their contradictory relationships. In part, our goal is to show how changes in some components do not guarantee particular changes in others. Class processes may be altered without power processes being changed in ways we see as vital. For example, a feudal class structure may be displaced by a communist one, while power relations remain sexist as women fear men's violence or disapproval, and so on. Alternatively, power or sexual processes may be altered without the class transformations we see as vital. For example, couples may share household property ownership and parenting equally, while surplus domestic labor is still performed by one partner for another. Women as well as men may obtain equal wages and political powers outside the household, yet still participate in a feudal class process inside it.

The social transformations we seek require close attention to all these different social processes. Their constitutions and interactions are always particular and always changing. For that reason, we do not use notions of patriarchy as a totality (nor, for parallel reasons, notions such as 'mode of production'). We concentrate instead on specific component processes such as gender and class.

We have no problem, then, with a notion of patriarchy that would be focused on certain power processes between women and men. Such an approach would elaborate how such power processes (and the oppressions they involve) interact with the class processes (and the exploitations they involve) and the gender processes (and the meanings and feelings they involve). In the context of such an approach, 'patriarchal' would be an adjective describing a particular power situation (men over women), while 'feudal' would be an adjective describing a particular class situation (one form of surplus labor production, appropriation, and distribution). A patriarchal feudal household would then describe a household where men appropriated the surplus labor of women in a feudal arrangement.

Folbre and Hartmann ask why they should use the term 'feudal' rather than 'patriarchal' (p. 59). That misses our point. It is not an either/or. Nor is it a matter for speculations about whether patriarchal power processes or feudal class processes have lasted longer historically or which one came first and served as a model for the other (pp. 59, 61). The point is to analyze the differences and varying interrelationships between them, and not to confuse or conflate them – as Folbre and Hartmann do, for example, when they refer to women as 'exploited not by a feudal class process, but by a publicly sanctioned patriarchy enforced by the state' (p. 61). Women are exploited by a feudal class process and oppressed by patriarchal state policies. Our point is that exploitation – a class phenomenon – should not be conflated with patriarchy – a political phenomenon. Nor should it be conflated with other equally important but different processes, such as inadequate state supports, nonpayment of child support by absent husbands, and price-gouging by merchants – all processes that overdetermine household lives.

Why do Folbre and Hartmann charge that we both 'overstate the uniqueness of [our] substantive claims' and produce 'inaccuracies in the characterization of Marxist-Feminist literature in general and our work in particular' (p. 58)? Regarding our claims, we could not and did not say that *we* discovered a crisis in families in the United States today. The Congress, the President, numerous media commentators, and various scholars have been 'discovering' that for a long time. The relevance of gender has been demonstrated by a vast number of Feminist writers before us, many of whom we cite. Chapter 1 likewise cites sources such as Blumstein and Schwartz (1983), Hite (1987), and Risman and Schwartz (1989) for the trend toward egalitarian couples. Nor did we claim to have discovered either surplus or feudal class structures there; our argument specifically acknowledges the Feminist writers who made those contributions.[15]

What we do claim is to have deployed overdetermination and some particular concepts of class and gender processes that have not yet been used to study households. Thus, our elaboration of the feudal, ancient, and communist class structures of US households and their interrelationships with gender processes is different from the few previous efforts to undertake comparable analyses of households. We admit that Folbre and Hartmann have a point about our remark that they, Eisenstein, and others 'apply class analysis only outside the boundaries of the household and chiefly to enterprises' (p. 2). Our remark is inaccurate: some of the authors we cite do work with concepts of surplus or exploitation. We should have been more careful to clarify that the few who do so understand these terms differently and that our analysis is thus different from theirs.

One of Folbre and Hartmann's examples of our overstating the uniqueness of our claims merits particular attention because of the number of issues it raises. 'Many Feminists have emphasized that men, as well as capitalists, benefit from control over women's labor power' (p. 58). We made no such claim, because that is not our view. Folbre and Hartmann are quite right to say of some Feminists what is true of them as well, namely that control, this time over labor power, is what they see as the central issue. As we would argue, a woman may be in a feudal class structure, yet still have control over her labor power (she may plan and control her cooking and cleaning). The parallel in a capitalist class structure would be productive laborers who produce surplus labor for their employers while exercising particular powers over various aspects of the labor process, their personal interactions, and other matters.

There is another problem with this view that they erroneously attribute to us. A man may control a woman's labor power in many ways: (1) he may do so by buying the fruits of her labor; (2) he may do so by lending her money and using her indebtedness for that purpose; (3) he may buy her labor power directly and put her to work making objects for his own consumption; (4) he may buy her labor power and combine it with purchased means of production to produce commodities for sale in the market; (5) he may marry her and establish a feudal household in which she performs surplus labor for him; and so on. Our point is that while all of these are examples of control, only situation (5) above qualifies as a feudal class process between woman and man and only (4) as a capitalist class process between them. In our theory, one cannot substitute class for control or link them mechanistically; they are just irreducibly different social processes that interact and connect in a myriad of different possible ways.

Folbre and Hartmann chastise us for painting 'a rosy picture' of newly formed ancient and communist households in which women exercise 'control over surplus.' They write: 'From our point of view, patriarchal inequalities have proved far more persistent. Increases in women's bargaining power in the household have been counterbalanced, in part, by men's increased freedom to avoid household responsibilities' (p. 61). In regard to communist class-structured households they write: 'No statistical data ... supports Fraad, Resnick, and Wolff's optimistic view that women and men can freely adopt all class positions in the household' (p. 61).

Yet one more time we confront the problem that Folbre and Hartmann conflate class and control or power. A change in the household's class process – say, from feudal to ancient – does not necessarily eliminate its patriarchal power processes. The picture we paint is not rosy – and is not subject to correction on that score – because we do not conflate or equate the change in class processes with a change in patriarchal power or control processes.

Our discussion of communist class processes in US households is not vulnerable to the criticism of Folbre and Hartmann for a quite different reason. They cite, by way of refutation, data about women and men, that is, heterosexual couples. However, we made no such restrictions. Our references to two-adult households or couples explicitly include gay and lesbian as well as heterosexual couples.

Zillah Eisenstein

Eisenstein's commentary is angry and dismissive: 'there are hardly any "knights" or "castles" in our discourse *or* our practice in the 1990s' (p. 49).[16] We regret her need to take up the invitation to respond to our work in this way. We are also amazed at her misreading of the basics of our argument.[17] Nonetheless, we feel a sympathy with some of her many resentments and would like to reply to them.

Eisenstein does capture an attitude towards Marxism shared by many Feminists, including, to varying degrees, Scheppele, Coontz, Matthaei, Folbre, and Hartmann. Those traditional Marxist theories that are informed by economic determinism offer only a secondary theoretical place and political role for Feminists concerned with patriarchy, gender, inequality, and, in general, the personal. Those kinds of Marxist theory are consequently unacceptable. They have had to be, as Eisenstein says, 'transformed by Feminism' (p. 50).[18]

That transformation has been and remains one of our goals as well. We want to build on Marxism's historic achievement of recognizing class as surplus labor production and distribution, yet we also want to jettison the role of class as causal essence in society. We fear that Eisenstein reads in our Marxism the former but not the latter objective.

Like Coontz and Matthaei, Eisenstein desires complexity in her analysis – a 'complicated mixture of processes' (p. 50) in analyses of different social sites in society. No site should be reduced to merely one of its processes. We agree with her objective here. The problem is: how do we combine analytically distinct processes – of class, gender, and power – to comprise each site as a nondeterminist complexity such that each process is constituted and transformed by all the others?

Eisenstein's solution – creating composite analytical entities – does not solve this problem. In one of her sets of composites women 'are a political class with a potential for consciousness as such. Women's "engendered" bodies make us a class. It is a biological and political construction that is formulated through history' (p. 50). In another set, she makes 'women constitute a political class, and we do this through very different economic and racial forms of household and family life' (p. 51). These compacted word groups agglomerate disparate terms operating at different levels of abstraction, and Eisenstein offers neither explanation or justification for such usages. Her composites beg the question of how their constituent processes are connected. Even if more could be made of them, she does not bother to do so.

We think that the notion of overdetermination does offer a solution to the problem, no matter which particular point of entry an analyst uses. Eisenstein, for example, could focus on the household, not in terms of its feudal character, as we do because of our class focus, but rather in terms of gender, political, or other nonclass processes. Her entry point, like ours, reflects what she deems to be especially relevant to and urgent for the analysis of the household. However, in elaborating her analysis, she would soon be forced, as we are, to specify how one's entry point process interacts with all the *other* processes that together comprise the site in question, the household. Overdetermination – our concept of this interaction – would give Eisenstein what she only vaguely gestures toward: a nonreductionist specification of social complexities such as households.

Perhaps Eisenstein became frustrated at the amalgamation of concepts in the complexities of her discourse and so opted, despite misgivings, for finding their essential core and presuming that we believe in such essential cores as well. Then what matters is 'whose core is the right one?' This might explain her remark that it is 'the politically engendered relations which are key' (p. 50). Eisenstein has thus made politics her privileged essential social cause as against what she presumes is our privileged economic cause. Missing what is at stake in overdetermination, she attributes to us the essentialism that we reject and that she, for lack of an alternative, embraces.

Conclusion

We are troubled that Chapter 1 did not successfully convey our excitement at the contributions made possible by applying a new Marxist-Feminism to social analysis. Our responsibility for not adequately communicating the uniqueness of the conceptual apparatus we constructed from the rich and diverse literatures of Marxism and Feminism is unavoidable. With the exception of Kim Lane Scheppele, the conceptualizations of class and gender as processes and of the connection among social processes in terms of overdetermination did not reach our commentators. Their praises were largely polite and summary, whereas their criticisms made clear their very different ways of theorizing and some considerable antagonisms to our project.

This reply aims chiefly to clarify our theoretical differences with Coontz, Matthaei, Folbre, Hartmann, and Eisenstein. Under current theoretical and political conditions, perhaps we underestimate the obstacles to obtaining a sympathetic hearing from Feminists for new formulations of Marxist thought.

Yet we think that Feminists and Marxists have far more to gain than lose by seriously engaging each other's work and actively seeking modes of theoretical and political partnership. We wonder and worry about how long the past sins of some Marxists in denigrating Feminists and Feminism will produce nothing more productive than the counterdenigration of Marxism. Our hope was and is to get beyond that primitive stage of retribution as soon as possible.

CHAPTER 3

The Reagan-Bush Strategy: Shifting Crises from Enterprises to Households*

Introduction

From many standpoints, the following analysis of Reagan-Bush economics was and still is proclaimed: a declining, problem-plagued economy in the 1970s was treated with an intensive dose of 'free-market' deregulation, tax-reduction, and entrepreneurial stimuli. The result was a classic turnaround, economic recovery and prosperity in the 1980s.

A crisis was averted and its causes dismantled. Reaganomics points the way forward clearly and triumphally. Conventional economics cheers on the sidelines.

The US recession of the early 1990s, in this view, merely reflects some regrettable backsliding toward tax increases by a weak President Bush. The excesses will be absorbed (self-correct in textbook fashion) and prosperity will resume unless the Clinton administration departs significantly from Reagan-Bush strategy.

From the Marxist-Feminist standpoint developed and utilized here, the analysis and prognosis could hardly be more different. Stressing a Marxist attention to class processes and combining it with a Feminist attention to gender and patriarchy outside as well as inside enterprises, the contradictions of Reaganomics are identified. Moreover, their consequences are shown to undermine and threaten what limited 'successes' it can claim. The result not only recasts the last 15 years of US history, it also illustrates dramatically the profound stakes in the struggles among alternative conceptions of society and social analysis.

Alternative Analyses

Non-Marxian economic theory typically divides the economy into three distinct parts or sites. One, the household, is a private locale of individual decisions about consumption, savings and supplying labor. Another, the firm,

* This chapter was prepared by S. Resnick and R. Wolff.

is also a private place, but here decisions about production and production itself occur. The third, the state, is the economy's public place where taxes are received (from households and firms) and collective expenditures and regulations are made to benefit everyone. Having specified (or, more likely, presumed as self-evident) this tripartite division of economic space, non-Marxian economic theory seeks a mechanism interconnecting the parts such that each, and the totality they comprise, will be reproduced. Markets are specified to be the key mechanism that plays this role. Markets are the economic bridge connecting the private decisions made in households and firms, while the state is assigned its roles of regulating and protecting, without at the same time jeopardizing, this web of private economic activity.

Whatever else Marxists might think of such a taxonomy and the analyses built upon it, they cannot but be struck by the total absence of any specification of class exploitation occurring at any of these sites of activity. This deafening silence about class (and indeed about a whole list of other dynamics such as gender, race, psychological and power conflicts) extends as well to the analysis of the market interactions among households, firms, and the state. It is particularly the absence of exploitation or, what is the same thing, the presence of nonclass analysis, that comprises the common heritage of non-Marxian economists over the last 100 years. Despite vast differences in their approaches, such economists nonetheless are very much alike in certain ways. They all affirm and elaborate kinds of social analysis that exclude class exploitation.

While we recognize the diverse complexity of processes occurring within and among enterprises, households, and the state, we concentrate here on class processes as defined in Chapter 1 – the processes of producing, appropriating, and distributing surplus labor. We focus on class processes not because they are any more determinant of social change than other processes (we do not think they are), but rather to remedy the neglect of class processes by other analysts. Marx focused on the existence and consequences of class processes within capitalist enterprises. Chapter 1 above extended that kind of analysis to the household. Elsewhere we have extended it to the state and to further work on enterprises (Resnick and Wolff, 1987, Chapters 4 and 5). In this chapter, we propose to combine the class analyses of these three social sites. We aim to show how their particular interaction during the Reagan-Bush regime resolved a crisis in US enterprises by intensifying the crisis of US households.

The Capitalist Enterprise

We begin with a traditional Marxian category, namely the capitalist commodity-producing enterprise. Parallel to feudal households, capitalist industrial enterprises are social sites in society where, among many other social and natural processes, the fundamental class process (producing and appropriating surplus labor) and the subsumed class process (distributing surplus labor) occur. Appreciating the differences between the fundamental class processes occurring in the household and the enterprise requires examining how each is constituted uniquely by its specific conditions of existence.

Doing this is like comparing any other distinct entities (or 'social sites'), including, of course, men and women. We understand differences between 'sites' in terms of how each is constituted uniquely by its component processes, including, as specified earlier, its unique class, gender, patriarchal, and biological processes. In all such comparisons, we stress how the addition of any one process not only adds its unique effectivity to the determination of that site, but also alters the determinations and interactions of all the other processes constituting it. That the addition of any one alters the entire nature of the site is worth remembering as we discuss differences between capitalist enterprises and feudal households.

As in feudal households, individuals labor in capitalist enterprises. There too they transform raw materials to produce use-values.[1] There too they are supervised, ordered, and commanded in their laboring activity. As women's laboring experience in households shapes them, individuals laboring in enterprises become complex products of their legal and hierarchal procedures, as well as of gendering, custom, religion, and even of the non-Marxian economic theory presented above. They are, as a result, consciously and unconsciously educated, trained, and motivated to labor productively and honestly for the capitalist who hires them; to receive orders from managerial supervisors hired by capitalists; and to perform unpaid surplus labor day after day for such capitalists. They may well be unconscious that they are willing to work, for perhaps considerable hours, for no pay whatsoever. Certainly in a competitive, private enterprise society like the US today, where individuals seem exquisitely sensitized to becoming victims of any sort, this continued and unacknowledged class victimization testifies to the power of ideology in structuring the work place.

Despite the common presence of labor, technological, class, power, legal, and ideological processes in both households and enterprises, the radically different forms assumed by them at each site dictate radically different sets of attitudes, feelings, ties, work habits, and, in general, class and nonclass behaviors. For example, unlike women laboring in feudal households, enterprise workers sell their labor power in the market, receiving wages from its buyer. Hence, unlike their serf counterparts in households, capitalist workers do not immediately obtain the fruits of their necessary labor; instead they have to purchase them in commodity markets by means of their wages. Additionally, although both household and enterprise workers produce use-values (physical goods and services), only those produced in enterprises also take on exchange values, i.e., become commodities by entering markets.

The presence of commodity exchange processes means, on the one hand, that the labor power of the capitalist worker has an exchange value, and, on the other, that the worker's products have exchange values. The presence of exchange processes and hence values implies a radically different social situation in the enterprise as compared to the household within which no commodity exchange occurs. For example, since surplus labor in the enterprise yields *surplus value* there, the enterprise is the site also of the process of the self-expansion of value, what Marx defines as *capital*. The presence of capital produces, in turn, a particular set of consequences impacting enterprises and the relationships therein – capital accumulation, technological innovation, product innovation, unemployment, and so forth. While the presence of capital in the enterprise differentiates it sharply from the non-capitalist household, the list of differences between enterprises and households hardly stops there.

The ideological, legal, emotional, moral, and economic ties that bind workers to capitalists are different from those binding household serfs to lords. These differences, combined with the presence of the exchange-à and capital processes, further define the uniqueness of capitalist as opposed to feudal behavior. For example, workers in enterprises are not tied to their capitalists in the same way as are household serfs to their lords. This difference may arise partly from the absence in the capitalist relationship of the legal, ideological, and patriarchal processes comprising marriage. It also derives, in part, from the presence in the feudal household of the ideology of love that can envelop feudal workers so pervasively and powerfully. Gendering, too, assigns its differential social, including class, roles to women and men in capitalist enterprises as compared to feudal households. In the latter, processes of gender help to determine that women become the producers of surplus for their men. In the former, these processes are linked more to discriminatory pay differences, unequal access to different jobs, and barriers to promotion.

Additionally, patriarchy is a powerful social force binding female serfs to male lords in households in ways that are different from the binding power used by capitalists over their workers. In contrast to feudal lords, capitalists' power over laborers derives partly from being buyers of their labor power. As with buyers of any commodity, capitalists have the right to consume what they have purchased: consuming labor power means setting laborers to work producing surplus. Since no purchase of labor power is involved inside households, the appropriation of feudal wives' surplus labor depends more on men's 'traditional' and 'natural' rights vis-à-vis women. On the other hand, the existence of patriarchy in society, regardless of its location, encourages an environment of control of the 'other,' wherever that individual may labor.[2] In that sense, patriarchy, like all the other social processes, impacts both social sites, albeit differently.

Generally, the inequality between men and women that rules the household is different from that in the capitalist enterprise. In the latter, as Marx showed in *Capital 1*, it is rather the socially contrived *equality* between buyers and sellers of labor power as contractual partners that becomes a condition of existence of capitalist exploitation. In household relationships, on the other hand, the differently contrived *inequality* between men and women helps to foster feudal exploitation.

Moreover, workers in capitalist enterprises typically lack (are separated from) sufficient means to reproduce themselves without entering a wage relationship. Feudal household workers are not so separated. This difference in access to means of production gives women in feudal households different kinds of control over their economic well-being from that of workers (male and female) in capitalist enterprises. The social constraints surrounding the power of husbands to eliminate feudal wives from the household are quite different from those limiting capitalists' freedom to fire workers. On the other hand, while the power of women inside households is constrained by gender, patriarchal, and ideological processes, that of workers in capitalist enterprises may be enhanced by unionization, statute law enforced by the state, and even by the freedom to leave and seek employment elsewhere. Thus, the effectivity of any process in each site is differently overdetermined both by the interaction among the other processes present at that site and by the processes elsewhere that impact on that site.

Capitalist enterprises typically have boards of directors appropriating surplus value from their productive laborers. These boards also distribute shares of this surplus value to secure certain conditions of existence of their continued ability to appropriate surplus value. In other words, just as the reproduction of the feudal household's appropriation of surplus labor depends on its distribution, the reproduction of the industrial enterprise's appropriation of surplus value also depends on its distribution.

The following equation (1) summarizes this argument for capitalist enterprises (Resnick and Wolff 1987, Wolff and Resnick 1987):[3]

$$(1) \qquad SV = SSCP_1 + SSCP_2 + SSCP_3 + \dots + SSCP_n$$

The SV term represents the surplus value appropriated by capitalist industrial enterprises' boards of directors. The several SSCP terms represent the different shares of appropriated surplus value distributed to those who provide various conditions of existence of those enterprises. We call these distributions of portions of appropriated surplus value the *capitalist subsumed class payments*. The boards of directors make such distributions with the goal of securing the conditions of existence needed to continue to appropriate surplus value.[4]

To illustrate the point, an industrial corporation needs to distribute a portion of appropriated surplus value in the form of taxes paid to the state to secure the production and dissemination of the powerful ideology described above (via schools and other institutions). Taxes also secure the laws and judicial infrastructure needed for capitalist exploitation. Another condition of existence of appropriating surplus value is the control or discipline of productive laborers' workplace behaviors. To secure this process, boards of directors make subsumed class payments to supervisory managers for their salaries and to buy their means of supervisory control. Still another condition of existence for the industrial enterprise's reproduction in a competitive environment is capital accumulation. Boards of directors will make subsumed class payments to managers charged with accumulation to enable them to purchase the requisite additional means of production and labor power. Other subsumed class payments include budgets for corporate research and development departments, dividends to corporate owners, rents to landlords and patent owners, fees to merchants, and interest payments to creditors (Resnick and Wolff 1987, 164–230).

A problem for capitalist industrial corporations arises when the following inequality (2) occurs:

$$(2) \qquad SV < \Sigma SSCP_i \text{ (where } \Sigma SSCP_i \text{ is the sum of all } SSCP)$$

The inequality signals that the quantity of surplus value appropriated is insufficient to make the distributions needed to secure the conditions of existence of the appropriation and hence of the enterprise's reproduction. If this problem is not solved, the capitalist enterprise's existence will be in jeopardy. A 'crisis' is at hand.

Analyzing Reagan-Bush

Here begins our tale of enterprise, state, and household interactions over the Reagan-Bush years. US industrial corporations faced very difficult problems at the end of the 1970s as certain of their conditions of existence were not being reproduced socially. If left unsolved, these problems might have generated a general crisis of US capitalism. Reaganomics represented one particular 'solution' to the problems of enterprises when Reagan took office. Reaganomic policies aimed to secure the reproduction of capitalist enterprises' jeopardized conditions of existence.

We wish to argue that an inequality – SV < $\sum SSCP_i$ – existed and grew among US capitalist enterprises across the 1970s. There was an increase in the number and size of distributed shares of surplus value (interest payments, dividends, managerial salaries, rents, taxes, etc.) demanded by those who reproduced capitalist conditions of existence. The costs of providing these conditions had risen faster than the surplus value available to many capitalist boards of directors at the beginning of Reagan's presidency.

In particular, prior to Reagan's election, we may point to several kinds of subsumed class demands which were pressing heavily on capitalists' appropriated surplus value. Two of them involved industrial capitalists having to use their surplus value to pay for input commodities whose prices had been raised above their exchange values. In these cases, as we shall see, certain groups had established the monopoly power enabling them to impose such prices and thereby obtain subsumed class distributions from capitalists who had to secure those inputs. A differently expanded subsumed class demand emanated from managers inside industrial corporations. They pushed capitalist boards of directors to allocate more of their surplus value for research and development budgets as well as to purchases of plant and equipment embodying new, productivity-raising technologies. These were argued to be indispensable defenses against the most severe foreign competition threatening US industry since at least the Second World War. Without distributing surplus value to these defensive uses, US enterprises in industry after industry – but especially in highly unionized industries such as steel and autos – faced a loss of appropriated surplus value to their more efficiently producing foreign competitors, in particular the Japanese and West Germans.[5]

Let us now examine these growing demands on capitalists' surplus values in detail. Some productive laborers were able to use the power of their unions or to take advantage of market conditions to raise the price of their labor power above its exchange value. Such laborers had, in effect, established monopoly positions in the labor power market. To gain access to this now monopolized commodity, industrial capitalists had to pay a premium equal to the difference between the price and value of the labor power they had to buy. That premium is a subsumed class distribution (for analytical convenience, let it be $SSCP_1$ in Equation 1). Productive laborers who receive such subsumed class payments do so as part of their wages. Thus, their total wage income comprises two parts – the value of their labor power (Marx's term V) plus a subsumed class share ($SSCR_1$ equal to enterprises' $SSCP_1$ in Equation 1) of the surplus value they produced for their employer.

The expanded wage incomes of productive workers ($V + SSCR_1$) not only helped to generate the post-Second World War expansion in US consumption expenditures. They also alleviated pressures on the traditional feudal family. Over these decades, such families formed a key part of the social structure of the major industrial, unionized cities of the Northeast and Middle West.[6] Capitalist heavy industry was most powerful just where it seemed the feudal family also had the strongest foothold. In this case, feudalism and capitalism supported one another. As suggested in Chapter 1, rising male workers' incomes (here specified as $V + SSCR_1$) tended to reduce the pressure on women in households to increase feudal exploitation. On the other hand, rising wages made life more difficult for industrial enterprises, for they only added to the demands on surplus value (the $SSCP_1$ distribution). While impaired, enterprises also benefited, for they were able to sell more and more of their commodities to these same workers.

Another subsumed class demand arose from those who established monopoly positions in raw materials, especially energy. Across the 1970s, the price of energy exceeded its exchange value, the so-called 'oil shock.' Consequently, US enterprises had to make significant subsumed class payments to such monopoly sellers ($SSCP_2$ on the right-hand side of Equation 1). Adding the latter subsumed class distribution to that made to productive laborers only put an additional strain on the ability of enterprises to reproduce themselves.[7]

Although the reason for both subsumed class payments can be found in the monopoly power deployed by specific commodity sellers, the timing of their impacts was different. Subsumed class payments to sellers of raw materials rose dramatically in the 1970s, especially with the creation of OPEC, whereas US industrial enterprises had purchased significant amounts of productive labor power at varying premiums for some time. A special relationship between the state and the unions had evolved since the 1930s. One of the conditions of existence securing workers' subsumed class position was the legal and ideological support received by them from the state. Indeed, the duration of that support and the subsumed class consequences of that state–union relationship made it an inviting target for Reagan's assaults, beginning with the air-traffic controllers' national strike in 1981.

Another subsumed class demand that surged upward derived from individuals inside capitalist industrial corporations, namely certain managers. They claimed that US industrial corporations had to increase their capital accumulation and research and development budgets to raise productivity. Expanded subsumed class distributions for these purposes were crucial to counter foreign competition, particularly since domestic companies were constrained by the high wages discussed above and by their inability to raise output prices because of the foreign competition.

The chorus of demands for increased productivity across the 1970s and 1980s offered various reasons for the slow productivity growth that was allegedly undermining US industry. Some stressed union-enforced work rules and attitudes. Others focused on an inability or unwillingness of managements to manage properly – to accumulate machines embodying improved technologies, rather than, say, to seek mergers that would enhance only short-run financial profits. Still others pointed to laws and regulations and to cultural attitudes fostered by an overly permissive educational system that together inhibited efficient private industry and its 'old fashioned American ingenuity.' Those who saw the problems in these terms generated corresponding solutions – weaken unions, induce managers to accumulate new technology, reduce state disincentives to such accumulation, and reaffirm traditional institutions such as conservative schools, nuclear families, orthodox religions. Indeed, these solutions effectively outline the basic social program of the Reagan and Bush administrations.

Across the 1970s, the cumulative impact of large and rising subsumed class demands exceeded the appropriated surplus value available to meet them. Because capitalist enterprises did not squeeze enough surplus value out of their workers to satisfy those demands, we may say that Equation 1 changed into Inequality 2. The associated problems foreshadowed a crisis. President Carter's policies were viewed as altogether inadequate to address the situation. Much like the more severe crisis of the 1930s, the crisis threatening in the 1980s called for a new and imaginative way of acting by the state. In this sense, it is no coincidence that both the Roosevelt and Reagan administrations inaugurated new paths for US capitalism.

For the 1980s, what was required was a new freedom for industrial capitalists both to search for new sources of surplus value and to reduce the demands of certain subsumed classes on their surplus value. However, the options were limited. It made no economic, political, or ideological sense for a newly elected, conservative, Republican administration to support reduced distributions to corporate managers for accumulation. Nor could the federal government do much about the monopoly positions of foreign energy sellers without risking at that time prohibitive political and military costs.

Thus, the Reaganomic solution to the specific problems of enterprises – the inequality between surplus value and the sum of subsumed class demands on it – centered on two priorities. The first aimed to arrange for certain conditions of existence to be reproduced for a much smaller subsumed class payment from industrial corporations than had previously been necessary. The second aimed to increase the quantity of surplus value appropriated by capitalist industrial enterprises and available for subsumed class distributions.

The State and Capitalist Enterprises Under Reaganomics

Reaganomics became a state policy that operated on both sides of Inequality 2 with the aim of reestablishing a balance between surplus value expropriated and surplus value distributed. In other words, by seeking to change Inequality 2 back into Equation 1, Reaganomics offered a solution to the class problems that beset enterprises. To develop this argument, we need first to specify how the state, as another site in society, is able to accomplish

such dramatic changes in the private sector. We begin with a class equation
for the state's own value flows (Resnick and Wolff 1987):

(3) $$SV + SSCR + NCR = \Sigma SSCP + \Sigma X + \Sigma Y$$

In this equation, SV stands for surplus value produced in state industrial
enterprises and appropriated by the state (for example, AMTRAK). SSCR
stands for the state's subsumed class revenues, i.e., taxes paid by industrial
capitalist enterprises out of their appropriated surplus values. NCR stands
for the nonclass revenues derived from all sources other than appropriators of surplus value (for example, personal taxes levied on the incomes of
productive and unproductive workers). Turning to the state's expenditures,
to the right of the equal sign, $\Sigma SSCP$ is the sum of subsumed class expenditures to secure the conditions of existence for state enterprises to
appropriate SV (for example, salaries to their managers). ΣX is the sum of
those state expenditures required to secure the state's receipt of taxes from
capitalist enterprises (SSCR) by providing certain conditions of existence
to them (for example, maintaining the police, court, and prison systems).
ΣY is the sum of the remaining state expenditures aimed to secure NCR
by providing services to those who are not industrial capitalists (for example,
building and maintaining public parks).

From the Marxian standpoint, part of Reaganomics focused on cheapening
the costs to enterprises of particular conditions of existence provided to
them by the federal government. These included military and police
security, subsidies, maintenance of economic infrastructures, adjudication
of contract disputes, control of the money supply, maintenance of public
health, etc. The means to accomplish this cheapening was a broad tax *shift*
which the Reagan administration publicized as a tax 'reduction.' The
point was to shift the cost of services delivered to enterprises onto the tax
bills of individuals. The numbers in the following table showing this shift
are striking:

Table 1: Federal Tax Receipts ($ Billions)

	1970	1980	1987
Total	196	519	886
Individual income taxes	104	288	465
Corporate income taxes	35	72	103
Corporate income taxes as Percent of total	17.9	13.9	11.6

Source: US Bureau of the Census, *Statistical Abstract of the United States 1990*, (110th edition)
Washington: Government Printing Office, 1990, p. 318. (Hereafter, this and other
editions of the *Statistical Abstract* will be cited as 'SAUS'.)

Returning to Equation 3, we can isolate one part of Reaganomics as relatively decreasing the state's SSCR on the left side while simultaneously increasing its NCR there. Reducing corporate (SSCR) relative to personal (NCR) taxes became one recurrent theme of the Reagan years. According to the numbers in Table 1, corporate taxes as a percentage of total tax receipts declined steadily over these years from 17.9 per cent of the total in 1970 to 11.6 per cent in 1987. Accomplishing these revenue changes in the state sector alleviated problems of industrial corporations; Inequality 2 was reduced by lessening the taxes demanded from corporate surplus values.

At the same time, the Reagan administration spent much more money on the military and less on social programs.[8] In this way, the state undertook a process – expanding defense commodity purchases – that secured a condition of existence of the corporations that produce weapons and inputs into weapons production. These corporations were thereby enabled to realize and indeed to expand surplus value. This, too, reduced Inequality 2.

However, this solution for industrial capitalists had its political risks. Reduced state expenditures for social programs directed to the non-corporate public coupled with increased personal taxes confronted the mass of US citizens with an attack on their living standards. One way to disguise and thus sell this pro-capitalist policy was to wrap it in a nationalist package. To restore US global hegemony, defended as necessary to national security, an expansion of the defense budget was required. Also required was a reduction of corporate taxes. That would strengthen US enterprises' international competitiveness by permitting them to use the money saved from taxes for technological progress via capital accumulation. Once these state changes were accomplished, the argument claimed, the *entire* US – not merely corporations – would reap the benefits.[9] To help convince Congress and public opinion, the administration added some reduction of individual tax rates also (a reduced NCR).

Carrying through these tax and expenditure changes (chiefly the reduced SSCR and NCR and the expanded ΣX) created the huge budget deficits and the resulting fiscal problems of the Reagan state, as detailed in Table 2:

Table 2: US Deficits and National Debts ($ Billions)

	Budget deficits	*National debt*
1970	2.8	380.9
1980	78.9	908.5
1989	161.5	2,868.8★

Source: *SAUS: 1990*, p. 309. ★ Estimated data.

Parallel to Inequality 2 that we specified to understand the problems of capitalist industrial enterprises, we may now specify a new Inequality 4 to illustrate the state's comparable problems:

$$(4) \qquad SV + SSCR + NCR < \Sigma SSCP + \Sigma X + \Sigma Y$$

Simply put, the expenditure demands to secure its conditions of existence – to satisfy its constituents – exceeded its revenues from them. Consequently, pressures now fell on the state's remaining revenue and expenditure variables – SV, ΣSSCP, and ΣY. Clearly, eliminating state industrial enterprises would have fit easily into the conservative ideology of the Reagan administration. However, few state enterprises existed that could be sold outright to private industry (thus eliminating both SV as revenues and ΣSSCP as expenditures, and generating, via their sale, a once and for all NCR for the state).[10] Thus, most of the pressure and congressional debate focused on the only remaining viable expenditure that could be cut, namely ΣY, the state expenditures directed to households and generally referred to as 'social programs.'

These social programs were cut, but never enough to eliminate the inequality in the state's equation. This necessitated the well-known Reagan solution of generating enormous deficits financed by ever new state borrowing, as revealed in the previous table. In the class analytical terms of Equation 3, these borrowings comprised a new NCR term, called by Marx (1967b, p. 465) 'fictitious capital,' added to the revenue side. However, such capital, while producing the necessary state budget revenues, produced as well a new set of contradictions for capitalist industrial enterprises, feudal households, and even for the state itself.

Vast increases in state borrowing pushed all interest rates higher. This meant even greater deficits, since the state had to pay more interest on its new debt. Higher interest rates meant that industrial enterprises also had to allocate increased shares (higher SSCP) of their surplus value to cover interest payments to their creditors. What the state gave on one hand to capitalists in the form of reduced corporate taxes, it took away on the other by fostering higher interest claims on their surplus value. Hence the state's aim of promoting technical progress by subsidizing private capital accumulation was being undermined by its own fiscal action. Moreover, higher US interest rates tended to attract foreign capital which strengthened the dollar vis-à-vis other currencies.[11] This improved position of the dollar compounded the severe competitive environment facing US industry, for it lowered the dollar prices of foreign imports and increased the foreign currency prices of US exports. Finally, a rise in interest rates created a particular burden on industrial workers and their households which we will analyze in the next section.

Rising federal deficits and their impact on interest rates reinforced the Reaganomic determination to pursue its solutions – constrain ΣY by eliminating state jobs and by cutting social programs directed to the poorest households. They also pushed the Reagan administration to raise new state revenues by increasing social security taxes on payrolls (the 'Trust Fund' balances of Table 3), while keeping public attention focused on personal income tax cuts.

Table 3: Federal Trust Fund Balances ($ Billions)

	Income	Outlay	Net
1980	94.7	84.8	9.9
1989*	250.2	184.3	65.9

Source: *SAUS: 1990*, p. 309. * Estimated data.

This Reagan strategy tended to limit government employment not only at the federal level, but also, through trickling down, at the state and local levels. From 1970 to 1981, civilian employment at all levels of government (federal, state, and local) rose from 13 to 16 million, an increase of 23 per cent. From 1981 to 1986, it rose only to 16.9 million, a rise of 5.6 per cent (*SAUS: 1989*, p. 293). New job entrants had to look to private rather than public employment. The deflection of the supply of labor power to the private sector, coupled with Reagan's assaults against unions, were two of the several forces that depressed real wages across the Reagan years. Another, discussed in the next section, was the exodus of women from feudal households into the capitalist wage-labor market. This, too, acted to increase the supply of labor power to the private sector. Since employers needed to pay productive workers less, more of the fruits of their increasingly productive labor accrued to those employers. Output per hour in the nonfarm private business sector rose 10.3 per cent from 1980 to 1987, while in manufacturing alone it rose over 30 per cent (*SAUS: 1989*, p. 403). Private industrial capitalists thus had more surplus to distribute to secure their various conditions of existence.

The Reagan strategy of increasing social security taxes while cutting social programs and government employment tended to reduce its overall deficit from what it would have been otherwise. However, the strategy's most important influence was probably felt by industrial enterprises in terms of the market in labor power that they confronted.[12]

The Carter years ended and the Reagan years began with a severe economic depression and, at least in terms of the post-Second World War period, relatively high rates of unemployment. Added to this were the state's new policy toward labor, signaled by Reagan's direct confrontation with the air-traffic controllers in 1981, and its effort to limit public employment at all levels. Relatively high unemployment rates depressed wages in many sectors over the Carter years and into the Reagan years. A growing supply of people looking for work in private industry (fed by the constraints on government employment and, as we will see, by housewives entering the wage labor market), coupled with a policy to limit the power of unions, broadened and deepened the pressure on wages across the 1980s. Table 4, measuring what could actually be bought for the money wages received (i.e., 'real' wages), shows the telltale pattern of this wage depression.

Table 4: Real Wages (Constant 1990 Dollars)

	Average weekly	*Average hourly*
1970	373.71	10.07
1973	397.58	10.77
1978	388.69	10.86
1980	367.93	10.42
1985	358.02	10.26
1989	347.18	10.03

Source: US House of Representatives, Committee on Ways and Means, *Overview of Entitlement Programs*, Washington: Government Printing Office, 1991, p. 552. (Hereafter cited as '1991 Green Book'.)

These pressures in the labor market eventually limited or removed the subsumed class payments ($SSCP_1$ in Equation 1) that many industrial capitalists had to make when labor market conditions enabled especially unionized labor to charge a price for labor power above its value. This further relieved the demands on industrial capitalists' surplus value.

Reaganomics had moved systematically toward solving the enterprise problems it confronted (Inequality 2) upon taking office. It had re-established a balance between the production/appropriation of surplus value (the capitalist fundamental class process), on the one hand, and its distribution to secure conditions of existence (the capitalist subsumed class process), on the other. In other words, it had averted a crisis for capitalist enterprises by changing Inequality 2 back into Equation 1. This success in treating the problems of capitalist enterprises occurred under the banner of a crusade against big, wasteful, inefficient, and intrusive government in the name of individual enterprise, freedom, initiative and prosperity.

The Crisis of Feudal Households

We can write the class structural equation for the feudal household as follows:

$$(5) \qquad SL = SSCP_1 + SSCP_2 + SSCP_3 + \ldots + SSCP_n$$

The surplus labor performed by the feudal wife, SL on the left of the equal sign, is appropriated by the husband. He distributes that surplus labor (or its products) to those individuals who secure conditions of existence of his feudal class position in the household. Each numbered SSCP term on the right-hand side of Equation 5 represents a portion of the surplus labor so distributed by the feudal husband. As discussed in Chapter 1, household feudal surplus delivered to a local church as contributions or to the municipality as, say, real estate taxes are examples of such distributions. Similarly, both the male, as the feudal appropriator of surplus, and the female, as its producer, may occupy, *in addition to their feudal fundamental class positions*, feudal subsumed class positions within the household as well. In other words, both may also appear on the right hand side of Equation 5 as receivers of the surplus distributed by the feudal husband. Thus, for example, if a husband and/or wife use a room to keep records of household affairs, the wife's surplus labor will be distributed to maintaining that room and/or keeping the records of the feudal class structured household.[13]

When Reagan took power in 1981, class problems afflicted households as well as enterprises. In other words, both feudalism and capitalism were experiencing difficulties reproducing their different class structures at their respective social sites. We may express the class problems of the feudal household in terms of the following inequality: its appropriated surplus labor (SL) was insufficient to meet the subsumed class demands upon it (all the SSCP needed to secure the continued appropriation of that feudal surplus):[14]

$$(6) \qquad SL < \Sigma SSCP_i \text{ (where } \Sigma SSCP_i \text{ is the sum of all } SSCP)$$

In feudal households, unlike capitalist enterprises, the locus of the problem lay less in subsumed class demands than in the reduced provisions of surplus labor by wives. Especially relevant in this regard were the women's liberation movement beginning in the 1960s; a male rebellion against family financial burdens (Ehrenreich 1983); downward pressures on family living standards in the 1970s; changing sexual mores; and changing attitudes toward children and childrearing practices such as daycare. These were all, in turn, complex products of the social upheavals of the 1960s.

The particular difficulties in the way of reproducing the feudal household concerned the women's inability and/or unwillingness to continue to perform any, or as much, surplus labor for their husbands. Women who took second jobs as wage-earners outside the home confronted physical and psychological limits to maintaining their full-time traditional positions as producers of household surplus labor (Hochschild 1989). Wage incomes earned outside the household lessened or removed the financial dependence conditioning women's feudal position inside. Similarly, the mental and cultural attitudes appropriate to wage laborers could and did often clash with those nurtured inside feudal households. The physical strain on women performing surplus labor at two social sites during the same day contributed to all sorts of household tensions among adults and children as well as to demands by women for relief from the burden of traditional deliveries of surplus labor to husbands. As the feudal surplus labor appropriated by husbands came under increasing pressure, the reduced surpluses threatened their ability to secure their conditions of existence as feudal appropriators. For some, the willingness to continue to meet their family obligations was eroded or undermined altogether.

On to this strained household class structure, Reaganomics fell like a bomb. Policies that had addressed and 'solved' the difficulties of capitalist class structures in enterprises only added intolerable pressures to the difficulties already undermining feudal households. On the one hand, the Reagan assault on governmental social programs and supports shifted many household expenses back on to families. Reduced maintenance of roads and bridges meant more family time and money to maintain, repair or replace vehicles. Reduced state provision of services to children, the sick, and the elderly directly and immediately placed added financial and caring responsibilities on the affected families. The list of other reductions – at federal, state and local levels – is similarly matched by the additional burdens shifted to family finances and family labor. At the same time, the other wing of the Reaganomic program for enterprises, exacerbating the long-term downward trend in private sector real wages, squeezed further the family's financial resources. Husbands often expected increased amounts of their wives' surplus labor to offset their reduced real wages.

Thus, the 'successes' of Reaganomics in the capitalist sphere helped to plunge American feudal households into a class crisis. In other words, a transitional conjuncture developed that threatened the survival of feudal class structures in US households. Thus, in many such households, new, nonfeudal class structures emerged and are still emerging.

To analyze this conjuncture, we begin by focusing on male productive workers who, in one social existence, produce surplus value for industrial capitalists, but who, in another, appropriate surplus labor from their wives. Such men are both exploited and exploiters. The following class structural equation is intended to illustrate summarily this complex contradiction of American life:

$$
\begin{aligned}
&\left[(V\,) + (SSCR_1)\right] + (SL\,) + (NCRst\,) + (NCRdbt\,) = \\
(7)\quad &\left[\left(\sum \frac{EV}{UV} UV \,\right) + (X\,)\right] + (\sum SSCP\,) + (Txp + Txss\,) + iNCRdbt
\end{aligned}
$$

On the left side of Equation 7, productive workers' incomes may now include three new additions to their previous categories of V and $SSCR_1$. The first, SL, signifies the surplus labor they may appropriate within a feudal household. The second, NCRst, is the value of goods and services workers receive from the state (the other side of the state's $\sum Y$ expenditures in Equation 3). The third, NCRdbt, comprises any credit they obtain. NCRst and NCRdbt are *nonclass* income flows because they are not directly part of either the production or distribution of surplus in any form. It is because such workers occupy *nonclass* positions (as citizens entitled to state benefits and as borrowers) that they receive these flows.[15]

The right hand side of Equation 7 specifies the worker's expenditure to reproduce each of these class and nonclass positions and their attendant income flows. First of all, male workers reproduce their capitalist existence outside the household (their status as V recipients) by purchasing commodities for consumption, means of subsistence. The term EV/UV denotes the exchange value per unit of such commodities, while UV is the number of such units purchased. Multiplied together, these terms amount to the value of what Marx called the 'means of subsistence necessary for the maintenance of the labourer' (1967a, p. 171). Secondly, their capitalist subsumed class position (the $SSCR_1$ that reflects any monopoly component of their wages) may require a payment of union dues indicated by the expenditure of an X. Then, the $\sum SSCP$ term is simply the sum of all the subsumed class distributions the feudal husband must make to secure the continuing receipt of his wife's surplus labor as elaborated in Chapter 1. Taxes paid to the state, Txp and Txss, representing personal and social security taxes respectively, help to secure NCRst, the value of benefits received from the state. Txp and Txss are, of course, sources of the state's NCR in Equation 3. Finally, iNCR represents the cost to workers' of interest payments they must make to secure their outstanding credit (expressed as total consumer debt, NCRdbt).[16] Analyzing Equation 7 reveals what we think is one of those particular moments in capitalist history when the rate of exploitation of the proletariat has shifted significantly. It rose *without* an increase in the length of the workday or in the intensity of labor, and *without* a decrease in the exchange value of means of subsistence. The process is worth detailing.

The depressed labor market continuing into the Reagan years combined with his attack on unions to reduce, if it did not eliminate, $SSCR_1$ as a part of workers' wage incomes. For many blue-collar workers, this meant the end of a traditional subsumed class position, held by many since World War Two. The labor power they supplied was no longer relatively scarce; hence it could no longer obtain a premium ($SSCR_1$). This not only lowered their standard of living but also portended major changes in their relationship with industrial capitalists that are still unfolding.

Capitalists were significantly strengthened: a hitherto necessary subsumed class payment was cut while leaving intact the condition of existence it had secured (namely access to labor power at its value). What was more, the eroded union power and depressed labor power market presented capitalists with an opportunity actually to reduce the value of labor power, to reduce the workers' notions of what was an acceptable standard of living. If capitalists could seize the opportunity, then reducing V would leave them that much more of the workers' daily labor as surplus labor for them to appropriate. In Marx's language, the rate of exploitation would have been raised. In our terms, the SV term on the left side of capitalist enterprises' equations would have been raised.

Added to the decline, if not elimination, of any premium on their labor power ($SSCR_1$) was likely a decline as well in the value of direct benefits derived from state expenditures (NCRst in Equation 7). State social programs hardly expanded under Reaganomics, and those directed to the poorest segments of the population declined. There was no dramatic rise in state expenditures benefiting workers to offset the fall in their subsumed class incomes. Moreover, while personal taxes (Txp) were cut as part of Reaganomics, this cut was more than offset, for many productive workers, by the rise in social security taxes (Txss). Most workers experienced, then, a net increase in their tax expenditures. Added to such an increased *net* tax burden was the rise in interest payments by workers – partly to pay for rapidly rising consumer debt (incurred because of the above-listed pressures on their standards of living) and partly to cope with a rising interest rate on consumer debt (itself linked to the budgetary deficits of the state's policies favoring industrial capitalists). Parallel to the experience of the state and of enterprises, rising interest rates (and debt) meant that workers too had to increase expenditures to service their debt.

Given the pressures generated by these changes damaging to workers' living standards, counterpressures developed to repair the damage or at least to reduce it. The workers could do little to force increases in their wages when they faced: (1) the unemployment produced by the business cycle that ended the Carter and began the Reagan administrations; (2) Reagan's attack on unions; (3) the mass near-hysteria endorsing a competitive necessity to lower wages to defend the US against the invasion of foreign commodities and consequent export of jobs; and (4) the entry of more women competitors into the labor force. Workers could and did complain about union dues and the inadequate *quid pro quo* they felt they were receiving in return; the secular decline in union membership accelerated.[17] Households incurred still more consumer debt (NCRdbt in Equation 7). Male workers from feudal households likely pressed their wives to do more surplus labor there (SL in Equation 7) and/or arrogated more feudal subsumed class payments (ΣSSCP in Equation 7) to themselves.

We suspect that these conditions together overdetermined one of those special conjunctures in US capitalist history when workers were forced over the Reagan years to accept, as a new long-run phenomenon, the lower real wages first experienced in the 1970s. No doubt reduced real incomes were explained to them as caused by the impersonal rules of international competition. Hence their only effective choice was to accept either reduced wages (and thereby maintain their jobs) or unemployment (no wages). More often than not, in their next rounds of wage bargaining, unions came to accept this 'new reality' of the American economy, this 'sharing of the burdens of global adjustment.' Putting this new reality in Marxian terms (1967a, p. 171), there was a change in the 'historical and moral element' determining the value of labor power.

Workers accepted a lower bundle of means of subsistence. Thus, V fell to a lower real wage without a shortened workday or workweek and without any lessened intensity of their labor; if anything, the reverse was more often the case. Industrial capital in the US now enjoyed a higher rate of exploitation of its workers. But the story is not yet over.

Male workers from feudal households who faced falling capitalist wages ($V + SSCR_1$), reduced state benefits (NCRst), and increased outlays on taxes and interest rates, often tried to maintain their standard of living by demanding more surplus labor from their wives and/or increasing their consumer debt. The latter only postponed and then ultimately intensified this demand on wives in the context of household 'debt crises.' At the same time, faced with the twin pincers of greater financial demands and reduced financial resources, many households tried to maintain living standards by means of an accelerated exodus of housewives into the wage labor market. Yet, falling wage levels, together with the systematically lower-paying jobs available to women, meant that their earnings did not much exceed the added costs of compensating for cut government supports plus the added costs of allowing women to leave homes for work (childcare expenses, prepared food expenses, increase clothing expenses, added transportation costs or a second car, etc.). In any case, the women's accelerated exodus undercut the provision of even the traditional amounts – not to speak of demands for increased amounts – of feudal surplus labor in additional millions of US households.

We can pose some of these contradictions by specifying a new class structural equation representing women who both perform feudal surplus labor in the household and sell their labor power to capitalists outside the household. They become part of the proletariat, but unlike their male counterparts, they are exploited at both sites in society:

$$(8) \quad \begin{aligned} &\left[(V) - (NCRmkt)\right] + (NL) + (NCRst) + (NCRdbt) = \\ &\left(\sum \frac{EV}{UV} UV\right) + Z + (Txp + Txss) + iNCRdbt \end{aligned}$$

V indicates income received from feudal wives' sale of labor power outside the household. To capture the reality of the lower-paying jobs taken by women, we subtract a nonclass revenue term (NCRmkt) from the value of labor power, V. Despite anti-discrimination laws in US society, women tend to receive a price for their labor power that is less than its value. In other words, they participate in an unequal exchange with industrial capital that reduces their income from selling their labor power from what it would have been otherwise.[18] Here, the term NCRmkt stands for the deviation in the labor market of women's market wages from the value of their labor power. NL stands for the feudal necessary labor performed and received by women in their feudal household position. Turning our attention next to the NCRst term in Equation 8, it refers to women's receipt of benefits from state expenditures and transfers in the forms of training programs, parental leave supports, etc.[19] Finally, revenues may accrue to such women by their incurring debt, expressed by the variable NCRdbt.[20]

On the expenditure side of Equation 8, the first term represents the commodity purchases made by women (food, clothing, shelter, etc.) needed to reproduce each day the labor power that they sell.[21] The second term, Z, stands for the expenditures they may have to make to reproduce their position as household feudal serfs receiving NL; depending on circumstances, this may include clothes, tools, etc. needed for their feudal household labor. A tax term, Txp + Txss, indicates that they too must pay personal and social security taxes to the state. Interest payments required by any debtor positions that they may occupy are captured by the final iNCRdbt term.

Like their husbands, women are caught in the dilemma of a falling V, and likely a falling NCRst too. However, added to their income problems is the negative NCRmkt. The magnitude of NCRmkt is likely becoming even larger in a market in which: (1) the labor supply is growing (women entering the labor power market in increasing numbers); (2) the demand for labor is falling (government pressure to reduce public employment);

and (3) union power is under attack. Given the additional and increasing net tax burdens and rising interest payments, the pressure on women's bundles of means of subsistence becomes intolerable.

To solve men's demands for increased feudal surplus, women could theoretically accept an increased feudal rate of exploitation either by reducing their necessary labor for themselves (NL) or by expanding their total hours of labor in the household, despite their working 40-hour weeks outside of it. Alternatively, their feudal rate of exploitation could remain unchanged, if expanded feudal hours could be found from additional household serfs – for example, children set to work as feudal serfs alongside their mothers.[22] Perhaps a more complex solution involves women reducing their commodity expenditures to reproduce their own labor power (the

$$\left[\Sigma \frac{EV}{UV} UV \right]$$

term in the above equation) and expanding household budgets for the benefit of their husbands (the ΣSSCP term in the comparable equation for males). Such a substitution serves to reduce women's real incomes even more and, consequently, may provoke a crisis in their capitalist existences as sellers of labor power. Spending less of her money on the food, clothing, and transportation needed for her wage employment will diminish her chances to rise within or even keep that employment.

The pressures caused by any one or more of these possibilities exploded feudal households over recent decades. The solutions that were found for the class problems afflicting capitalist industries and the US state (summarized by Inequalities 2 and 4 above) created major disruptions in the income and expenditure equations for laboring men and women.[23] Consequently, feudal households in the United States literally broke apart under the weight that Reaganomics added to the already heavy pressures – cultural and political as well as economic – that had accumulated across the 1970s.

The statistics on household living conditions suggest much about this explosion.[24] The number of divorces and annulments rose from 708,000 in 1970 (roughly one-third the number of marriages that year) to 1,213,000 in 1981 (roughly one-half the number of marriages); then, the 2:1 ratio of marriages to divorces/annulments continued across the 1980s (*SAUS: 1990*, p. 86). Reports of domestic abuse and violence among adults and children soared. For example, the number of child maltreatment cases reported to officials in the US rose from 669,000 in 1976 to 1,225,000 in 1981 and to 2,086,000 in 1986 (*SAUS: 1990*, p. 176). Drug and substance abuse became even more of a national epidemic; for example, the value of narcotics seizures by the US Immigration border patrols rose from $3.9

million in 1970 to $10.2 million in 1981 and to $582.4 million in 1987 (*SAUS: 1989*, p. 118). Women's eating disorders (see Chapter 4) became an epidemic. Psychological depression and suicides, as well as a widespread sense of deepening emotional distances between parents and children, provoked alarms and anxieties on all sides.

The organizational forms of desperate people's searches for solutions to the critical problems of households took new forms or returned to forms associated with salvation in times of crisis. Revivalism and fundamentalism intensified across all existing religious movements. New organizations modeled after Alcoholics Anonymous proliferated (Adult Children of Alcoholics Anonymous, Overeaters Anonymous, Gamblers Anonymous, Narcotics Anonymous, Cocaine Anonymous, Relationships Anonymous, Eating Disorders Anonymous, and many others).

Increasingly, the feudal household class structures could not survive the pressures. Those who sought divorces to escape these pressures often chose not to recreate new feudal households with new partners. Instead, as argued in Chapter 1, households with different, nonfeudal class structures were established. One rapidly growing option, as we argued previously, was the single adult or, in class terms, the ancient household. Households with communist class structures represented another option to which some escapees from household feudalism were drawn. In this case, a group of adults – linked by varying possible kin or affective relations – collectively produced and collectively appropriated their own surplus labor. Such communist households have qualities different from both their feudal and their ancient counterparts. In the latter two household class structures, the surplus is *privately* appropriated, whether by the *individual* male in the feudal or by the *individual* adult in the ancient. In the communist household, the surplus is *collectively* appropriated as well as produced by the adults.

Conclusion

The impact of Reaganomics on the already mounting difficulties of feudal households exploded millions of those households. This was accomplished notwithstanding, and indeed under the cover of, a barrage of 'pro-family' rhetoric and posturing that were ideological constants across both the Reagan and Bush administrations. Reaganomics thus provoked a transitional conjuncture at the social site of the household. Feudalism in US households is giving way especially to ancient and perhaps even to communist class structures instead. This class transformation, like all others, is the product of cultural and political as well as economic causes. Our Marxian focus in this chapter has been on the class dimensions of and interactions among households, state, and enterprises because there has been a lack of attention to their respective class structures in existing discussions of household and family transformations in the United States today.

It is far too soon to determine whether this class transition will continue, stop, or reverse direction to reestablish household feudalism. It is possible that ancient and communist households will also prove vulnerable to the cultural, political, and economic pressures that undermined feudal households. In any case, the general crisis and transitional conjuncture in feudal households will surely react back upon the 'solution' Reaganomics brought to capitalist enterprises. In that reaction, at least from the Marxian perspective, lie important root causes of class conflicts and changes in the immediate future. There, too, lie important opportunities for political activity aimed at basic social change.

The questions to be answered concern whether and how the household crisis will produce a fall in worker productivity, changes in mass consciousness, alterations in market and savings behaviors, etc., that could well undermine the successes attributed to that solution. These are questions that the Reagan and Bush administration apologists never answered because they never asked them. Nor is there any sign that the Clinton administration will do so any time soon.

To assess Reaganomics, or indeed *any* established official policy of the federal government, requires attention to more than capitalist industrial enterprises. Such attention suggests that whatever its 'successes' at the enterprise level (an increased rate of exploitation as a means to achieve one of the longest expansions in US history), these have to be set against the additional difficulties Reaganomics heaped upon the millions of US households with feudal class structures. Thus, increased rates of exploitation of all productive workers in enterprises were accompanied by increased exploitation of women workers in households and increased violence, despair and disruption of family life generally with perhaps special negative impacts on children. Such rising exploitation and the social implosions it ignites may well come to threaten the very enterprises that Reaganomics was meant to protect and support – far more urgently and critically, perhaps, than any other threat. The feedback effects of the class and other crises of households will have to be factored into any overall judgement on the success of Reaganomics when evaluated even on its own terms.

From a Marxian perspective, what is perhaps most significant is the strategic lesson to be learned from the peculiar trajectory of Reaganomics and its social consequences. Class conflicts in enterprises were partially and temporarily mollified, but at the cost of displacing them on to households. There they have become extremely intense. These conflicts are often taking directly violent forms and radically altering people's perceptions of social life. Many are experimenting with nonfeudal and even communist class structures at household sites. The renewal of a broadly-based socialist movement in the United States presupposes understanding and addressing the new sites of class conflict and class changes in the country. The point is not, of course, to dismiss or demote class analysis, conflict, and change at the sites of enterprise or state. It is rather to integrate them into a systematic application of Marxian theory to changing class structures at other social sites such as households. We believe that such an integration can and should be an important component of the reconstruction of Marxism, theoretically and in terms of practical politics, over the years ahead.

CHAPTER 4

Anorexia as Crises Embodied: A Marxist-Feminist Analysis of the Household*

Introduction

Marxism's tools were originally designed to chisel meaning out of the military industrial blocks of society. They were rarely rigorously applied to the intimate arena of private life. Because class was considered by many Marxists to be the determining essence of social understanding, Marxian tools could not easily be applied to areas such as gender and race without rendering them secondary. However, the kind of Marxian theory utilized in this book views class, gender, and race as each having a unique impact on people and society with no one of them more important than any other. Each particular process operates in its own ways. This approach permits us to combine Marxian understandings of class theory with Feminist conceptions of gender, psychoanalytic ideas of psychology, and new Marxian theories of race. All of these different understandings may be interpreted so as to complement each other and create unique windows of meaning within a non-essentialist methodology. The result is a kind of Marxism that considers class, race, gender, psychological and an infinite variety of other processes as distinct strands in a complex tapestry, each transforming and transformed by all the other strands in the tapestry.

In Chapter 1 we brought our analysis to bear on one intimate area, the household. Here, I explore a different intimate site, that of the female body. On the one hand, I attempt to integrate class, gender, and race with the psychoanalytic theory that traditionally neglects them. On the other, I attempt to integrate race, gender, psychological, and sexual processes with the Marxian theory in which they were considered secondary. The female body is a site on which these different processes reinforce and contradict each other in constant interaction. Parallel to the argument in the previous chapter – that household class and gender processes are in a period of revolution-

* This chapter was prepared by H. Fraad.

ary transformation – here we trace those revolutionary transformations that shape the current epidemic of eating disorders playing themselves out on the stage of women's bodies.

Each person can be thought of as a unique site, a special cross-section of particular biological, cultural, political, economic, and psychological processes.[1] At certain historical moments, these processes interact so as to create diseases of epidemic proportions such as hysteria in Freud's time and eating disorders in our time. In both cases the female body is the theater, the stage on which contradictory social, biological and unconscious forces play. It is my contention that eating disorders are one way that women express the impossibility of managing our contradictions within and between the profoundly and rapidly changing class and gender processes which shape our lives.

Feminist theorists (Orbach 1986; Chernin 1981 and 1985; Bordo 1988; Lawrence 1987; and Spignesi 1983) have explored and illuminated the powerful role of traditional gender ideology and its psychological and sexual consequences in the genesis of anorexia. It is Feminists who connected anorexia to contemporary demands on women to be simultaneously traditional housewives and glamorous, slender, liberated and 'virtuous' sexual objects. Feminists have been pioneers in an endeavor to understand anorexia in order to stop the suffering it expresses. I add overdeterminist Marxian theory to Feminist theory to present a way of understanding anorexia as a means of coping with complex contradictions produced by the wide range of processes in which women participate. In particular while developing an understanding of gender and sexual processes in the tradition of Feminist work on the subject, I introduce some new understandings of psychological processes, and a new analysis of the relevance of racial and class processes to anorexia. As a result, anorexia, a woman's eating disorder, is understood to be constituted not only from effects emanating from gender, sexual, and psychological processes, but also by effects flowing from class and racial processes as well. Thus the class part of North American life – the production, appropriation, and distribution of surplus labor – plays a unique role in helping to produce this modern disorder attacking so many women in today's society.

Eating disorders are psychophysiological symptoms. They are a system of signs of an unconscious disturbance that cannot be spoken and is therefore expressed in symptomatic behavior. There are three main kinds of eating disorder: anorexia, bulimia, and obesity. Each expresses a different kind of adjustment to society's contradictory demands on women.

Anorexia nervosa, or anorexia is the relentless pursuit of thinness, and, at the same time, a delusional denial of thinness (Bruch 1973). The anorectic is a living proof that all perception is interpretation. She may weigh 60 pounds and be a living skeleton but nonetheless she appears to herself as fat and needing to lose weight. Anorexia is controlled rejection of all but

meager amounts of food often combined with uncontrollable urges to gorge
followed by self-induced purging. It is an obsession with food and diets
accompanied by planning rituals related to which foods and what quantities
one can consume at which intervals. It may include compulsive preparation of food for others. An anorectic may plan a daily intake of 300 calories.
This might involve eating an apple divided into quarters and eaten in total
secrecy every three and one-half hours, an egg quartered and eaten at four
other intervals with water, and a few ounces of yogurt eaten at two other
intervals. These foods are often eaten only in particular locations and in
complete privacy. Food controls may be combined with another form of
body control, compulsive exercise. Anorexia literally means without
appetite, but anorectics have appetites which they rigidly control.[2]

Bulimia is similar to anorexia but with regular uncontrollable bingeing
followed by regular self-induced purging. Anorectics may also induce
vomiting or use excessive laxatives if they exceed their calorie intake.
However it is starvation, not bingeing and purging, that chiefly characterizes anorexia. Both anorectics and bulimics tend to be ambitious women
competing or preparing to compete in prestigious, previously 'male' occupations. In marked contrast, obesity, the best known of the eating disorders,
is the compulsive eating of great quantities of food without physical hunger.
It is accompanied by obsessive thinking about food and fatness and feeling
and indulging out of control 'desires' for particular foods. Obesity is not
exclusive to, but is more often found in poorer, less career-ambitious
women (Bruch 1973, 19–21; Lawrence 1988, 40). Eating disorders are
variations on one theme; a compulsive preoccupation with food. They
involve either obesity or 'obesophobia' (Brumberg 1988, 32), a terror of
becoming fat.

Anorexia Nervosa

Eating disorders have become an epidemic among American women and
anorexia is a woman's disorder. There is some debate as to whether any
males at all have typical anorexia. Many authors of books on anorexia write
their books on the subject without any discussion of male anorectics (Bruch
1988; Brumberg 1988; Chernin 1981 and 1985; Orbach 1986; Spignesi
1983; Szekely 1988). Statistics vary as to the proportion of women who
are anorexic. Most writers agree that females constitute at least 90 per cent
of anorectics (Brumberg 1988; Orbach 1986; Lawrence 1987; Bordo
1988).

As many as 20 per cent of college women have some form of anorexia
or bulimia (Brumberg 1988, 13; Chernin 1985, 13). Most American
women are in some way obsessively obesophobic and diet compulsively

(Brumberg 1988, 32–4). Food is women's 'normative obsession' (Wolf 1989). The overwhelming majority of American women in the 1980s had some kind of eating disorder (Chernin 1985; Orbach 1978 and 1986; Szekely 1988). This chapter focuses on anorexia because it is the most dramatic of eating disorders; it is quite often fatal. Like all disorders, anorexia represents a difference of degree, not of kind. It is an exaggerated example of the torment experienced by most contemporary women.

Whom does it strike? The profile of 'a typical anorectic' is changing. White prosperous women were previously the prime candidates for the disorder. Now it is moving across income and color lines (Lawrence 1987, 209; Garfinkel and Garner 1982, 102–13). Anorexia usually strikes women from the ages of 15 to 40. Although it is no longer restricted to the daughters of the wealthy, it appears in families for whom there is no scarcity of food. Palazzoli (1974) points out that because of the severe food shortages in Italy during the Second World War, there were no hospital-izations for anorexia. However, once those shortages were over and affluence and food abundance returned to Italy, so did hospitalizations for anorexia. It seems to strike women in families whose sufficient food supplies transform the meaning of food from an immediate guarantor of survival to a primarily symbolic substance. Anorexia strikes: (1) women preparing to become 'modern women', moving out of the traditional female household gender roles; (2) young high school students, usually with excellent records; (3) college-age women facing a changed female environment at college; (4) women entering professions or competing in what were once male pro-fessional spheres; and (5) older women returning to school or the job market. Anorexia often afflicts women who have ambitious educational plans or accomplishments (Lawrence 1987, 207–25).

Anorexia is a disorder that captures and acts out for its victim the con-tradictions of modern women's social position. It is a disorder whose symptoms are paralytic and wildly contradictory. As all the previous chapters document, North American women are in a period of class and gender transition. For women with employed husbands, current conditions permit neither our former full-time domestic positions in the male supported household nor our new positions in the household and the marketplace simultaneously. For women without employed spouses, this dilemma is deepened by the absence of supports for the now weakened extended families which once made it possible for single women to manage the double burdens of mothering and jobs outside of the home.[3] For white women and women of color, career expectations have risen without the social underpinnings that make those expectations reasonable. [4]

Anorexia is a disorder that permits its sufferer to express dramatic con-tradictions. The anorectic rejects her body's needs. She rejects all 'input', 'hunger', or desire for or dependence on other things such as food and, ultimately, other people. Anorexia is a desire to be in total control of the female body and totally autonomous. Yet, it is a control that is out of control: a control that renders its victim so debilitated and helpless that she is forced into the hospital dependent on the care of others, to be fed like an embryo through an intravenous tube. It is a disorder of women who often become demanding and controlling. They 'demand their space', and 'throw their weight around'. Yet they 'reduce' themselves until they have no weight to throw and occupy very little space indeed. It is a disorder of women who are often obsessed by physical fitness and yet become totally weak. It involves a rejection of food and yet is often accompanied by a compulsive need to feed others. Anorectics often force food on others as well as cook and serve food as an attempt to control the food intake of others as well as themselves.

Anorexia, like other psychological disorders, meets simultaneous, contradictory needs. It is an obsession with food and a powerful rejection of food. It is a disorder of a woman asserting her will-power and mastery over her needs and yet becoming anything but strong and autonomous. Anorectics are women desperate to 'measure up' who radically 'reduce' themselves. They follow the current maxim for women, 'One can never be too thin or too rich,' to the point of parody.

Why anorexia now? Why does anorexia almost exclusively affect women? Given that the disorder has been recorded as early as the middle ages (Brumberg 1988, 2), why is it currently a part of an epidemic of eating disorders? Why is it, with other eating disorders, a mass phenomenon, paralleling hysteria in Freud's time? What social conditions in modern North America foster anorexia as an epidemic? Most particularly how do class, race, psychological and gender processes interact (reinforce and contradict each other) in ways that contribute to an anorexia epidemic?

Gender Processes as Conditions of Existence for Anorexia

Gender processes are ways of representing women to ourselves, to each other and to men. They are, as argued in Chapter 1, ways of producing the socially contrived facts of 'women' and 'men', and, thus, of their differences from one another. One of anorexia's cultural conditions of existence is a particular kind of gender ideology that represents women as the sex-objects in and of society. Such an ideology acts upon us as a kind of Foucauldian discipline (Bordo 1988). It helps to create us. We tweeze the hair in our eyebrows, shave our underarms and legs, or use hot wax to rip hair out by the roots. We apply hot curling or straightening irons to our hair. We painstakingly apply creams and make-up to our faces and eyes. On continuous diets, we starve ourselves and push our bodies to slenderness with strenuous exercise or conceal our flesh in tight confining underwear. These are disciplines for whose infractions the very real punishment is personal, sexual rejection. The woman who will not wear make-up, or shave her legs, or be slender, may sometimes maintain or regain her job when threatened, but she may nonetheless lose friendship (of both men and women), social acceptance, and sexual approval. Our bodies are usurped through a thousand Lilliputian disciplines typically presented as harmless routines of self-care. Thus our desire to please others is confused with our need to care for ourselves. Our fear of rejection is enmeshed with our desire for self-pride.

Consider the following description of our lives: '*Men act* and *women appear*. Men look at women. Women watch themselves being looked at. This determines not only most relations between men and women but also the relation of women to themselves' (Berger 1972, 47). Women in our culture learn to experience our bodies as if we were the male spectators to ourselves. 'The surveyor of woman in herself is male: the surveyed, female. Thus she turns herself into an object – and most particularly an object of vision; a sight' (Berger 1972, 47). We learn via television, movies, magazines, and advertisements what we should look like rather than how to feel and know the sensations of our bodies. We are dependent upon external reinforcement for being attractive and sexy. Attractiveness is verified by those one attracts. Women's own sexuality, our own desire, is not cultivated as our own experience, but the experience of being desirable to someone else. 'Women are there to feed an appetite, not to have any of their own' (Berger 1972, 55). Food does not experience its own consumption. Thus food may become a medium that represents our alienated situation. Food, like female sexuality, may become something consumed by others, not by a woman for herself. Our appetite for approval as desirable women contributes to our shaping ourselves as objects to be consumed by others' hungers rather than subjects to experience our own desire.

On the one hand anorectics reject food to gain approval for being a slender sex-object for another. Yet at the same time, it is this taste for approval which anorectics disavow. Craving for status as a body for male consumption is seen by the anorectic as an abandonment of her independent self. In the words of an anorexic girl, 'I can at the same time be choosing to live as the self and choosing to die as the body' (MacLeod 1981, 88). Margaret Atwood captures this female condition in her tale of *The Edible Woman* (1969) who is an object of everyone's needs (hungers) but her own. Anorexia is thus a deeply contradictory relation to food: controlling and rejecting it both to fulfil the stereotype of the attractive woman and simultaneously to deny and denounce that stereotype.

Women's work on creating 'delectable' external images is often understood as narcissism. Based on my psychotherapeutic practice, it is rather a hopeless attempt to reconnect with a personal sense of physical self and sexuality by imagining oneself as one's own consumer. Because attractiveness depends on others, one can never be sure of one's looks. The resulting sense of insecurity makes women particularly vulnerable to social standards of beauty including external standards for slenderness.

The culture's idealized images of women's bodies are plastered everywhere. Women's bodies sell everything from cars to cigarettes to video cassettes. The idealized omnipresent images are all slim; they have no cellulite. Many female models appear androgynous with bodies resembling the bodies of adolescent males (Chernin 1985). Their already striking images are further artificially corrected and perfected in photographic studios. They present standards that women can never actually achieve. Nonetheless, they present the objective standard for female beauty. There are considerable social pressures to conform to requirements for female success and sexiness by achieving and maintaining slenderness. Fat is failure as a woman.

Trying desperately to regain control of their own bodies from which they as women are alienated, anorectics act out their contradictory relationship to food. They become parodies of the social demand for slenderness by becoming hideously slender while they ostensibly strive to be perfectly beautiful. They strive for a body image as a way to experience personal power and social acceptance, yet their anorexia debilitates and isolates them. They often exercise compulsively, partly trying to feel in command of bodies with which they are out of touch and partly trying to convert their bodies into super ideals of fit slenderness. Yet anorexia undermines their physical strength. They mimic yet they also mock the media's impossible standards for them.

One of many long prevalent female gender processes is the creation and dissemination of the definition of woman as nurturer. Women are to feed men and children. Women's bodies sustain children in the womb and their breasts nourish most people when they emerge. Beginning in infancy, memories of food and feeding are attached to women. The household kitchen is defined as women's sphere. For family events and holidays women shop, cook, and serve food, and then clean up its remains. Women are the overwhelming majority of parents who feed and of professional food service workers who serve. Not surprisingly, women are society's symbolic nurturers as well. They 'feed' people through mothering, teaching young children, social work, and nursing, to list but a small selection among women's nurturing professions. One part of the female feeder role is being the one who gives, while not demanding to be sustained in return. In times of food scarcity, women tend to feed their families, while they themselves go hungry (Edwards 1987; Wolf 1989).

On the one hand, the anorectic rebels against such gender processes by starving herself to the point where she loses female characteristics. Anorexics become emaciated to the point of losing all female curves, becoming amenorrhoeic, and developing body hair.[5] On the other hand, the anorectic so identifies with the plight of women that her emaciated form represents the emotional, intellectual, and spiritual starvation of women driven to extremes in nurturing and serving others (Spignesi 1983). Anorexia is at once a reflection of the contradictions involved in being female today and an attempt, also contradictory, to cope with them.

Another established gender process defines a particular kind of 'womanly behavior.' Women should be the ones who absorb family tensions and obligingly take orders. Anorectics usually start out life as extraordinarily good girls, obedient and 'sweet'. They take what is 'dished out' to them, including food, and 'swallow' it without complaint. Anorexia is in part a rebellion against compliance. Anorectics often feed (sometimes coercively) others, but they will not eat. They refuse any more 'input' from others. They eat their meager portion only in circumstances under their own control. When they break discipline and eat more than their strict controls allow, they reject and purge that food. It is as if they can no longer 'swallow' or 'stomach' submissive roles. They enact in the realm of food the impossible cultural demand on women, that they sustain ('feed') others and are not themselves sustained ('fed'). They obediently follow the gender rule that 'has them by the throat'; they keep their mouths shut. At the same time their starvation is a hunger strike (Orbach 1986) against such restrictions.

Another gender process stereotypes women's realm as the body, the flesh, and not the mind or soul. This is an aspect of femaleness that anorexics strenuously reject. The anorectic is not (to use the significant vernacular) a 'dish, peach, chick or tomato' to be served up for sexual consumption. The anorectic's starved body is a rejection of female sexuality. Anorexia has a long history of being a rebellion against the notion of woman as flesh. From at least the middle ages to the present, fasting has been widely considered a noble path to spiritual purity. The ascetic nuns and 'miraculous fasting girls' that we would now call 'anorectics' were revered for going beyond the flesh to a spiritual existence (Brumberg 1988, 41–100; Bell 1985, 20, 54–81). Only in this century has what we know as 'anorexia' been considered a disorder. As she fasts, the anorectic is obsessed by food and fear of the flesh to the point where she can think of nothing else. Her escape route from woman as flesh leads right back to the flesh in an obsession with flesh.

Anorexia is a rejection of the gender process that defines the relationship between male and female bodies to be one in which agency and desire are allocated to masculinity and receptivity and passivity to femininity. It is an unconscious rejection of being the sex that Jacques Lacan refers to as 'that sex which is not one.' Lacan presents the woman as a kind of female impersonator acting out male fantasies of the mysterious 'other' to men. In herself, she is no one (Lacan 1975, 138–48, and 162–71). The belief that women are somehow not fully human, and resemble the characters in males' fantasy lives, not only robs women of our own agency. It also sets the stage for men taking power over women in ways that one can do only if one considers the victim not human, but 'other'. Anorexia is a rebellion against those gender and power processes which express themselves socially in male control of women's bodies in rape, incest, pornography, prostitution, and restrictions on birth control and abortion.[6]

When a painfully thin woman looks at her reflection in the mirror and mourns over what she perceives as her fat, she sees and grieves over the body of a fat woman because for her to be a woman is to be fleshy, fat, and thus needy, passive, and helpless. She is possessed by a wish to be active and in control, wishes she often considers male. The inner voice that commands anorexic women to drive themselves and starve is described by them as a male voice: 'The little man who objects when I eat' (Bruch 1978, 55), 'An armed man' (Bruch 1978, 251), 'A man with a drawn sword' (Bruch 1978, 258), 'The little man inside me who says "No!"' (Bruch 1988, 124–5). Here the anorectic rebels against male power while submitting to it.

Alongside the prevalent traditional gender processes which I have discussed are conflicting, quite opposite, modern gender processes. Today's successful business woman or professional is hardly passively awaiting orders. She is supposed to be at the creative edge, innovating and initiating those programs that will offer her or her employer the competitive edge. Nurturance of her professional clients or her employer may well be in order, but compassion for and nourishment of her competitors will not be tolerated. She is to look out for herself and her employer only. Sacrifice for the company or her private clients may be encouraged, if it is lucrative, but sacrifice of the client and the corporation to the needs of a husband and children will not be suffered. An asset of the 'modern' woman is a slender body that is simultaneously sensual and severe in a stylish business suit. She should be sexual but not sexually needy or dependent. She should use her sex, which often counts against her, as a business asset. She should use her body like her head for the purpose of getting ahead.

Current gender processes inspire women as well as define women as capable of becoming the 'head' of the corporation, rather than the humble wife who performs the daily labor that attends the bodily and emotional needs of her family. Modern women can be the spiritual leaders of the flock in those religions which permit women to be leaders. They should 'head' the churches rather than remain in their traditional roles as the body of the faithful. These are roles that today's gender processes compel young anorectics to try to attain alongside of their traditional opposites.

Anorectics are trapped within contradictory Feminine roles – defined by opposed and changing gender processes that they can no longer 'stomach'. They are literally 'fed up' with being women. They are 'sick to death' of the contradictory roles they see ahead of them. They are traumatized by having to be characterized as the body while they strive to get ahead and be the head of the company. They feel the need to be the desirable object and also the desiring subject. They agonize over their own desire to be passive and to be active, to be what was traditionally female and also, increasingly in today's world, what was male.

Political and Social Processes as Conditions of Existence for Anorexia

The women's liberation movement that started in the 1960s is an example of a political development which provided certain other conditions of existence for the development of anorexia. When women began to 'throw their weight around,' the campaign for thinness accelerated markedly (Chernin 1985). At that same time, women themselves began to want to lose the weight that marked them as women in a society in which women were considered socially and politically inferior. It was in the 1960s that the current androgynous ideal began to be celebrated. This ideal of the woman without those curves that mark her clearly as a female is taken to extremes in anorexic women.

It is interesting that anorexia has been a highly visible, widely recognized disorder of the 1980s. This timing may be connected to the recent history of the Feminist movement in the United States. From the late 1960s to the middle 1970s, the Feminist movement existed as a militant voice for all women expressing outrage at the totality of women's oppression. However, by the 1980s the women's movement had become for the most part a series of separate, issue-oriented groups and institutions such as: reproductive rights groups, anti-pornography groups, rape crisis centers, and battered women's shelters. Those umbrella groups that remain no longer capture women's imaginations and energies as they once did. Militant voices of fury at all the interconnected processes oppressing women have become significantly muted.

Ironically enough the women's liberation movement which militated for expanded job possibilities for women has suffered in part from many former activists and potential new Feminists pouring their energy into career advancement for themselves at the expense of collective struggle. It is possible that the anorectic's *private* protest against the future offered to her reflects the relative absence of the *public, social* protests that a militant women's movement had earlier made possible and even popular. The political processes that helped to dislodge women from our domestic oppression have changed, leaving us without an aggressive social or political voice in which to express collective protest.[7] Anorexia may have stepped into the void as an unconscious enactment of our outrage.[8]

As explained in Chapter 1, the decline in the male wage, and men's increasing refusal to provide economic support to women and children combined with a myriad of other processes to push women out of full-time positions in feudal households and into exploitation outside of the household. The Feminist movement was one of the political processes whose effect was to push women out of full-time household labor and traditional gender roles. From the 1960s the movement struggled to achieve women's economic, intellectual, and psychological equality with men. The Feminist movement participated in increasing female political and economic power as well as strengthening some of the conditions of existence for women's exploitation in capitalist enterprises. We won some extension of women's job possibilities, some protection against discrimination in hiring, some small protection against sexual harassment on the job, and some greater means for women to control our own bodies through legislation concerning rape, birth control and abortion. Most importantly, the women's movement combined with the male rebellion against supporting families and with economic pressures forcing women into the labor force, to achieve changed expectations for women.

Although the goals of the women's movement have been at best partially won, the scope and expectations for women's professional achievement have been dramatically extended, particularly among the ambitious, educated women who are typical candidates for anorexia. The former roles of full-time feudal housewife and mother are now often perceived as insufficient, and, in any case, financially impossible. The goals for women have been extended far further than have the social and political supports enabling us to reach these goals. The resulting pressures on women are staggering. We should successfully compete against men on the job and at the same time be Feminine and non-competitive sexual objects, and feudal household serfs. We can no longer return to the familiar female role of feudal full-time homemaker symbolized by food and the kitchen and yet are unable to assume all the different (and often contradictory) additional roles required of us. Demands on women are out of control. Anorexic women respond by taking control of the one thing in life they seem able to control, their own female bodies.

A political process that demands that women be treated as the equals of 'ruggedly individualistic' men has driven many women to reject – like many men – the realm of human need, of dependence on others. Instead of being acknowledged as the human condition, dependence is part of a half shameful private life, assigned to women and children. Caught up in rugged individualism, the anorectic desperately denies her needs: most dramatically and symbolically, the need to eat. She would rather starve than need.

Anorexia is a revolt against being relegated to the private world of regressive neediness. It is a protest against and a withdrawal from a society that drives males to pose as without need while women are representatives and fulfillers of everyone's needs. It is a rebellion against and an expression of the impossible, thrice contradictory demands on women: (1) that we be 'Feminine,' need-centered, and domestically focused in a society in which needs are an embarrassment; (2) that we be simultaneously centered on competition and achievement in the social and political realms in which we operate at a disadvantage; and (3) that we also be sex-centered and glamorous in a public world in which just such behavior is unsafe.

In the contemporary United States individual sites of personal nurturing atrophy. The phenomenon of the housewife caring for her own children as well as those of neighbors is replaced by the working woman who struggles for time with her own children and cannot give to her neighbors. The nurturant interactions between small shopkeepers and their patrons is increasingly replaced by the anomie of huge chain-stores. The society becomes more threatening as drugs and crime force people indoors, locked away from their neighbors. It falls to women to compensate for this disintegration of the United States' social fabric. We need to be concurrently super nurturant, and super tough to succeed in the capitalist work world. Anorexia is partly a resistance against and withdrawal from a predatory work world in which changed social expectations require women to be in control and without apparent personal need at the same time as it is a protest against the simultaneous social processes requiring women to be, more than before, household nurturers, needers and administrators to others' personal needs.

Anorexia is also, in part, a revolt against political and other social processes which push women into a sexually predatory public sphere. American females are increasingly subjected to sexual molestation and rape. Sexual assaults are increasing four times faster than the overall crime rate.[9] Approximately one out of every four United States women is raped, while one out of five women is date raped while at college (Estrich 1987, 12). The influential *Playboy* philosophy of appropriating women's sexuality without long-range commitments to support wives and children has enhanced women's sexual and economic vulnerability. Women are pushed to enter political and social life within a rape culture which sexually harasses us. The anorectic rejects the flesh that marks her as a target for sexual oppression.

Within their social positions as helpless children, many anorectics have experienced childhood sexual abuse fueling desires to escape the female bodies that have made them sexual prey (Bordo 1988, 88). The anorectic repossesses the body that her childhood abuser usurped for his pleasure. She starves her body to the point where its sexuality is invisible to potential predators. Yet again, contradictorily, she joins her abusers in 'reducing herself' to a body by channeling her desires and ambitions into an abusive form of body control.

Psychological Processes as Conditions of
Existence for Anorexia Nervosa

Anorexia is an exaggeration of the obesophobia experienced by most North American women. We may therefore look at the psychology of women to gauge some of its psychological conditions of existence. Women in our society are the primary and often almost exclusive carers for children. Children spend their earliest formative years in a virtual matriarchy presided over by mothers, female daycare workers, grandmothers, nurses and baby-sitters (Dinnerstein 1976). Because of the relative social isolation of US families, mothers become awesomely powerful figures in this matriarchy.[10] In order to be separate people, children need to differentiate themselves from their seemingly powerful and often overwhelming mothers. The project of separation is enhanced for boys by the realization that they are different from mother because they are a different sex (Chodorow 1978; Dinnerstein 1976). Parents tend to push their male children towards independence faster than they push their female children (Fraad 1985, 22–3). Their different sex and childrearing norms help both boys and their mothers see males as distinct from mother and as separate people.

Girls do not have these opportunities to separate. Many girls try to turn to fathers as models and ways out of a dominant mother/subordinate daughter fusion, but that way out is often barred. Families often lack a genuinely involved father figure. Other families include involved fathers who are seductive, who treat their daughters as sexual objects rather than identify with them as people (Chodorow 1987).[11] Closeness to these seductive fathers is often and quite reasonably perceived by daughters as too dangerous to pursue. Another obstacle may be the presence of fathers whose male identity is a negative identity based upon their not being female. Threatened by identification with their daughters, such fathers discourage their daughter's identification with them and encourage its opposite. They treat their girls as cute little creatures very different from themselves (Bernstein 1983). Girls' relationships with their mothers as both the same sex and the sex that is encouraged to be more dependent, tend to encourage empathy, merging, and continuity at the expense of individuality and independence (Benjamin 1988; Chodorow 1978).

It is also the case that mothers, particularly mothers who do not have satisfying independent lives in which they are needed at work and desired by their partners, i.e., most mothers, need their daughters to need them. Daughters enact their mothers' needs by staying dependent upon their mothers. Such unsatisfied mothers are rarely capable of articulating their own needs and asking that they be satisfied. Part of the daughter's identi-fication (and often fusion) with the mother follows from the daughter's learning to intuit her mother's needs and learning to become the voice for those needs. Often mothers are so fused with their daughters and so determined to serve others rather than themselves that they attribute their needs to their daughters and meet their own needs in the guise of caring for their daughters' needs. At the same time, daughters, following their mothers' leads, also confuse their mothers' needs with their own. What begins as the daughter's normal infantile need for maternal nurturing symbolized as food becomes a dangerous fusion in which the daughter's need traps her into a confusion between her desires and her mother's in which she loses a separate identity. Her separate self feels as if it is starving.

Since mothers are markedly associated with food, feeding, and love, women may try desperately to control suffocating neediness for their mothers or others whom they love by rigidly controlling what they eat. Thus they may become anorexic. They act out their starvation as independent selves by literally starving themselves. The attempt at such total control represents a desperate attempt to break dependency on the mother. This dependency is experienced as a threat to the daughter's existence as a separate person. Ironically, literal starvation becomes a strategy for psychological survival. It permits the anorectic at once to express her mother's starvation for a separate self and her own starvation for a separate self, her need both to separate from the mother and to fuse with her. The anorectic becomes obsessed with her desire for food in her denial of it just as she becomes obsessed with her mother by denying her need for her mother. Anorexia is a disorder of women starved for recognition of their own separate personhood. It is a disturbance among women whose boundaries are particularly unclear; women who have little practice in knowing their own needs outside of the one need to please others. It is a disorder of women who are very practiced in anticipating and fulfilling their mothers' and others' needs.

Female children feel keenly the loss of subjectivity and agency from which many mothers suffer. In Lacanian terms, the woman is the 'Not all,' the 'other' to male fantasies: 'Man acts as the relay whereby the woman becomes this other for herself as she is the other for him' (Lacan 1964, 93). Women cut off from their own desire and agency are often pained and angry. Mothers frequently vent their self-hatred as women on their daughters who are like them. Many seem particularly to resent the sacrifices they make to care for daughters. Studies indicate that daughters are fed less well and less sensitively than are sons (Orbach 1978, 18). This feeding behavior extends to emotional feeding and empowerment as well.

Anorexic daughters partly identify with their mothers' pain and rage. They combine empathy for their mothers with a resentment at both the unspoken and the articulated demands that they follow maternal examples of self-sacrifice. The anorexic daughter becomes the skeleton that compassionately acts out the death in her mother's life, a life dedicated to service nurturing others (Spignesi 1983). Yet, contradictorily, the anorectic renounces her mother's life and her mother by giving up her lifeline to her mother through food.

Anorexia is a disturbance of guilt. The daughter who has seen and felt the pain of her mother's sacrificed independence has tremendous guilt about realizing independence. The possibilities for modern women lead them away from the lives their mothers have led. Often a daughter fears that if she leaves to make an independent life her mother will not survive the separation. Many daughters feel that if they go on to have careers and love-lives and possibilities their mothers either did not have or could not allow themselves, then they will have benefited at their mothers' expense and will be responsible somehow for victimizing their mothers. They will prosper for their mothers' sacrifice. They may then sacrifice their futures for their mothers as a way of repaying their mothers' sacrifices and expiating their guilt over their mothers' wasted possibilities. Anorexia may then involve such a compelling obsession with food preparation and exercise that it prevents the daughter from leaving her mother and moving on to her own life. Its end result is total helplessness and being cared for, often by the mother.

With perceptiveness, Rosalind Coward refers to inviting, exquisite, stylized food illustrations as women's pornography (1985, 99–106). She attributes food's pornographic appeal to the fact that our diet-conscious culture and slim ideals for women punish women for indulging ourselves as they exhort women to create oral pleasure for others. Women are to serve others, not to indulge themselves. Food may be women's 'cheesecake' in other ways as well. One important attribute of male pornography is that it allows its male viewer to appropriate the object of his desire without being vulnerable to her or him. Pornography fans are often men who are terrified by their dependency needs. With pornography, the needs of the viewer are not exposed to anyone but himself. Food may be tied in to women's desires and needs for mothering, desires of which they too are terrified. Women, like men, may want to appropriate their objects of desire without being vulnerable to them. Women's 'cheesecake' may be an attempt to appropriate mothering without paying the fearful price of dependency and fusion.

Racial Processes as Conditions of Existence for Anorexia

Following Gabriel (1990, 69–78) we may consider racial processes as the systems of meaning attached to people of color. My argument here is that changes in these racial processes have interacted with changes in other social processes to enable minority women to join white women as anorexics

(Garfinkel and Garner 1982, 102–103). From the mid 1950s to the end of the 1970s, the civil rights movement helped to create some increased possibilities for North Americans of color, particularly those whose economic privilege or extraordinary talent and tenacity permitted them access to elite educations. However, by the 1980s the energy for a broadly-based civil rights movement had markedly decreased. The unabashed racism of the Reagan and Bush administrations, the murders of African-American leaders, the wholesale introduction of drugs into minority communities, and systematic cuts in opportunities and supports for the dispossessed combined with the disintegration of a broad civil rights constituency to remove many of the conditions for hope among North Americans of color. As with women as a whole, the combination of just enough new opportunities with newly raised expectations placed heavy pressures on minority women to add new social roles in addition to their traditional roles.

Many women of color had never experienced the ostensible luxury of serfdom in feudal households supported by men. Feudal households depend on the wages of the male lord of the manor to pay for the rent or mortgage and the raw materials, cleaning agents, raw foods, etc. which the serf housewife transforms into cleanliness and edible meals. Systematic racism often excluded African American and other minority males from the steady jobs and/or the levels of wages necessary for sustaining feudal households. Many women of color have thus always carried the double burden – low wage employment plus childcare without a husband or with a husband unable or unwilling to provide support – that the mass of white women now bear. Many minority women, whether they lived in ancient or communal or feudal households, have for generations worked both inside and outside of their homes. What has changed is that with a small new window of opportunity came a powerful pressure on significant numbers of minority women to do more than sustain themselves and often children while working in and outside of their homes. For ambitious educated women, there is now an additional imperative, to succeed in a high power, professional career in a white, male, capitalist, world while caring for children and doing the domestic labor for their own households. It is among those minority women who aspire to professional success that anorexia strikes. Racial processes here combine with gender, class, psychological, political, and economic processes to push minority women to join their white sisters in anorexic disorders.

Economic Processes as Conditions of Existence for Anorexia

The economic process of selling labor power yields for women systematically lower wages than men obtain. Although the gap between women's

and men's earnings has very slowly decreased, we still have a long way to
go before earning three-quarters of what men earn for full-time work.[12]
Women's overwhelming responsibility for childcare and our preponder-
ance in the lowest paid jobs, i.e., part-time work without benefits (Beechey
and Perkins 1987), combine to make the escape from poverty part of what
induces us to attract men and their wages. Women's attractiveness, defined
in terms of slenderness, becomes a means to economic security for women.
Thus, economic considerations may contribute to women's dieting, a
regimen that can then, for other reasons, become excessive.

Both legal and illegal pornography are multi-billion dollar industries
devoted to portraying woman as bodies and desirable women as slim. The
diet industry is a five billion dollar industry (Brumberg 1988, 253) convincing
women that happiness can be achieved through slenderness. The advertising industry is a multi-billion dollar industry feeding women's insecurities
about our looks and bodies in order to sell products. Fashions are designed
for slender women with the standard shapes that fit mass-produced clothing
styles. With sales in mind, the cosmetics industry seeks to convince women
that their looks are crucial to future happiness. From home and family
magazines at supermarket check-out counters to fashion or career oriented
women's magazines, the stress is upon pictures of idealized and slender models
and celebrities, the latest diets, recipes for low-calorie foods, and special
exercises designed to help women lose weight. The fashion/cosmetics/
magazine industries combine with the legal and illegal pornography
industries to create a chorus of different voices extolling slenderness as female
success and defining fat as failure. The anorectic takes this barrage of diet
advice to heart. Believing that her problems will diminish with her flesh,
she can become relentless in pursuit of that slenderness that will make her
the person of her dreams. At the same time, these economic processes help
to create the terror of 'measuring up' which sends the anorectic in flight
from her projected and impossible standards of physical beauty.

The economic processes that provide conditions of existence for anorexia
include certain class processes that also interact with the gender, political,
and psychological processes developed above to overdetermine anorexia.
The role of class processes and their interaction with other processes in conditioning anorexia have not received the attention they deserve for their
contribution towards explaining the anorexia epidemic.

Our first chapter described the feudal, communal and ancient class
processes in the household. It is important to note that none of the
household class processes we have described is a capitalist class process. All
take place outside of the capitalist marketplace in which, for a wage,
surplus is created by some and appropriated and distributed by others.

As young women develop in households they define themselves in
terms of the values and behaviors they perceive. Most young women

model themselves in part on the feudal, ancient or communal value systems their mothers adopt in relation to their household class situations. These values often are a detriment to success in the capitalist marketplace. Young women are caught between their deep identification with their mothers, whose noncapitalist models they learned to follow as unconscious young children, and the demands made upon them to play capitalist roles for which they may be educated, but for which they are not emotionally prepared. They are unconsciously functioning within one set of psychological, gender and class processes, while they consciously try to live within a different set. They are wrenched between two worlds each with a different, contradictory set of values. One attempt to resolve this conflict is anorexia.

Currently, as ever more women in the United States take regular jobs outside of their feudal or other noncapitalist households, they join their poorer sisters who have always had double shifts inside and outside. They function within different class structures at home and at work. Their adjustments to the different class processes in which they participate are overdetermined in part by the self-definitions and attitudes of the women involved. If a woman defines herself as what we call a feudal housewife, and sees her work outside the home as an extension of her work within it, she may define her capitalist job as a temporary family duty assumed until no longer necessary. In this case, she may work outside of the home *without* forming either a commitment to her job or any kind of deep identification as an extra-household worker. In such a case, the woman's self-definition is not split by dual identification.

On the other hand double demands are particularly contradictory in the case of the educated women who become anorexic. These are women whose identities are split between the demands for dependency, sacrifice, and nurture in feudal or other noncapitalist households and ruthless competition in the capitalist work world. It is these women who are expected to work both a psychological and a physical 'double shift'.[13] These women expect themselves to compete successfully in the capitalist world of exchange-value outside the home as well as to maintain their feudal, ancient, or communal use-value producing roles within the home.

In the particularly feudal household world of women, the ties that both bind and choke are symbolized by food and its preparation. Anorectics refuse the need for food and with it the need to belong to the noncapitalist world of the household. However anorexia's victims obsess on the food they cannot have. In this way the disorder enacts the need for connection and continuity with a frequently feudal past, symbolized by need, food and mothering. Anorexia also enacts the drive for personal independence and control in capitalist careers with little tolerance for personal need. Anorexia denies and controls women's needs for two contradictory roles, each impossible fully to achieve or to relinquish.

To compete in the capitalist world in the contemporary United States, women need to have vastly different characteristics from those needed within feudal, ancient or communal households. Career oriented, educated anorectics will be competing for executive roles like their male peers. For these roles they need to get others to serve them and their corporations. If they become industrial capitalists, they appropriate the surplus labor of others. If they become capitalist managers, they order others to produce surplus labor. They must be concerned not that each person receive her or his due, but rather that the corporation successfully exploits its laborers. In fact, their corporate executive success depends upon insuring that employees receive little or nothing of the surplus they create. They need to deny needs both to nurture and be nurtured while they foster their needs to exploit and compete. They need to think in terms of production for exchange and not production for use.

Highly motivated intelligent women often try to escape from the feudal household in part to evade control by the demands of others on them. But their escape is to careers, whether as industrial capitalists, managers, or wage workers, in which they are controlled by others in another class system.[14] They leave their homes and feudal or communal value systems in order to be independent and find themselves dependent once more, but in a different, if not so emotional, hierarchy. As we show in Chapter 1, the households from which modern women emerge are themselves contradictory. Anorectics focus on controlling diet as a displacement for controlling the competing, contradictory foci within and between career advancement and feudal or communal nurture. In extreme cases, anorexic women end up so distracted and physically exhausted that they are forced to drop out of both class processes and to die. In this way they opt out of both controlling class systems, the one at home and the different one at work. They literally sacrifice their lives to gain control of themselves.

The anorectic is acting out on her own body the need to be in command. She must stop both the urge to fill others' needs and also the urge to fill or even to experience her own. In order to get 'ahead' (a head) on the job, she imagines she must stop being sexualized flesh with its symbolism as a vehicle for male pleasure and female neediness. She wishes to be 'disembodied' in order to be able to compete with men as equals in the capitalist marketplace while she also flees the controls imposed by that marketplace. The anorectic's identification with her mother and needs for nurturing tie her to the familial role of woman preoccupied with food and family within noncapitalist household values and class structures. Her identification as a successful, ambitious, career woman ties her to the capitalist structures and values of the marketplace. Anorexia is a protest against being trapped by two untenable, contradictory, capitalist and noncapitalist class positions. It is a strike against having to assume contradictory gender, race, psychological, political, economic, and class roles currently expected of so many women.

Anorexia has become an epidemic as the demands on women to perform as men in the capitalist workplace have escalated without creating the social services that would relieve women of their role as nurturers in non-capitalist households. The seeming contradictions in anorexic behavior express the conflict between current expectations of women and a largely feudal past with which we are now breaking. For hundreds of years, women's primary labor has been socially defined as the production of household goods, services, and nurturing (household surplus) for men. Generations of women raised their daughters to fill their feudal household roles. Now women are expected to maintain their roles as homemakers, while succeeding at labor in the marketplace, all the while disciplining ourselves to fit media images of feminine attractiveness. Whereas formerly we had one feudal master, the male lord of the household, now we have three masters: men, bosses, and the media, all giving simultaneous contradictory directives. The radical break in the ambitious, modern woman's three-ring life erupts in the form of eating disturbances expressing the rupture between generations of daughters and their mothers whose noncapitalist home-circumscribed lives can no longer serve as viable models.

Anorexia is an expression of women's agony as we grapple painfully, and with few supports, with the contradictions crowding in on our lives. Eating disorders are a social metaphor: the stage on which women, defined as bodies, act out on the site of our own bodies the revolutionary transformations of our age.

Notes

Editor's Preface

1. See for example Katherine Gibson 'Hewers of Cake and Drawers of Tea: Women, Industrial Restructuring, and Class Processes on the Coalfields of Central Queensland,' *Rethinking Marxism* 5:4 (Winter 1992), and Richard McIntyre and Michael Hillard, 'Stressed Families, Impoverished Families: Crises in the Household and in the Reproduction of the Working Class,' *Review of Radical Political Economy* 24:2 (Summer 1992).

Chapter 1

1. Marxist-Feminist and Socialist-Feminist contributions are too extensive to document fully here. The following items were especially useful to us: Barker and Allen (1976); Barrett (1980); Barrett and McIntosh (1982); Bebel (1971); Beneria and Stimpson (1987); Beechey (1987); Beechey and Perkins (1987); Benhabib and Cornell (1987); Eisenstein (1979); Folbre (1987); Fox (1980); Goldman (1910); Hayden (1981 and 1984); Kollontai (1971, 1972, 1977a,b); Kuhn and Wolpe (1978); Malos (1980); Reiter (1975); Rosaldo and Lamphere (1974); and Westwood (1985).
2. People may or may not participate in class processes, or they may participate in several different forms of class process (i.e. different forms of producing, appropriating and distributing surplus labor such as the feudal, slave, capitalist, and other forms discussed below).
3. Some others who share this approach are: Delphy (1984); Elshtain (1982); Hartsock (1979); Gardiner (1979); MacKinnon (1982); O'Brien (1982); and Seecombe (1980).
4. Although the following are Feminists who have embraced Marxian class analysis and extended it to sites other than enterprises, none has undertaken a class analysis of the internal structure and dynamic of the household itself: Kuhn and Wolpe (1978); Vogel (1981, 1983 and 1986); Petchesky (1979 and 1984); Rowbotham (1973 and 1974); G. Rubin (1975); Rosaldo and Lamphere (1974); O'Laughlin (1974); Schwarzer (1984); Nicholson (1987); Barrett (1980); Beechey (1987); Beechey and Perkins (1987); Benhabib and Cornell (1987).

5. This perspective on gender is shared by several Marxist–Feminist theorists: see Barrett (1980); Kuhn and Wolpe (1978); Sokoloff (1981); Jaggar (1985); Ortner (1974); Ortner and Whitehead (1981); Rosaldo and Lamphere (1974); Reiter (1975); Benhabib and Cornell (1987); de Beauvoir (1973); Badinter (1980); and Risman and Schwartz (1989).

6. As far as we can ascertain, Margaret Benston was the first to apply the concept of feudalism to the household in her article for *Monthly Review* (Benston 1969). While she did not develop any systematic class analysis of the household such as we attempt here, she did use the feudal analogy to describe women's use-value production in the household and generally to compare women in households to serfs.

7. If the husband uses his wages to buy the raw materials and means of production (or passes his wages to the woman to enable her to buy them), that does not detract from the feudal form of the fundamental class process in this household. Indeed, feudal lords in medieval Europe also often made available the raw materials (land) and means of production (animals and tools) to their serfs. How raw materials and means of production are made available to the direct producer is a different and separate issue from whether and how surplus labor is produced and appropriated. Here we focus on this latter issue, and we consider the former issue only in so far as it pertains to the latter.

8. Here we disagree with such authors as Dalla Costa and James (1980); Coulson, Magav and Wainwright (1980); Seecombe (1980); and Gardiner (1979).

9. These figures represent an average of the data cited by several different sources. Vanek (1980, 82–90) finds that full-time homemakers spend 52 hours per week on household tasks. Berch (1982, 96–9) agrees, while Cowan (1983, 200) estimates that full-time homemakers work 50 hours per week. Hartmann (1981a, 366–94) estimates 60 hours per week, while Oakley (1973) works with the statistic of eleven hours per day for seven days per week for London housewives. Walker (1970, 85) finds that women who do not work outside the home spend 57 hours per week on housework.

10. For further clarification of nonclass processes and their complex relationships to class processes, see Resnick and Wolff (1987, esp. 149–58 and 231–53).

11. Such nonclass processes may be secured without any subsumed class distribution to them. For example, the man may act as record keeper for himself without demanding a share of the appropriated surplus labor. Likewise, the woman may supervise herself without a distribution, as is discussed in the text below. Which conditions of existence of the household's feudal fundamental class process require surplus distributions depends on all the historical circumstances of time and place.

12.   Paradoxically, such motivation can become counterproductive from the standpoint of the surplus-distributing husband. Believing that a carefully run household is not only the measure of her success but also of his, she may demand even more of the surplus from her husband to manage well. For him to comply would jeopardize other kinds of subsumed class distribution needed to reproduce the household, for example, contributions to religious institutions that propound the very gender processes that helped to produce her self-motivation.

13.   Women may perform labor, give products, and donate cash to religious institutions without a feudal subsumed class process being present. To take one example, the institution may itself occupy a position as an appropriator of surplus labor within one or another form of the fundamental class process. Alternatively, no class process may be involved at all, as women donate their own labor time to the Church. In our theoretical approach, the processes of labor are distinct from the processes of class: they may or may not occur together in any relationship. Concrete analysis of the context of each relationship is needed to answer the theory's questions about its exact class aspects.

14.   Of course these positions do not go uncontested. The *New York Times* (12 April 1988) includes both an article about and excerpts from a draft pastoral letter on women by American Catholic bishops. The letter urges wider church roles for women. The article and the excerpts indicate that the bishops were inspired by Catholic women protesting sexism within the churches. Some of the many Catholic groups protesting sexism in the Church are Catholics for a Free Choice, the Women's Ordination Conference, Association for the Rights of Catholics in the Church, the New Ways Ministry, the Christic Institute, and the Women's Alliance for Theology, Ethics and Ritual (Koepke 1989, 16).

15.   The most romanticized aspect of women's domestic role is childrearing. In Simone de Beauvoir's words:

> Given that one can hardly tell women that washing up saucepans is their divine mission, they are told that bringing up children is their divine mission. But the way things are in this world, bringing up children has a great deal in common with washing up saucepans. In this way, women are thrust back into the role of a relative being, a second class person (Schwarzer 1984, 114).

16.   There is an ongoing debate over psychoanalytic versions of biological determinism as applied to the traditional or, as we would argue, feudal role of women. Below is a brief sketch of some key works in the extensive literature generated by that debate (all French works are cited in their English translations). The debate began in 1924, continued to 1935, and then lay dormant until 1968. Since then it

has attracted wide attention and intense participation. Freud's biological determinist explanation for women's alleged inferiority was opposed by some early students of Freud: Adler (1927); Jones (1922, 1927, and 1935); Horney (1967); and Muller (1932). The debate was reopened in France in 1968 by the Feminist group, 'Psychoanalyse et Politique,' and has continued there ever since: Cixous and Clement (1986); Irigaray (1985); Chasseguet-Smirgel (1970); Montreley (1978); and Moi (1987). The debate also spread to England and the United States. For major contributors there, see Mitchell (1974); Mitchell and Rose (1983); Chodorow (1978); Gallop (1982); Bernheimer and Kahane (1985); Strouse (1974); and Miller (1973).

17. A variation on this theme presumes that women are the embodiments of sex. Billboards, television and magazine advertisements, films, and so on, portray women as sex objects. As such they need to be protected from the desires their nature provokes.

18. We are indebted to Professor Kim Scheppele, Department of Political Science, University of Michigan, for this point.

19. Women's exploitation within the household haunts them when they work outside of it. Females are overwhelmingly employed in capitalist class positions that parallel their roles in their feudal households. In 1982, more than half of employed women worked in occupations that were more than 75 per cent female; 22 per cent worked in occupations that were 95 per cent female. Women account for 99 per cent of secretaries, 97 per cent of typists, and 96 per cent of nurses (Hewlett 1986, 76). These professions all involve women's traditional role as the subordinate helper to a man. Other professions in which women dominate are social work and elementary school education. These involve women's sex-role stereotyped position as nurturer (Kahn-Hut et al. 1982, 39–88, 101–10, and 202–66; and Pietrokowski 1980).

20. The United States has fewer of these supports than any other industrialized nation excepting South Africa (Hewlett 1986, 51–230).

21. Professor Kim Scheppele suggested to us that some of the apparent toleration here may be attributed to the legal difficulty in sorting out 'fault' in cases of domestic violence.

22. Violence against wives is estimated to occur in two-thirds of American marriages (Roy 1977).

23. We are indebted to Professor Kim Scheppele for this point.

24. In 1985, 54.7 per cent of women aged 16 years or more worked outside of the home (the *Wall Street Journal*, 25 September 1986).

25. In spite of the massive increase in female paid employment over the past 20 years, there has been no appreciable increase in male participation in housework (Pleck 1982, 251–333). Even if a husband is unemployed, he typically does less housework than his wife who is working a 40-hour week outside the home (Blumstein and Schwartz

1983, 145). According to the US Department of Labor, in 1985 sixty percent of mothers with children between the ages of three and five were in the paid labor force (the *New York Times,* 14 January 1987).

26. In 1985, fewer than 14 per cent of American divorced women were granted alimony payments. A 1980 study showed that only a third of those women who were granted alimony payments actually received the full amount granted (Hewlett 1986, 60; Weitzman 1985, 143–83).

27. According to a 1982 Census Bureau survey, 60 per cent of fathers contribute nothing to their children's financial support (Hewlett 1986, 62).

28. This situation is beginning to be addressed for the first time. In 1987, a law was passed allowing the courts to deduct illegally-withheld child support payments from men's paychecks. In addition, there are now interstate means of forcing men to pay child support after they have left the state in which the mother and children are living. However, these means remain inadequate, and men can still evade the law without being punished. According to 1982 Census Bureau statistics, only 41 per cent of custodial mothers were even awarded child support (Hewlett 1986, 62). A study of child support payments in Denver in 1980 revealed that those mothers who did receive child support payments got an average of $150 per month which was less than the average car payment and less than the cost of monthly sustenance for a child at that time (Hewlett 1986, 63). Weitzman (1985, 262–322) elaborates on these statistics.

29. Statistics for 1982 indicate that one out of every four female murder victims is killed by her husband or lover (US Department of Justice, Federal Bureau of Investigation 1982). Men commit 95 per cent of all reported assaults on spouses (US Department of Justice 1982).

30. Mounting divorce rates illustrate the growing strains on the feudal household. The United States shows a doubling of the divorce rate between 1965 (25 per cent) and 1985 (50 per cent) of marriages ending in divorce. The US divorce rate is the highest in the world (the *Wall Street Journal,* 26 September 1986).

31. Although the following historians do not use Marxist class analysis, we believe that their findings support a thesis of the widespread nature of feudal households in the United States: Komarovsky (1962, 49–72); Kelly (1981); Coontz (1988).

32. As of 1986, the United States labor force was 45 per cent female (Hewlett 1986, 72). Arlie Hochschild's 1989 study of households is tellingly entitled *The Second Shift.*

33. The notion that women's unpaid household labor is universally supportive of and positive for the capitalist system in general is shared by many, including, among others: Delphy (1984); Seecombe (1980);

Dalla Costa and James (1980); Hartmann (1981b); and Coulson, Magav and Wainwright (1980).

34. We are indebted to Professor Frank Annunziato for this point.
35. In this example, the man occupies three very different class positions. One is the feudal fundamental class position of appropriator of his wife's surplus labor, while the other two are capitalist class positions. Of the latter, one is the capitalist fundamental class position of producer of surplus value for an industrial capitalist. The other is a capitalist subsumed class position in which the worker provides the capitalist with access to labor power in a tight labor market in return for a fee (a kind of premium over the value of the worker's labor power). The capitalist distributes some of the surplus value appropriated from the workers to pay this fee to the workers. Hence the recipient of such a distribution occupies a capitalist subsumed class position by providing a condition of existence of the capitalist fundamental class process in return for a distribution of the resulting surplus value. In the example discussed in the text, it is this subsumed class receipt (the male worker's cut of a portion of the surplus value which he helped to produce) that enables him to maintain his standard of living, despite the reduced use-value bundle (feudal surplus labor) he receives from his wife.
36. In this case, the creditors occupy feudal subsumed class positions – providing a condition of existence (credit for the household's feudal fundamental class process) in return for distributions of feudal surplus labor in the form of interest payments.
37. Ironically, communist household class structures in which many families share household appliances and other household costs, might well economize on them and thereby lessen wage pressures on capitalists from wage-earners wishing to purchase such appliances and other household means of production.
38. Dramatic examples of this struggle abound in English and American literature. Two particularly powerful examples may be found in Susan Glaspell's 1917 story, 'A Jury of Her Peers,' and in Mary Wilkins Freeman's 1893 story, 'The Revolt of Mother.' Glaspell's story details how a symbolic jury of women acquits Minnie Foster of her husband's murder because he denied her the minimum emotional and physical support needed to maintain a feudal household. Freeman's story follows an old mother as she removes her entire household into the barn to protest her husband's priority of a new, expanded barn over a new, expanded home.
39. Women's fears of losing economic security are well founded. In a 1976 study of 5,000 American families, researchers found that over a seven-year period, divorced fathers' living standards rose 17 per cent

while divorced mothers' living standards fell 29 per cent (Weitzman 1985, 337). In a similar 1985 study of California families, Weitzman found that the divorced fathers' living standards rose by 42 per cent while the divorced mothers' living standards fell by 73 per cent (1985, 338–43). These effects of divorce on mothers are corroborated in two studies of American women's economic position in the 1980s (Sidel 1986, 24–47; Hewlett 1986, 51–70). The deterioration for mothers and children between 1976 and the mid 1980s reflects the impact of no-fault divorce laws (Weitzman 1985, 15–51). These laws set new standards for alimony and property awards based on treating both sexes 'equally' rather than taking into account the economic realities of women's and children's actual financial opportunities and needs (e.g., the impact on women's lifetime salaries of maternity leaves that are unpaid for most women and damaging to the earnings of those who do receive some compensation: see Hartmann and Spalter-Roth 1988).

40. Rowbotham (1974, 34) cites an eighteenth-century poem of rebellion against a man who will not fulfil his obligation (as household feudal lord) of bringing home his paycheck to sustain the household:

> Damn thee Jack, I'll dust thy eyes up.
> Thou leeds a plaguy drunken life;
> Here thous sits instead of working
> Wi' thy pitcher on thy knee;
> Curse thee thou'd be always lurking
> And I may slave myself for thee.

41. Children's participation in domestic labor has attracted little scholarly attention. However, some recent studies indicate that when wives work outside of the home, it is children, rather than husbands, who increase their participation in housework (Thrall 1978; Walker and Woods 1976; Hedges and Barnett 1972).

42. These numbers are based on a variety of published studies as well as our own adjustments of their findings. According to Joann Vanek (1980, 82–90), who bases her estimates on several formal statistical studies, full-time homemakers spend an average of 52 hours a week on housework, whereas homemakers who also accept full-time paid employment spend an average of 26 hours a week on housework after completing a 40-hour paid work week. Cowan (1983, 200), who also surveys other studies, finds that full-time homemakers spend 50 hours a week doing housework whereas employed women spend 35 hours on housework after a 40-hour paid work week. Several recent studies surveyed in the *New York Times* (20 August 1987) found that time spent on housework had fallen to six hours per week for full-

time employed women. However, those recent studies did not include what has become the most time-consuming set of modern household chores – shopping, household management, childcare, and travel connected with household tasks.

43. All women in the paid labor force are not participating in capitalist class processes. A woman who is running her own small business with only herself employed, or a woman working as a self-employed doctor, lawyer, nurse, craftsperson, domestic servant, and so on, would participate in the ancient class process outside the household.

44. The *Wall Street Journal* (26 January 1988) reported that 77 per cent of working mothers prepare dinner alone and 64 per cent clean after dinner alone. These findings are reinforced by others: Hartmann (1981a, 366–94); Blumstein and Schwartz (1983, 144–5); Cowan (1983, 200); and Pleck (1982, 251-333).

45. This is well documented by Sallie Westwood (1985, 159–81). Ironically, the independent bonds and support systems among the factory women whom Westwood describes are built largely around women's shared domestic lives, specifically, their lives in feudal households. Women return to work in part to escape the isolation and usual financial dependency of feudal domestic lives. However, they often build support and solidarity on the job through a celebration of feudal female rites of passage – marriage, birth, the advent of grandchildren. They also commiserate on the problems they have with their men.

46. We have used the phrase 'female co-workers' because the expression 'fellow workers' refers to males. This, in itself, is a telling comment on gender divisions.

47. According to the Hite survey (1987, 23), 82 per cent of American women report that the greatest loneliness in their lives is being married to someone with whom they cannot talk. Although Hite's research methods have been criticized by some for the usual sorts of flaws in data gathering and processing, other studies have confirmed their significance. While her responses from the questionnaires which she had sent to 4,500 women may not be indicative of the opinions of all American women, they are consistent with other less dramatic findings: see Rubin (1976); Westwood (1985); Blumstein and Schwartz (1983). Researchers have also found that approximately one-third of women married for five years or more have extra-marital affairs (Hochschild 1987).

48. Marx's discussions of the ancient class process are scattered: see Marx (1963, 407–9; 1971, 530–31; 1973, 471–514; and 1965). For examples of how Marxists have developed and applied the concept of the ancient class process, see Hindess and Hirst (1975, 79–108) and De Ste.

Croix (1981, 31–277). For the most theoretically developed study of the ancient class process currently available, see the doctoral dissertation, 'Ancients: A Marxian Theory of Self-Exploitation' by Satyananda Gabriel (1989).

49. This has been true from the inception of the women's liberation movement (Friedan 1963; *Radical Feminism* 1968).

50. Widely read magazines such as *Playboy, Penthouse* and *Hustler* stressed sexual gratification outside and instead of marriage. Spokespersons of the 'beat' movements such as Jack Kerouac, William Burroughs, and Allen Ginsburg condemned the American dream of the male providing for a wife and children and accumulating household possessions. Self-realization therapies and the 'human potential movement' associated with Abraham Maslow, Paul Goodman, Fritz Perls, and others often encouraged 'creative divorce' among other means to the ultimate goal of self-realization. Writers such as Paul Goodman and Charles Reich made statements rejecting marriage as the road to conformity and financial burdens which crush male adventure and creativity. In the 1960s, the 'hippie' and 'yippie' movements frequently rejected the male breadwinner role in favor of 'doing your own thing.'

51. Playboys can escape the trap of sexual neediness and dependence by reifying women. Sexually inviting pictures stress the sexuality of women as optimal and hence preferable when outside the context of marriage, household, or virtually any lasting, complex relationship. The recent increase in pornography may result partly from a need to become a voyeur to escape from requests for intimacy and to escape vulnerability in one's need to become intimate with others. Pornography presents sexually exposed people whom one can view without being vulnerable in the request to see their naked bodies. It presents sexual intimacies without the viewer having to expose himself or herself to anyone. Within some pornography, sexual need is associated with loss of freedom or entrance into bondage. It is humiliating like all need which requires dependency. As need becomes degraded and as people hate themselves for their needs, they also may hate the people whom they need. Their hateful, degraded needs are translated into hateful, degraded portrayals of those whom they need. Male pornography abounds with such portrayals. Pornography may thus be related to the suppression of friendship, emotional intimacy, and vulnerability between the sexes. This pattern is less apparent in women's magazines. Even *Playgirl*, which features a naked 'hunk of the month,' does not disparage relationships or marriage. Both *Playgirl* and *Cosmopolitan* magazines reject the financial dependence of women on men. They champion sexual pleasure and career achievement for women, but they do not reject heterosexual emotional intimacy.

52. 'The Equalizer' is television's ex–CIA man who is critical of injustice to specific individuals and who therefore makes an individual choice of which individual case of individual problems he will individually resolve.

53. Hite (1987, 665) uses 20 per cent as the proportion of couples who succeed in having relationships of equality. The description she gives of such relationships corresponds, albeit roughly, to our communist class processes in the household. Although Hite's figures in this case too were challenged, they also corresponded rather well with the uncontested figures of Blumstein and Schwartz (1983, 57 and 144). The 20 per cent figure remains rough because neither Hite nor Blumstein and Schwartz nor others have yet studied either class processes in households generally or the communist class process in the household in particular.

54. This is a greatly simplified and abridged sketch of a communist class structure. The literature on communist class structures summarized and developed by Amariglio (1984) and Resnick and Wolff (1988) indicates that complex, variant types of communist class processes can exist. A full discussion of household communist class structures would then have to consider the corresponding variant forms of household communism. That level of detail is not possible or necessary here. Our goal is limited to showing the relevance of a general notion of household communism for a class and gender analysis of the United States today.

55. There remains a key problem now that both feudal and communist class processes exist simultaneously within a capitalist social formation. State officials find themselves caught in a contradictory situation: fostering certain of the conditions of existence of one of these fundamental class processes undermines the others and vice versa. Struggles within the state may be expected as officials respond to the contradictory pressures emanating from differently class-structured households seeking to secure their conditions of existence.

56. Freedom from rape is not actually a right in the United States. Only in 1984 did the New York Court of Appeals strike down the marital exemption in that state's rape law. As of 1987, there are only three states in the United States in which a husband can be prosecuted without restrictions for raping his wife (*New York Times*, 13 May 1987). Yet a recent estimate affirms that one wife in ten experiences a rape by her husband (Finkelhor 1987).

57. Not surprisingly, conservative and reactionary forces in the United States – especially the 'religious right wing' within the 'born again' Protestant movements and their counterparts among Roman Catholics and Jews – have mounted a fierce offensive against changing the class

processes in the household (although not, of course, in such terms). They systematically attack the conditions of existence of the ancient and communist class households through their assaults against the following: abortion rights, access to birth control, gay and lesbian rights, protections against the sexual harassment of women, antidiscrimination and equal rights amendment movements, and so on.

58.   These conflicts within the Roman Catholic Church are documented especially in the following reports published in the *New York Times*: 'Bishops' Panel Asks Widening Role of Women' (12 April 1988); 'Excerpts from Draft Pastoral Letter on Women by Catholic Bishops in U.S.' (12 April 1988); 'Compromise Sought at Catholic University on Teacher Censure by Vatican' (8 April 1988); 'Catholic U. Curbs Theology Teacher' (14 April 1988); 'Cardinal Won't Allow Instruction on Condoms in Programs on AIDS' (14 December 1987); 'Two Divided Camps of Bishops Form Over Catholic AIDS Policy Paper' (17 December 1987); '11 Are Arrested in Gay Protest at St. Patrick's' (7 December 1987).

Chapter 2

1.   For a presentation and critique of current Marxist-Feminist theory, see Matthaei (1992). For a collection of many of the central US Marxist-feminist writings, see Sargent (1981).

2.   See, for example, Part 2 of Matthaei (1982).

3.   See, for example, Blau and Ferber (1986, 126), which presents an overview of recent time-use studies and finds that, in the 1970s, husbands with non-employed wives averaged 8.3–8.9 hours of total work per day, compared to an average of 6.5–6.8 for non-employed wives.

4.   See, for example, Matthaei (1988, 141–50) and Miller (1981).

5.   See Amott and Matthaei (1991) for a more detailed analysis of these theoretical issues, as well as an examination of the interaction of race, class, and gender in women's economic history.

6.   An excellent analysis of the interactions between structural pressures and psychological adaptations can be found in Merton (1976).

7.   See Fraad, Resnick, and Wolff (1989) and the comments published in the same issue.

8.   Coontz sometimes caricatures us: 'The authors' explanation of women's religious activities as resulting from a man's distribution of his feudal surplus is clearly inadequate here' (p. 67). What disturbs us here is the failure to grasp the antireductionism of our theoretical commitment to overdetermination.

9. She consistently renders our work as reductionist: we construe 'relations in the feudal household as class relations' (p. 44); we conceptualize 'gender relationships within marriage as a class relation' (p. 43); and we understand 'the essence of gender oppression within marriage as an issue of surplus labor extraction' (p. 46). Yet, paradoxically, she applauds us for our nonreductionist 'stance' (p. 44). Perhaps these basic terms, too, have meanings different for Matthaei from the one they have for us.

10. Matthaei also criticizes us for silence about the fact that the wife may be living off the paid labor of the husband in the feudal household. She sees this as undermining our description of the household as feudal. Now, we do specifically address that point. In any case, because medieval serfs lived off the land, water, etc. provided by their lords, we do not therefore conclude that there was not a feudal class structure present. How the lord acquired those means of feudal production (inheritance, theft, labor, etc.) is a different matter from the particular class process in which they are deployed. Parallel reasoning applies to the feudal household. Wives can 'live off' their husbands' earnings in households exhibiting different class structures; Chapter 1 is concerned with those structures and their differences.

   Chapter 1 also explains that wives may not participate in any class process within households if, for example, either the husband or hired personnel perform household labor. Our overdeterminist approach studies each particular situation to see which, if any, class processes are present and who participates in them. A wife who does not participate in household class processes is one of the many possibilities that we discuss. All reality is not class reality for us; we do not squeeze everything into class categories. Class processes, we repeated, are only some of the many that comprise social life.

11. See the differing perspectives of Hartmann (1981) and Young (1981). Our approach is more compatible with the following idea: 'dual systems theory, by making the issue of women's oppression separate and distinct from that which is covered by Marxism, reinforces the idea that women's oppression is merely a supplemental topic to the major concerns of Marxism' (Nicholson 1987, 28). Our Marxist-Feminism departs from dual systems theory in part because we directly inquire into women's exploitation (a matter of class) as well as their oppression (the different matter of power) and the overdetermined relations between them *at all social sites*.

12. Thus we do not and could not argue that unequal wages for equal work 'are not gender related' as Matthaei claims we do (p. 45). Overdetermination means that wages and gender are different processes in a relation of mutual constitutivity with one another and with all

the other processes in their environment. The analytical issue is rarely whether two processes are related but, rather, just how to think their relationship.

13. In the opening section of Chapter 1, we distinguish between exploitation (which concerns class) and oppression (which concerns power). We explain there why we feel it to be important to keep these notions distinct (so as to explore their interrelation and mutual constitution). Of course, Matthaei need not agree with us. However, she seems not to register the importance of the distinction for us and for our entire argument. Perhaps this contributes to her reading into us an intention of deriving oppression from exploitation – as unacceptable as the reverse.

14. Coontz's essentialist epistemology finds an echo in Matthaei's assertion (77) that 'we *cannot understand* the household, consistently, in terms of labor extraction' (italics ours). We are told that our theory is wrong (rather than different from hers); it cannot capture the essential truth of its object, the household. We also find attributed to us again a goal we do not have – to understand a complexity – the household – by reducing it to a simplicity, labor extraction. Our goal is rather to bring class and gender processes, as we define them, into the discussion and debates over the many, diverse dimensions of households.

15. Benston (1969), whom we cited, did use the term feudalism in regard to households. However, the dramatic differences between her understanding and ours are not seen by Folbre and Hartmann. For Benston, a 'pre-industrial production unit' – for example, a feudal household – means the production of goods and services for use rather than for exchange. By contrast, for us feudal is defined not by the presence or absence of a market for outputs, but rather by the particular manner in which the production, appropriation, and distribution of surplus labor is organized. For example, it would still be a feudal household if the husband took the fruits of his wife's surplus labor and sold them in a market (in the same sense that medieval manors did not cease being feudal when they marketed some of their serfs' surpluses). Benston's and ours are very different notions of the word 'feudal' and our elaborations of households are correspondingly different.

16. Is it really necessary to explain that these terms are metaphorical and, as such, appropriate? As argued in Chapter 1, 'feudal' simply designates one kind of surplus labor production and distribution system. It makes its historical appearances in many forms according to the times and places where it occurs.

17. Eisenstein writes of us: 'they define class as any site wherever surplus labor is produced, appropriated and distributed' (p. 50). Actually, we define class as processes and distinguish sites as distinct sets of particular, different processes which may or may not include class processes (pp. 3–4). She refers to our feudal 'model' as assuming 'the stance that all women are similar' (p. 50). We will not list here all the pages in Chapter 1 – and all our other published works – that argue otherwise.

18. Of course, Feminism's critiques of economic determinist Marxism encouraged and were encouraged by other critiques. Thus, it is a new and different kind of Marxism – one focused on overdetermination as an alternative to economic and all other determinisms – that comprises our Marxist-Feminism.

Chapter 3

1. Of course, the use-values produced in capitalist enterprises are destined not for immediate consumption, but rather for market sale. They must pass through an exchange process *before* they are consumed. Hence they possess exchange value as well as use value; this makes them commodities. In contrast, the use-values produced within households lack such exchange value and are thus not commodities.

2. We are indebted to Claire Sproul for this point.

3. The purpose of this and the following equations is to clarify the arguments offered in the text. However, since we well understand how and why equations can mislead as much as they clarify, our narrative is designed to convey our arguments with or without reference to the equations.

4. In this and subsequent equations and inequalities, we assume that all variables are denominated in terms of abstract labor hours. This permits us to ignore the otherwise important issue of deviations of prices of production from values, since that is not directly germane to the argument here.

5. What we are describing here is an example of a redistribution of surplus value from less to more efficient enterprises operating within the same industry. Called a competitive search for super-profits, it resulted in US enterprises experiencing a lower profit rate than their foreign competitors in the same industry selling the same commodities. For theoretical discussion, see Part IV in Marx 1967a and pp. 192–200 in Resnick and Wolff (1987). For a compelling discussion of the US steel industry's loss of SV to foreign competitors, see McIntyre (1989).

6. There were, of course, many exceptions to this generalization. For example, minority men and women were often excluded from the positions earning such relatively high wage incomes.

7. Parallel to the analysis of productive workers as sellers of labor power, sellers of energy receive as a monopoly revenue (SSCR) what capitalist enterprises must pay to them (SSCP) as the premium over the exchange value of the needed inputs. Such monopoly revenues can lead to an expansion of the monopolists' own spending, and thus can serve indirectly to benefit the economy, including the very enterprises paying the monopoly prices for energy. A well-known example of this occurred over these years in relation to foreign sellers of monopolized oil. In class terms, those sellers received a considerable SSCR from US capitalist industries. However, their subsumed class revenues were then returned as a major new source of foreign investment in the US economy.

8. Reagan's military expansion (more ΣX) was only offset partially by reduced state spending on social programs (less ΣY). It also required massive state borrowing (an increase in NCR). Both of these aspects of Reagan's and indeed also of Bush's policies are discussed further below.

9. Such arguments also touted the enhanced employment that would follow from technological investments and from the growing exports and falling imports that such investments would surely cause.

10. In contrast, the British equivalent of Reaganomics, the economic policies of the Thatcher regime, involved the systematic sale – 'privatization' – of formerly state-owned and operated enterprises in many industries.

11. The aforementioned expansion in SSCR's of foreign suppliers of oil became a major source of foreign demand for the US state's debt. Such a capital inflow helped to finance this contrived solution to industrial capital's crisis, while, as the next few sentences in the text suggest, it also undermined it.

12. While our focus is on productive laborers – those who produce surplus value for their capitalist employers – we can rely for our argument here on general data for all US workers to see the relevant trends.

13. This is the feudal analog to the capitalist using a portion of surplus labor appropriated from workers to hire and equip a staff of book-keepers, managers, etc.

14. This household feudal inequality is directly analogous and comparable to the enterprise's capitalist inequality that was discussed above.

15 Once again, we are measuring all variables (flows, etc.) in abstract labor hours.

16 To simplify matters, we ignore repayment of any principal. Such repayments, however, could easily be added to the expenditure side of the equation. We further assume that debt can be used for either of two reasons – to help reproduce the male's feudal position in the household or to reproduce his capitalist position as seller of labor power. In the former case, interest payments would form a part of feudal subsumed class expenditures and thus be included as one of the SSCP's on the right-hand side of the equation. Lenders, as recipients of such payments, would occupy a feudal subsumed class position outside the household. In American life, officials in commercial banks and department stores typically occupy such positions as major providers of credit to reproduce feudal households. Where debt is used to help reproduce a worker's capitalist existence, then payments of interest would appear as they do now in the equation, i.e., as iNCRdbt, since they clearly are not a commodity expenditure, and thus are not a part of the worker's means of subsistence expenditures. In this case, suppliers of credit and receivers of interest would not occupy any class position whatsoever.

17. Given that union dues represented only a small portion of workers' expenditures, successfully reducing them would hardly provide the help needed to alleviate their class structural problems. On the other hand, the pressure on dues and declining memberships further pushed US unions to secure their dues, and indeed their survival, by delivering goods and services *other* than the collective bargaining which they could not accomplish as successfully as earlier. Thus, unions moved aggressively in the direction of providing credit cards, discounts for merchandise purchases, etc. to dues-paying members (Annunziato 1990).

18. Of course, men may also find themselves in a similar situation. For example, nonwhites may experience a loss of NCRmkt from the value of their labor power because of racism, or a religious or ethnic group may be comparably situated socially.

19. Such receipts by women workers appear in the state's equation as components of the state's Y expenditures.

20. Such debt would presumably require interest payments. This necessarily introduces another term into Equation 8, iNCRdbt, representing the interest payments required of an indebted woman.

21. The UV stands for the use-values (meals, clothes, etc.) purchased, while the EV/UV stands for the cost per use-value; multiplying them together yields the total cost of women's expenditures to reproduce their labor power. These expenditures represented new markets for industrial capitalists. They sometimes involved entirely new use-values – special working women's clothing – to secure

women's capitalist existence. In either case, the expansion of women into the capitalist labor force expanded the demand for capitalist commodities and thus the surplus value produced and embodied within those commodities. This once again suggests how the pressures on the feudal household, unleashed under Reaganomics, helped to produce a new source of industrial capitalist expansion over those same years.

22. Formerly, single women had such limited economic opportunities that capable maiden aunts or widows would join feudal households of their relatives as additional feudal serfs. Currently, it is more likely to be elderly, widowed and incapacitated relatives that become such additional feudal serfs.

23. While our analysis focuses only on laboring women who are exploited both in the household and enterprise, we could have extended it to include the much rarer situation in which women remain in a feudal serf position within a traditional household, but now take on a capitalist position of exploiter of both men and women outside the household. Their class structural equation would change to include, on its left-hand side, an appropriation of surplus value (SV) while dropping (V − NCRmkt) and, on the right-hand side, to include the distributions of surplus value to various capitalist subsumed classes while eliminating expenditures on means of subsistence. One interesting analysis suggested by this approach would examine women's behavior when men, in response to a higher exploitation rate outside of the household, pressure women to perform more surplus in the households. In one part of their lives, then, women would be benefiting from increased (capitalist) exploitation, while in another, they would suffer from increased (feudal) exploitation. As women move from one site to another over the same day, they move from being the capitalist exploiter to being the feudally exploited.

Perhaps one strategy to deal with some of the contradictions produced would be to hire household servants (see the comments on this point in Chapter 2) in order to reduce if not eliminate wives' feudal existence as surplus producers within the household. There is no necessity for their feudal existence to disappear in the case when servants are hired (servants could simply share in wives' feudal labors). However, a servant situation that seems to be of current interest concerns women who occupy relatively high paying jobs outside the household − perhaps as occupants of capitalist fundamental and/or subsumed class positions − and also replace their own surplus labor by buying instead the services of women servants. We may presume that the latter are self-employed individuals selling service commodities such as cooking, cleaning, etc. − what Marx referred to as individuals involved in the 'ancient class process' appropriating their own surplus labor individually.

In this situation, feudal household exploitation of women by men has ended. In its place we have women's self-exploitation there – women as both exploited and exploiter. However, such women laboring – within an ancient class process – in these now no longer feudal households may themselves be involved in their own feudal households in which they provide surplus for their husbands or in ancient households (no husband present) where they provide surplus for themselves.

24. We use the word 'suggest' here because there are a host of well-known difficulties involved in the interpretation of such statistics (of which perhaps the most intractable concerns whether changes in the numbers reflect changes in events or in the official reporting of events). Not proof, but rather suggestion, is what we derive from the statistics cited.

Chapter 4

1. Here there is a parallel between the household of the first chapter and the human being of this chapter. The household site contains contradictory entities with multiple dimensions while the human being contains multiple contradictory personal needs that express themselves in anorexia.

2. Because food disorders are so prevalent, the term 'anorexic' is now used colloquially as an adjective describing a very slender person. The term 'anorexic' or 'anorectic' used in this paper refers to a person with the life-threatening psycho-physiological disorder described above.

3. Some of the conditions that previously made it easier for some single women to manage follow. There was the availability of a family wage for many men whose wives were enabled and even pushed to be at home with dependent children. These homebound women were able to watch the children of their relatives. There existed a tradition of collectivity that gave many families a sense of responsibility for their close relations. The practice of living close to family made collective familial childcare possible. The practice of taking in retired or widowed parents gave families a live-in caretaker for their children. (Of course this also gave those families the obligation of caring for those same relatives when they became ill.) The less predatory street life allowed children to spend a good deal of time playing outside so that they were less of a burden to their caretakers.

4. Some of those 'social underpinnings' would be paid maternity and paternity leaves; quality, affordable daycare; after-school, summer-camp, and evening programs for children of all ages; safe neighborhoods; availability of nutritious, affordable meals; national healthcare; enforcement of regulations against sexual harassment; living wages for women; etc.

5. Amenorrhea is the inability to menstruate. Anorectics become amenorrheic because they lack the sufficient body fat which is a prerequisite to menstruation. They develop a soft downy covering of hair called lanugo which seems to be the body's attempt to create extra warmth.

6. Of course it is not only the anorexic disorder which is contradictory. As we argue in Chapter 1, society gives contradictory directives to women. The discussion of anorexia as both a rebellion against, and an acquiescence to, male domination is reflected in the contradictions around a blatant form of reduction of women to a position of 'others' whose purpose is to serve male sexual appetites. Prostitution is the reduction of women to the status of sexual commodities. While there is social pressure on women to be active equals competing with men for high salaries in the workplace, there is enormous pressure on women to become sexual objects. In fact, the society rewards prostitutes with the highest earnings that the vast mass of young women can actually earn in the workplace. The role of women as sinful flesh is ostensibly punished by making prostitution illegal while it is most lucratively rewarded. Other pink-collar trades which are not socially condemned as is prostitution are noteworthy for their poor salaries.

7. This is not only true of the women's liberation movement. The 1980s have sapped the vitality of most progressive movements. Therefore, it is important to understand that neither the women's liberation movement nor any other single group alone could explain a change in political processes.

8. I am indebted to Susan Kaufman for this point.

9. This figure is from a Senate Judiciary Committee Study released 21 March 1991 as reported in the *San Francisco Chronicle*, 22 March 1991, p. 11.

10. In African-American families where nuclear families are often less isolated and males are also less often present, children grow up in more extended matriarchies.

11. This is reflected in the statistics on incest in which fathers are the most frequent perpetrators (Russell 1986, 10, 71, 72, 74; Ward 1985, 77–100).

12. In 1960 women earned a median full-time wage that was 59 per cent of men's; by 1980, the figure was 60 per cent, and by 1990, it was 72 per cent (Bloom 1986; Hartmann and Roth 1991, 3).

13. Arlie Hochschild (1989) captures the anguish of these professional women.

14. I am indebted to Richard Lichtman for this point.

References

Abraham, K. 1920. 'Manifestations of the Female Castration Complex.' In Strouse 1974, 131–61.

Adams, E. and Briscoe, M., eds. 1971. *Up Against the Wall Mother.* Beverly Hills: Glencoe Press.

Adler, A. 1927. 'Sex.' In Baker-Miller 1973, 39–50.

Amariglio, J. 1984. 'Economic History and the Theory of Primitive Socio-economic Development.' PhD dissertation, University of Massachusetts, Amherst.

Amott, T. and Matthaei, J. 1991. *Race, Gender, and Work: A Multi-cultural Economic History of Women in the United States.* Boston: South End Press.

Amsden, A., ed. 1980. *The Economics of Women and Work.* New York: St Martins Press.

Annunziato, Frank. 1990. 'Commodity Unionism.' *Rethinking Marxism.* 3:2 (Summer), 8–33.

Ardrey, R. 1961. *African Genesis.* New York: Atheneum.

Atwood, M. 1969. *The Edible Woman.* New York: Warner books.

Badinter, E. 1980. *Motherhood.* New York: Macmillan.

Baker-Miller, J., ed. 1973. *Psychoanalysis and Women.* New York: Penguin.

Barash, D. 1982. *Sociology and Behavior.* New York: Elsevier.

Barker, D. and Allen, S., eds. 1976. *Dependence and Exploitation in Work and Marriage.* New York: Longman.

Barrett, M. 1980. *Women's Oppression Today.* London: Verso.

Barrett, M. and Hamilton, R., eds. 1987. *The Politics of Diversity.* London: Verso.

Barrett, M. and McIntosh, M. 1982. *The Anti-social Family.* London: Verso.

Bebel, A. 1971. *Women Under Socialism.* Trans. D. DeLeon. New York: Schocken.

Beechey, V. 1987. *Unequal Work.* London: Verso.

Beechey, V. and Perkins, T. 1987. *A Matter of Hours.* Minneapolis: University of Minnesota Press.

Bell, R. 1985. *Holy Anorexia.* Chicago: University of Chicago Press.

Beneria, L. and Stimpson, C., eds. 1987. *Women, Households and the Economy.* New Brunswick: Rutgers University Press.

Benhabib, S. and Cornell, D. 1987. 'Beyond the Politics of Gender.' In *Feminism as Critique*, eds. S. Benhabib and D. Cornell, 1–15. Minneapolis: University of Minnesota Press.

Benjamin, J. 1988. *Bonds of Love*. New York: Pantheon.

Bennett, H. S. 1971. *Life on the English Manor*. Cambridge: Cambridge University Press.

Benston, M. 1969. 'The Political Economy of Women's Liberation.' In *The Politics of Housework*, ed. E. Malos, 119–29. London: Alison and Busby.

—— 1971. 'The Political Economy of Women's Liberation.' In *Voices from Women's Liberation*, ed. L.B. Tanner, 279–91. New York: New American Library.

Berch, B. 1982. *The Endless Day: The Political Economy of Women and Work*. New York: Harcourt, Brace, Jovanovich.

Berger, J. 1972. *Ways of Seeing*. London: BBC and Penguin Books.

Bergmann, B. 1986. *The Economic Emergence of Women*. New York: Basic Books.

Berik, G. 1989. 'Born Factories: Woman's Labor in Carpet Workshops in Rural Turkey.' New School for Social Research, Working Paper 177.

Bernheimer, C. and Kahane, C., eds. 1985. *In Dora's Case*. New York: Columbia University Press.

Bernstein, D. 1983. 'The Female Superego: A Different Perspective.' *International Journal of Psychoanalysis*, no. 64: 187–202.

Blau, F. and Ferber, M. 1986. *The Economics of Women, Men, and Work*. Englewood Cliffs, NJ: Prentice-Hall.

Bloom, D. 1986. 'Women and Work' in *American Demographics*. Unpaged reprint September 1986.

Blumstein, P. and Schwartz, P. 1983. *American Couples: Money, Work and Sex*. New York: William Morrow.

Bonaparte, M. 1934. 'Passivity, Masochism and Femininity.' In Strouse 1974, 279–88.

Bordo, S. 1988. 'Anorexia Nervosa: Psychopathology as the Crystallization of Culture'. In *Feminism and Foucault*, eds. I. Diamond and L. Quinby, 87–117. Boston: Northeastern University Press.

—— 1989. 'The Body and the Reproduction of Femininity: A Feminist Appropriation of Foucault'. In *Gender Body Knowledge*, eds. A. Jaggar and S. Bordo, 13–34. New Brunswick and London: Rutgers University Press.

Brown, C. 1981. 'Mothers, Fathers and Children: From Private to Public Patriarchy.' In *Women and Revolution. A Discussion of the Unhappy Marriage of Marxism and Feminism*, ed. L. Sargent, 239–68. Boston: South End Press.

Brownmiller, S. 1975. *Against Our Will*. New York: Simon and Schuster.

Bruch, H. 1973. *Eating Disorders*. New York: Basic Books.

—— 1988. *Conversations with Anorectics*, eds. D. Czyzewski and M. Suhr. New York: Basic Books.

Brumberg, J. 1988. *Fasting Girls*. Cambridge, Massachusetts and London: Harvard University Press.

Caskey, N. 1986. 'Interpreting Anorexia Nervosa.' In *The Female Body in Western Culture,* ed. S.R.Suleiman, 175–89. Cambridge, Massachusetts and London: Harvard University Press.

Chapman, J. and Gates, M., eds. 1978. *The Victimization of Women*. Beverly Hills: Sage Publications.

Chasseguet-Smirgel, J. 1970. *Feminine Sexuality*. Ann Arbor: University of Michigan Press.

Chernin, K. 1981. *The Obsession*. New York: Harper and Row.

—— 1985. *The Hungry Self*. New York: Harper and Row.

Chesler, P. 1972. *Women and Madness*. New York: Doubleday.

Chodorow, N. 1978. *Mothering*. Berkeley: University of California Press.

Cixous, H. and Clement, C. 1986. *The Newly Born Woman*. Trans. B. Wing. Minneapolis: University of Minnesota Press.

Coontz, S. 1988. *The Social Origins of Private Life*. London: Verso.

Coontz, S. and Henderson, P., eds. 1986. *Women's Work, Men's Property*. London: Verso.

Coulson, M., Magav, B., and Wainwright, H. 1980. 'The Housewife and Her Labour Under Capitalism.' In Malos 1980, 218–34.

Cowan, A.L. 1989. 'Women's Gains On The Job: Not Without A Heavy Toll.' *The New York Times*. 21 August A14.

Cowan, R. 1983. *More Work for Mother*. New York: Basic Books.

Coward, R. 1985. *Female Desires*. New York: Grove Press.

Crispell, D. 1990. 'Workers in The Year 2000.' *American Demographics*. March 1990, 36–40.

Dalla Costa, M. and James, S. 1980. 'The Power of Women and the Subversion of the Community.' In Malos 1980, 160–95.

Dawkins, R. 1976. *The Selfish Gene*. New York: Oxford.

de Beauvoir, S. 1973. *The Second Sex*. Trans. P. O'Brian. New York: Warner.

Delaney, J., Lupton, M.J., and Toth, E. 1976. *The Curse: A Cultural History of Menstruation*. New York: E.P. Dutton.

Delphy, C. 1984. *Close to Home: A Materialist Analysis of Women's Oppression*. Trans. D. Leonard. Amherst: University of Massachusetts Press.

De Ste. Croix, G.E.M. 1981. *The Class Struggle in the Ancient World*. London: Duckworth.

Deutsch, H. 1944. *Psychology of Women* vol. 1. New York: Grune and Stratton.

Dinnerstein, D. 1976. *The Mermaid and the Minotaur*. New York: Harper and Row.

Dobash, R. and Dobash, E.R. 1979. *Violence Against Wives*. New York: Free Press.

Duby, G. 1968. *Rural Economy and Country Life in the Medieval West*. London: Edward Arnold.

Edwards, G. 1987. 'Anorexia and the Family.' In *Fed Up and Hungry*, ed. M. Lawrence, 61–74. New York: Peter Bedrick Books.

Ehrenreich, B. 1983. *The Hearts of Men*. New York: Anchor Doubleday.

Eichenbaum, L. and Orbach, S. 1983. *What Do Women Want*. New York: Berkley Books.

Eisenstein, Z., ed. 1979. *Capitalist Patriarchy and the Case for Socialist Feminism*. New York: Monthly Review Press.

—— 1979. 'Developing a Theory of Capitalist Patriarchy and Socialist Feminism.' In *Capitalist Patriarchy and the Case for Socialist Feminism*, ed. Z. Eisenstein, 5–40. New York: Monthly Review Press.

Elshtain, J.B. 1982. 'Feminist Discourse and Its Discontents: Language, Power and Meaning.' In Keohane 1982, 127–46.

Engels, F. 1962. *Anti-Dühring*. 3rd edition. Moscow: Foreign Languages Publishing House.

—— 1975. *The Origin of the Family, Private Property and the State*. Moscow: Foreign Languages Publishing House.

Erikson, E. 1964. 'Inner and Outer Space: Reflections on Womanhood.' *Daedalus* 93: 582–606.

Estrich, S. 1987. *Real Rape*. Cambridge, Massachusetts and London: Harvard University Press.

Finkelhor, D. 1987. *License to Rape: Sexual Abuse of Wives*. New York: Free Press.

Firestone, S. 1972. *The Dialectic of Sex*. New York: Bantam.

Folbre, N. 1982. 'Exploitation Comes Home: A Critique of the Marxian Theory of Family Labour.' *Cambridge Journal of Economics* vol. 6: 317–29.

—— 1985. 'The Pauperization of Motherhood: Patriarchy and Public Policy in the United States.' *Review of Radical Political Economics* vol. 11 no. 4: 72–88.

—— 1987. 'A Patriarchal Mode of Production.' In *Alternatives to Economic Orthodoxy: A Reader in Political Economy*, ed. R. Albelda, C. Gunn, and W. Waller. Armonk, New York: M.E. Sharpe.

Fox, B., ed. 1980. *Hidden in the Household*. Toronto: The Women's Press.

Fraad, H. 1985. 'The Separation-Fusion Complex: A Dialectical Feminist Revision of the Freudian Oedipus Complex.' Discussion Paper no. 21, Association for Economic and Social Analysis, University of Massachusetts, Amherst.

Fraad, H., Resnick, S., and Wolff, R. 1989. 'For Every Knight in Shining Armor, There's a Castle Waiting to be Cleaned: A Marxist-Feminist

Analysis of the Household.' *Rethinking Marxism* vol. 2 no.4 (Winter): 10–69.

Freeman, M.E.W. 1983. 'The Revolt of Mother.' In *Selected Stories of Mary E. Wilkins Freeman,* ed. M. Pryse, 293–313. New York: W.W. Norton.

Freud, S. 1925. 'Some Physical Consequences of the Anatomical Distinction Between the Sexes.' In Strouse 1974, 17–26.

—— 1933. 'Femininity.' In Strouse 1974, 73–94.

—— 1977. 'Female Sexuality.' In *Sigmund Freud on Sexuality*. Trans. J. Strachey, 367–91. London: Penguin.

Friedan, B. 1963. *The Feminine Mystique*. New York: W.W. Norton.

'Full-time Wage and Salary Workers – Number and Median Weekly Earnings by Selected Characteristics: 1983 To 1988' Table 671 (*Statistical Abstract of the United States: 1990*).

Gabriel, S. 1989. 'Ancients: A Marxian Theory of Self-Exploitation.' PhD dissertation, University of Massachusetts, Amherst.

—— 1990. 'The Continuing Significance of Race: An Overdeterminist Approach to Racism.' *Rethinking Marxism* vol. 3, no. 3–4 (Fall–Winter).

Gallop, J. 1982. *The Daughter's Seduction: Feminism and Psychoanalysis*. New York: Macmillan.

Gardiner, J. 1979. 'Women's Domestic Labor.' In Eisenstein 1979, 173–89.

Garfinkel, P. and Garner, D. 1982. *Anorexia Nervosa: A Multidimensional Perspective*. New York: Brunner and Mazel.

Gilligan, C. 1982. *In a Different Voice*. Cambridge: Harvard University Press.

Glaspell, S. 1917. 'A Jury of Her Peers.' In *Images of Women in Literature*, ed. A. Ferguson, 370–85. New York: Houghton Mifflin.

Glazer, N. and Youngelson, H. 1977. *Women in a Man Made World: A Socioeconomic Handbook*. New York: Rand-McNally.

Goldman, E. 1910. 'The Tragedy of Women's Emancipation' and 'Marriages and Love.' In E. Goldman, *Anarchism and Other Issues*. New York: Mother Earth Publishing.

Harrison, J. 1973. 'The Political Economy of Housework.' *Bulletin of the Conference of Socialist Economists* vol. 4 no. 1.

Hartmann, H. 1974. 'Capitalism and Women's Work in the Home.' PhD dissertation, Yale University.

—— 1976. 'Capitalism, Patriarchy, and Job Segregation by Sex.' *Signs: Journal of Women in Culture and Society* vol. 1 (Spring): 137–69.

—— 1979. 'The Unhappy Marriage of Marxism and Feminism: Towards a More Progressive Union.' *Capital and Class* vol. 8 (Summer): 1–33.

—— 1981a. 'The Family as the Locus of Gender, Class and Political Struggle.' *Signs* vol. 6 no. 3 (Spring): 366–94.

—— 1981b. 'The Unhappy Marriage of Marxism and Feminism.' In Sargent 1981, 1–42.

—— 1987. 'Changes in Women's Economic and Family Roles.' In Beneria and Stimpson 1987, 33–64.

Hartmann, H. and Spalter-Roth, R. 1988. 'Unnecessary Losses: Costs to Americans of the Lack of Family and Medical Leave.' Washington: Institute for Women's Policy Studies.

—— 1991. *Improving Employment Opportunities for Women*. Washington, DC: Institute for Women's Policy Research.

Hartsock, N. 1979. 'Feminist Theory and the Development of Revolutionary Strategy.' In Eisenstein 1979, 56–82.

Hayden, D. 1981. *The Grand Domestic Revolution*. Cambridge: MIT Press.

—— 1984. *Redesigning the American Dream*. New York: W.W. Norton.

Hays, H.R. 1965. *The Dangerous Sex: The Myth of Feminine Evil*. New York: Putnam.

Hedges, J.N. and Barnett, J.K. 1972. 'Working Women and the Division of Household Tasks.' *Monthly Labor Review* vol. 95 (January): 9–14.

Hewlett, S. 1986. *A Lesser Life*. New York: William Morrow.

Hindess, B. and Hirst, P. 1975. *Precapitalist Modes of Production*. London: Routledge & Kegan Paul.

Hite, S. 1987. *Women and Love*. New York: Alfred A. Knopf.

Hochschild, A. 1987. 'Why Can't a Man be More Like a Woman?' *New York Times Book Review* vol. 15 November: 3–4.

—— 1989. *The Second Shift*. New York: Viking.

Horney, K. 1967. 'The Flight from Womanhood: The Masculinity Complex in Women as Viewed by Men and Women.' In *Feminine Psychology: Previously Uncollected Essays by Karen Horney*, ed. H. Kelman, 54–70. New York: W.W. Norton.

Inman, M. 1946. *Facts for Women*. Los Angeles: Committee for the Advancement of Women.

—— 1949. *Thirteen Years of CPUSA Misleadership on the Woman Question*. Los Angeles: Committee for the Advancement of Women.

Irigaray, L. 1985. *This Sex Which is Not One*. Trans. C. Porter. New York: Schocken.

Jaggar, A. 1985. 'Towards a More Integrated World: Feminist Reconstructions of the Self and Society.' Paper presented at Douglas College, Rutgers University.

Jensen, R. 1981. 'Development and Change in the Wolof Social Formation: A Study of Primitive Communism.' PhD dissertation, University of Massachusetts, Amherst.

Jones, E. 1922. 'Notes on Dr. Abraham's Article on the Female Castration Complex.' *The International Journal of Psychoanalysis* vol. 3.

—— 1927. 'The Early Development of Female Sexuality.' *The International Journal of Psychoanalysis* vol. 8.

—— 1935. 'Early Female Sexuality.' *The International Journal of Psychoanalysis* vol. 16.

Kahn-Hut, R., Kaplan, A., and Colvard, R., eds. 1982. *Women and Work.* Oxford: Oxford University Press.

Kelly, J. 1981. 'Family Life: An Historical Perspective.' In *Household and Kin,* ed. A. Swerdlow, R. Bridenthal, and P. Vine. New York: McGraw-Hill.

Keohane, N., Rosaldo, M., and Gelpi, B., eds. 1982. *Feminist Theory: A Critique of Ideology.* Chicago: University of Chicago Press.

Koepke, M. 1989. 'Catholic Women Challenge Church.' *New Directions For Women* vol. 18 no. 16 (May–June).

Kollontai, A. 1971 (1919). *Communism and the Family.* London: Pluto.

—— 1972 (1919). 'Sexual Relations and the Class Struggle' in Kollontai, 1977b, 237–49.

—— 1972 (1919). *Love and the New Morality* (pamphlet). Bristol, England: Falling Wall Press.

—— 1975 (1926). *The Autobiography of a Sexually Emancipated Communist Woman.* Trans. S. Attanasio. New York: Schocken Books.

—— 1977a (1923). *Love of Worker Bees.* London: Virago.

—— 1977b. *Alexandra Kollontai: Selected Writings.* Trans. A. Holt. New York: Norton.

—— 1981 (1927). *A Great Love.* Trans. C. Porter. New York: Norton.

Komarovsky, M. 1962. *Blue Collar Marriage.* New York: Vintage.

Kovel, J. 1981. *The Age of Desire.* New York: Pantheon.

Kuhn, A. and Wolpe, A., eds. 1978. *Feminism and Materialism.* London: Routledge & Kegan Paul.

Lacan, J. 1964. 'Guiding Remarks for a Congress on Female Sexuality.' In J. Lacan. *Feminine Sexuality.* 1983, ed. J. Mitchell and J. Rose. Trans. J. Rose, 86–98. New York: W.W. Norton.

Lawrence, M. 1987. 'Education and Identity: The Social Origins of Anorexia.' In *Fed Up and Hungry,* ed. M. Lawrence. New York: Peter Bedrick Books, 207–225.

—— 1988. *The Anorexic Experience.* London: The Women's Press.

Lenin, V.I. 1919. *Women and Society.* New York: International.

Lerman, L. 1981. *Prosecution of Spouse Abuse: Innovations in Criminal Justice Response.* Washington: Center for Women's Policy Studies.

Lerner, G. 1986. *The Creation of Patriarchy.* New York: Oxford University Press.

Lichtman, R. 1982. *The Production of Desire.* New York: Free Press.

Lumsden, C. and Wilson, E. 1981. *Genes, Mind and Culture.* Cambridge: Harvard University Press.

MacKinnon, C. 1982. 'Feminism, Marxism, Method and the State.' In Keohane et al. 1982, 1–30.

MacLeod, S. 1981. *The Art of Starvation*. London: Virago.

Malos, E., ed. 1980. *The Politics of Housework*. London: Allison and Busby.

Marx, K. 1963. *Theories of Surplus Value*. Part 1. Trans. E. Burns. Moscow: Progress Publishers.

—— 1965. *Pre-capitalist Economic Formations*. Trans. J. Cohen. Intro. E.J. Hobsbawm. New York: International.

—— 1967a. *Capital, Vol. 1*. New York: International Publishers.

—— 1967b. *Capital, Vol. 3*. New York: International Publishers.

—— 1971. *Theories of Surplus Value*. Part 3. Trans. J. Cohen and S.W. Ryazanskaya. Moscow: Progress Publishers.

—— 1973. *Grundrisse*. Trans. M. Nicolaus. Harmondsworth: Penguin.

Marx, K., Engels, F., Lenin, V. I., and Stalin, J. 1951. *The Woman Question*. New York: International.

Matthaei, J. 1982. *An Economic History of Women in America: Women's Work, the Sexual Division of Labor, and the Development of Capitalism*. New York: Schocken Books.

—— 1988. 'Political Economy and Family Policy.' In *The Imperiled Economy*, Book 2, 'Through the Safety Net,' ed. R. Cherry et al., 141–50. New York: Union for Radical Political Economics.

—— 1992. 'Marxist-Feminist Contributions to Radical Economics.' In *Radical Economics*, ed. S. Feiner and B. Roberts, 117–144. Boston: Kluwer Academic Publishers.

Matthews, G. 1987. *Just a Housewife*. New York: Oxford.

McCrate, E. 1987. 'Trade, Merger and Employment: Economic Theory on Marriage.' *Review of Radical Political Economics* vol. 19 (Spring): 73–89.

McIntyre, Richard. 1989. 'Theories of Economic Growth, Economic Decline, and Uneven Development in the U.S. Steel Industry: A Marxian Critique.' PhD dissertation, University of Massachusetts, Amherst.

McNulty, F. 1980. *The Burning Bed*. New York: Harcourt, Brace, Jovanovich.

Merton, R.K. 1976. *Sociological Ambivalence*. New York: Free Press.

Middleton, C. 1983. 'Patriarchal Exploitation and the Rise of English Capitalism.' In *Gender, Class and Work*, ed. E. Barmonikow, D.H.H. Morgan, J. Purvis, and D.E. Taylorson, 11–27. London: Heinemann.

Milkman, R. 1987. *Gender at Work*. Urbana: University of Illinois Press.

Miller, A. 1981. *The Drama of the Gifted Child*. Trans. R. Ward. New York: Basic Books.

Miller, J. 1973. *Psychoanalysis and Women*. Harmondsworth: Penguin.

Mitchell, J., ed. 1974. *Psychoanalysis and Feminism*. New York: Random House.

Mitchell, J. and Rose, J., eds. 1983. *Feminine Sexuality*. New York: Pantheon.

Moi, T., ed. 1987. *French Feminist Thought*. Oxford: Basil Blackwell.

Bringing It All Back Home

Montreley, M. 1978. 'Inquiry into Femininity.' *M/F* vol. 1.

Morris, D. 1968. *The Naked Ape*. New York: McGraw-Hill.

—— 1969. *The Human Zoo*. New York: McGraw-Hill.

Muller, J. 1932. 'A Contribution to the Problem of Libidinal Development in the Genital Phase of Girls.' *The International Journal of Psychoanalysis* vol. 13.

Nicholson, L. 1987. 'Feminism and Marx.' In Benhabib and Cornell 1987, 16–30.

Oakley, A. 1973. *The Sociology of Housework*. New York: Pantheon.

O'Brien, M. 1982. 'Feminist Theory and Dialectical Logic.' In Keohane et al. 1982, 99–112.

O'Faolin, J. and Martines, L., eds. 1973. *Not in God's Image*. New York: Harper and Row.

O'Laughlin, B. 1974. 'Mediation of Contradiction: Why Mbum Women Do Not Eat Chicken.' In Rosaldo and Lamphere 1974, 301–20.

Orbach, S. 1978. *Fat Is A Feminist Issue*. New York: Berkley Books.

—— 1986. *Hunger Strike*. New York: W.W. Norton.

Ortner, S. 1974. 'Is Male to Female as Nature is to Culture?' In Rosaldo and Lamphere 1974, 67–88.

Ortner, S. and Whitehead, H. 1981. 'Introduction: Accounting For Sexual Meanings.' In *Sexual Meanings,* ed. S. Ortner and H. Whitehead, 1–28. Cambridge: Cambridge University Press.

Pagelow, M. 1981. *Women Battering: Victims and Their Experiences*. Beverly Hills: Sage Publications.

Palazzoli, M.S. 1974. *Anorexia Nervosa*. London: Chaucer.

Petchesky, R. 1979. 'Dissolving the Hyphen: A Report on Marxist Feminist Groups 1-5.' In Eisenstein 1979, 373–90.

—— 1984. *Abortion and Women's Choice*. Boston: Northeastern University Press.

Pietrokowski, C. 1980. *Work and the Family System*. New York: Free Press.

Pleck, J. 1982. 'Husband's Paid Work and Family Roles: Current Research Issues.' In *Research in the Interweave of Social Roles,* eds. H. Lopata and J. Pleck, 251–333. Greenwich, CT: JAI Press.

Prusack, B. 1974. 'Woman: Seductive Siren and Source of Sin?' In Reuther 1974, 89–116.

Radical Feminism. 1968. *Notes From the First Year*. New York.

Rapping, E. 1987. 'Media on a Marriage Kick.' *New Directions for Women* (July/August).

Redstockings. 1975. *Feminist Revolution*. New Paltz, New York: Redstockings.

Reiter, R., ed. 1975. *Toward an Anthropology of Women*. New York: Monthly Review Press.

Resnick, S. and Wolff, R. 1987. *Knowledge and Class: A Marxian Critique of Political Economy*. Chicago: University of Chicago Press.

—— 1988. 'Communism: Between Class and Classless.' *Rethinking Marxism* vol. 1 (Spring): 14–42.

Reuther, R. 1974. *Religion and Sexism*. New York: Simon and Schuster.

Rich, A. 1976. *Of Woman Born*. New York: W.W. Norton.

Risman, B. and Schwartz, P. 1989. *Gender in Intimate Relationships*. Belmont, CA: Wadsworth Publishing.

Rosaldo, M. 1974. 'Women, Culture and Society: A Theoretical Overview.' In Rosaldo and Lamphere 1974, 17–42.

Rosaldo, M. and Lamphere, L., eds. 1974. *Women, Culture and Society*. Stanford: Stanford University Press.

Rowbotham, S. 1973. *Hidden from History*. New York: Random House.

—— 1974. *Women, Resistance and Revolution*. New York: Vintage.

Roy, M., ed. 1982. *The Abusive Partner: An Analysis of Domestic Battering*. New York: Van Nostrand-Reinhold.

—— ed. 1977. *Battered Women: A Psychosociological Study of Domestic Violence*. New York: Van Nostrand-Reinhold.

Rubin, G. 1975. 'The Traffic in Women: Notes on the "Political Economy of Sex."' In Reiter 1975, 157–210.

Rubin, L. 1976. *Worlds of Pain: Life in the Working Class Family*. New York: Basic Books.

Rush, F. 1980. *The Best Kept Secret: Sexual Abuse of Children*. Englewood Cliffs, New Jersey: Prentice Hall.

Russell, D. 1986. *The Secret Trauma: Incest in the Lives of Girls and Women*. New York: Basic Books.

Saffioti, H. 1978. *Women in Class Society*. Trans. M. Vale. New York: Monthly Review Press.

Sargent, L., ed. 1981. *Women and Revolution: A Discussion of the Unhappy Marriage of Marxism and Feminism*. Boston: South End Press.

Sayers, J. 1986. *Sexual Contradictions*. New York: Tavistock Publications.

Schwarzer, A. 1984. *After the Second Sex: Conversations with Simone de Beauvoir*. Trans. M. Havarth. New York: Pantheon.

Seecombe, W. 1980. 'Domestic Labour and the Working Class Household.' In Fox 1980, 25–100.

Showalter, E. 1985. *The Female Malady*. New York: Pantheon.

Sidel, R. 1986. *Women and Children Last*. New York: Penguin.

Simmel, G. 1950. 'The Triad.' In *The Sociology of Georg Simmel*, ed. K. Wolff. New York: Free Press.

Smart, C. and Smart, B. 1978. *Women, Sexuality and Social Control*. London: Routledge & Kegan Paul.

Sokoloff, N. 1981. *Between Money and Love*. New York: Praeger.

Spignesi, A. 1983. *Starving Women*. Dallas: Spring Publications.

Stacey, W. and Schupe, A. 1983. *The Family Secret: Domestic Violence in America*. Boston: Beacon Press.

Strasser, S. 1982. *Never Done*. New York: Pantheon.

Strober, M. 1980. 'Wives' Labor Force Behavior and Family Consumption Patterns.' In Amsden 1980, 386–400.

Strouse, J., ed. 1974. *Women and Psychoanalysis*. New York: Dell.

Szekely, E. 1988. *Never Too Thin*. Toronto: The Women's Press.

Thorne, B. and Yalom, M., eds. 1982. *Rethinking the Family*. New York: Longman.

Thrall, C.A. 1978. 'Who Does What? Role Stereotyping, Children's Work, and Continuity Between Generations in the Household Division of Labor.' *Human Relations* vol. 31: 249–65.

Tiger, L. 1969. *Men in Groups*. New York: Random House.

United States Bureau of the Census. 1983. *American Women: Three Decades of Change*. Washington: Government Printing Office.

—— 1987. *Statistical Abstract of the United States: 1988*. Washington: Government Printing Office.

—— 1989. *Statistical Abstract of the United States: 1989*. Washington: Government Printing Office.

—— 1990. *Statistical Abstract of the United States: 1990*. Washington: Government Printing Office.

—— 1990. 'Full-Time Wage and Salary Workers – Number and Median Weekly Earnings by Selected Characteristics:1983 To 1988' Table 671 in *Statistical Abstract of the United States: 1990*.

United States Commission on Civil Rights. 1982. *Under the Rule of Thumb: Battered Women and the Administration of Justice*. Washington: Government Printing Office.

United States Department of Justice. 1982. *Report to the Nation on Crime and Justice*. Washington: Government Printing Office.

United States Department of Justice. Federal Bureau of Investigation. 1982. *Uniform Crime Reports, 1982*. Washington: Government Printing Office.

United States House of Representatives, Committee on Ways and Means. 1991. *Overview of Entitlement Programs: 1991 Green Book*. Washington: Government Printing Office.

Vanek, J. 1980. 'Time Spent in Housework.' In Amsden 1980, 82–90.

Vogel, L. 1981. 'Marxism and Feminism: Unhappy Marriage, Trial Separation or Something Else.' In Sargent 1981, 195–218.

—— 1983. *Marxism and the Oppression of Women*. New Brunswick: Rutgers University Press.

—— 1986. 'Feminist Scholarship: The Impact of Marxism.' In *The Left Academy: Marxist Scholarship on American Campuses* vol. 3, eds. B. Ollman and E. Vernoff, 1–34. New York: Praeger.

Waldrop, J. 1989. 'Inside America's Households.' *American Demographics* vol. 11 (March): 20–27.

Walker, K. 1970. 'Time Spent by Husbands in Household Work.' *Family Economics Review* vol. 4: 8–11.

Walker, K. and Woods, M. 1976. *Time Use: A Measure of Household Production of Family Goods and Services*. Washington: American Home Economics Association.

Walker, L. 1979. *The Battered Woman*. New York: Harper and Row.

Ward, E. 1985. *Father Daughter Rape*. New York: Grove Press.

Washburn, S. and Lancaster, C. 1968. 'The Evolution of Hunting.' In *Man the Hunter*, ed. R. Lee and I. DeVore. Chicago: Aldine.

Weideger, P. 1975. *Menstruation and Menopause*. New York: Alfred A. Knopf.

Weitzman, L. 1981. 'The Economics of Divorce: Social and Economic Consequences of Property, Alimony, and Child Support Awards.' *UCLA Law Review* vol. 28 (August): 1181–1268.

—— 1985. *The Divorce Revolution*. New York: Free Press.

Westwood, S. 1985. *All Day Every Day*. Chicago: University of Illinois Press.

Wilson, E. 1976. *Sociobiology: The New Synthesis*. Cambridge: Harvard University Press.

—— 1978. *On Human Nature*. Cambridge: Harvard University Press.

Wolf, N. 1989. 'Hunger Artists.' *Village Voice Literary Supplement*. (December): 20–1.

Wolff, R. and Resnick, S. 1987. *Economics: Marxian vs. Neoclassical*. Baltimore: The Johns Hopkins University Press.

Young, I. 1981. 'Beyond the Unhappy Marriage: A Critique of the Dual Systems Theory.' In *Women and Revolution*, ed. L. Sargent, 43–70. Boston: South End Press.

Index

Inman, Mary, 73
interest payments, 104, 105, 107–8
interest rates, 99, 105
isolation, 35, 56

Jaggar, A., 4(n5)
James, S., 26(n33), 27

Kaufman, Susan, 122(n8)
Kelly, J., 25(n31)
Kollontai, Alexandra, 2(n1), 73
Komarovsky, M., 25(n31)
Kuhn, A., 2(n1), 4(n5)

labor
  appropriation of, numbers/proportions involved in, 55–6
  household, 6, 8, 52
    as devalued, 14–15, 60
    division of, 17, 21(n25), 29, 31, 32, 108
    law and, 16
    nature of, 73
    numbers/proportions of appropriators, 55–6
    relatives (other than nuclear family) and, 29, 108(n22)
    responsibility for, 13
    time spent on, 8, 21(n25), 32(+n42)
    wages and, 26–9
  necessary, 3, 8, 73
  scarcity value, 105
  sexual division of, class and, 66
  surplus, 3, 8, 73
    changes in amount, 28–9
    extraction, marriage and, 45–9
    time spent on, 32, 45–6, 78
    oppression and, 47
    see also under household labor *in this entry*
Lacan, Jacques, 119–20, 125
Lamphere, L., 2(n1), 4(n5)
Lawrence, M., 113, 114, 115
laws, 9, 15–16
  anti-discrimination, 107

contradictions, 21
feudal analysis and, 53
and household labor, 16
and male power, 47
and property ownership, 17
on rape, 39–40
Lenin, V.I., 73
lesbian couples/households, 48, 80, 85
Lichtman, Richard, 130(n14)
living standards
  divorce and, *see* divorce, financial effects
  and tensions, 29–31
  see also earnings
loneliness, 35, 56
love, ideology of, 12–13, 19, 56–7, 66

McCrate, E., 58
McIntosh, M., 2(n1)
McIntyre, Richard, 94(n5)
MacLeod, S., 117
Magav, B., 26(n33), 27
magazines, 37(+nn50–1), 128
Malos, E., 2(n1)
managers, 10, 95
marriage(s)
  contracts, 22, 24
  ease of leaving/ending, 24
  rights and obligations in, 22–4
Marx, Karl, 68, 72, 92, 94(n5)
  on ancient class structure, 35(n48), 36
  on capital, 91
  on communism, 38
  on modes of cooperation, 70
Marxism, 53–4, 57–8, 70
  and Feminism, *see under* Feminism
  and historical specificity, 62
  and individuals, 112
  views on male domination within, 62
Matthaei, Julie: contribution by, 42–9; response to, 75, 77–80
media, 37, 117, 118, 128

Published by Pluto Press

Changing Our Lives
Women In/to Women's Studies

GABRIELE GRIFFIN

☐ *Ideal for anyone entering Women's Studies courses.*

Women's Studies is now an established course subject in many universities and colleges. This history of the development of Women's Studies offers both lay readers and those specialising in the subject a unique overview of the discipline.

Gabriele Griffin covers the establishment of Women's Studies as a discipline; its relation to feminism and to liberation movements; a discussion of its institutional status; its contents and methodologies with special emphasis on the personal–political dimension and an outline of the issues raised by students on Women's Studies courses.

A feature of the book is a series of interviews providing an integrated personal narrative of the interviewees' experiences of Women's Studies.

Gabriele Griffin teaches English and Women's Studies at Nene College, Northampton.

ISBNs hardback: 0 7453 0752 3   softback: 0 7453 0753 1

Order from your local bookseller or contact the publisher on
081 348 2724.

Pluto Press 345 Archway Road, London N6 5AA